ALSO BY CHRISTOPHER McKITTRICK

Can't Give It Away on Seventh Avenue:
The Rolling Stones and New York City

SOMEWHERE YOU
FEEL FREE

SOMEWHERE YOU FEEL FREE

TOM PETTY AND LOS ANGELES

CHRISTOPHER McKITTRICK

Post Hill
PRESS

A POST HILL PRESS BOOK

Somewhere You Feel Free:
Tom Petty and Los Angeles
© 2020 by Christopher McKittrick
All Rights Reserved

ISBN: 978-1-64293-511-0
ISBN (eBook): 978-1-64293-512-7

Cover art by Cody Corcoran
Interior design and composition by Greg Johnson, Textbook Perfect

Post Hill Press
New York • Nashville
posthillpress.com

Published in the United States of America

Cheers to Donna and Kevin

CONTENTS

"WHO KNOWS WHERE THEY ARE FROM?"

After claiming in interviews during the Heartbreakers' 40th Anniversary Tour that it would be his band's last full-scale tour, Tom Petty departed the stage of the Hollywood Bowl on September 25, 2017, the final show of the five-month celebration of the band's incredible history. Mike Campbell, the Heartbreakers' lead guitarist and bandmate of Petty's since they were both twenty years old, was doubtful, telling *Rolling Stone* in a June 2017 story presciently titled "Inside Tom Petty and the Heartbreakers' Last Big Tour:" "I've been hearing that for 15 years. We'll see." It certainly wasn't the first time that Petty had talked about scaling back the band's touring schedule, but this being another false declaration (or a cynical marketing ploy) seemed less likely than before.

For one, Petty was finally starting to look his age, moving across and off the stage that night with a noticeable limp. The sixty-six-year-old bandleader was not known for being particularly acrobatic on stage since the Heartbreakers' late 1970s run to superstardom, but footage from the Hollywood Bowl concerts shows a Petty whose performances are every bit as powerful, if not more reserved in movement. Still, like Campbell, the Los Angeles audience had reason to doubt Petty's words about the finality of touring, particularly on the Heartbreakers' home turf. Even when touring Europe, Petty never seemed far from Southern California. Most of the Heartbreaker tours either began or ended at venues not far from Petty's Malibu home, and almost half of the dates played on Petty's previous tour with Mudcrutch—his before-he-was-famous band that he revived in 2008—had been in the Golden State. Many of Petty's older musical heroes, like Bob Dylan and Byrds' bassist Chris Hillman—whose album *Bidin' My Time* was produced by Petty and released on September 22, the day of the second of Petty's three Hollywood Bowl concerts—still maintained active touring schedules. In fact, shortly after the Heartbreakers ceased serving as Dylan's backup band in October 1987, Dylan embarked on a touring cycle critics and fans have dubbed "The Never-Ending Tour." By Dylan's standard, the Heartbreakers were practically in semi-retirement already.

Sadly, that third Hollywood Bowl show was indeed the final concert by Tom Petty and the Heartbreakers. Petty died at the UCLA Medical Center in Santa Monica, California, on October 2, 2017, the consequence of an accidental overdose of pain medication he had been prescribed in part to treat knee and hip issues that plagued him before and during that final tour.

At a cursory glance, an artist with the voice of Tom Petty—both in terms of his artistic voice and the unmistakably Northern Florida inflection in his vocals—seems like an odd fit for Los Angeles, especially when one has the erroneous point of view that the Heartbreakers' music falls under the umbrella of Southern rock, or, even more off-base, whatever critics mean by the label "Heartland rock." When Tom Petty and the Heartbreakers released their self-titled first album on November 6, 1976, nobody quite knew what to make of them. The Los Angeles-based band didn't fit comfortably in any of the categories of music popular in 1976. Petty certainly didn't look or sound like a hard rocker, and the band didn't sound like punk, even if they were a bunch of skinny twenty-somethings in casual dress and leather jackets. Their songs certainly weren't disco or arena rock or anything that involved prominent synthesizers. Nonetheless, the *Billboard* review of their debut album dismissed Petty on one hand as "another punk rock, black leather jacketed offshoot," while on the other stating that the album "gains impact on its second spin." In the opening line of his review of the album for *Rolling Stone*, famed rock critic Dave Marsh asked, "Who knows where they are from?" He went on to say in his short comments that "No part is particularly special—songs, singing, playing are all kind of primordial L.S. rock, like Love or the Seeds." Still, he followed that lukewarm criticism with an extremely prophetic line: "But it's such a Sixties throwback, you can't help but fall in love." It demonstrated that the only people who really thought of the Heartbreakers as "punk" didn't actually listen to the record. The desire of the establishment to put any label other than rock 'n' roll on the Heartbreakers' music makes it no surprise that Petty, in the cover story of the November 1977 edition of *Back Door Man* magazine, declared the oft-repeated line, "Call me a punk and I'll fucking cut you." (It even became the article's subtitle.) Petty continued, "I'm fucking serious. I don't fuck around. From the beginning, I think because I have a leather jacket on (on the album sleeve) they called me a punk. Don't fucking call me one. I don't like that. I ain't joining nobody's club, I've got my own club. I'm in a rock 'n' roll band."

Tom Petty and the Heartbreakers was released by independent label Shelter Records and distributed by ABC Records, which by then was in the first stages of being on its last legs. (The label would be sold to MCA Records in 1979, leading to the first of Petty's many battles with record labels.) As a result, the album received little promotion stateside. The Heartbreakers were not a magic combination that instantly unlocked music industry success for Petty. The band's 1976 debut was mostly overlooked. In contrast, Petty's labelmate on Shelter, Dwight Twilley, had a top 20 hit with his band's debut single "I'm On Fire," which peaked at #16 in August 1975, before the Dwight Twilley Band had even recorded an album. The Heartbreakers didn't have the same luck. Of the singles from the self-titled debut album, only "Breakdown" charted in the US, crawling to #40 in February 1978. That nominally gave the group its first US Top 40 hit, but it utilized every bit of industry clout that ABC's Vice President of Album Promotion Jon Scott had, in a Herculean effort. The album wasn't certified as a gold record by the Recording Industry of America until January 1988, almost a dozen years after it was released.

Yet, just a few years later, more people would have heard the Dwight Twilley Band's Phil Seymour singing background vocals on "Breakdown" and "American Girl" than on any Dwight Twilley Band album. That Petty and the Heartbreakers survived and later thrived is doubly impressive viewing their collective accomplishments through the changing face of Los Angeles and the entertainment industry as a whole.

One doesn't need much of a deep dive on Tom Petty to realize that Los Angeles is the only place that could have produced a musician like him and a band like the Heartbreakers, which was formed from the remnants of Petty's Gainesville band Mudcrutch. Los Angeles had molded Petty before he and fellow Mudcrutch member Danny Roberts and roadie Keith McAllister crossed the Florida state line on their way to Hollywood in pursuit of a record deal in 1974.

Petty's childhood in Gainesville, Florida, has been extensively documented, often focusing on his difficult relationship with his father, his teenage years playing in a variety of successful local cover-bands, and his crowning youthful achievement of establishing Mudcrutch, the locally famous band that drew hundreds to its music festival-like performances at the farm where the band crashed, affectionately called the Mudcrutch Farm.

While Petty was shaped by his early years in Northern Florida, he was also molded by the mid-century pop culture that he consumed. Born at the dawn of the 1950s, Petty was a child of the Television Age. In an interview for *Petty: The Biography*, Petty recalled being enchanted by the idealism of Los Angeles at an early age. "What I did come to notice was that everything really great seemed to be coming from California," remembered Petty. "The television announcers would say, 'From Television City, in Hollywood, it's the *Red Skelton Show*!' And I thought, 'Television City? Man, that's where I need to be.' This is when

I was still a little kid. Television turned me on to a whole different idea of living, and I was a sponge. But pretty soon you start wondering if there isn't something between what you see on television and the shit you're dealing with at home." He also said, "I knew I didn't want to grow up and be an insurance salesman. That looked really dull to me. And I think it was television that saved my life, that raised and educated me." Petty also developed a deep love for movies, especially older ones from the golden age of Hollywood—in later life he claimed to have watched three or four movies a day and, while touring, preferred staying in hotels that offered the Turner Classic Movies channel on their televisions.

It seems incredibly appropriate then that Petty's first of many encounters with a rock 'n' roll icon happened not through a jukebox or at a concert, but on a movie set. While those early glimpses of Hollywood on television had grabbed Petty's interest, Petty was really bitten by the entertainment bug in one of the most mythological ways possible—by meeting Elvis Presley on a movie set when Petty was ten years old. As if to push fact into an even more unbelievable territory that rock 'n' roll legend occupies, the title of the movie Elvis was filming was 1962's *Follow That Dream* ("I've always thought [it] was a cosmic title," Petty would later say in *Conversations with Tom Petty*).

How the preteen Petty came to encounter the King of Rock 'n' Roll seems like a setup to a Hollywood screenplay. Petty's uncle, Earl Jernigan, regularly helped scout locations for filmmakers working in Florida. Jernigan had scouted the courthouse in Ocala, Florida, about forty miles south of Petty's hometown of Gainesville, for a scene in Elvis' movie. Jernigan's wife, Petty's Aunt Kitty, asked the boy if he'd like to go on a trip to meet Elvis, and Petty went without really knowing who Elvis was.

Whenever an impressive looking man walked by, Petty asked his aunt if *that* was Elvis. Finally, the man himself appeared. In a piece Petty wrote for *Esquire* decades later, he recounted of that moment, "When I met Elvis, we didn't really have a conversation. I was introduced by my uncle, and he sort of grunted my way. What stays with me is the whole scene. I had never seen a real mob scene before. I was really young and impressionable. Elvis really did look—he looked sort of not real, as if he were glowing. He was astounding, even spiritual."

With this combined taste of rock stardom and Hollywood, Petty saw his future. Shortly thereafter, he traded his Wham-O slingshot for a box of Elvis 45s. Three years later, Petty would receive another cosmic nudge when he saw the Beatles make their American debut on *The Ed Sullivan Show* and realized that if he could get a few guys from the neighborhood together to play in a band, they could be rock stars like the four young men on television. "That was when the world turned to color from black and white. All of a sudden Technicolor," Petty said in an interview with *Billboard* in 2005. "I was 13 or 14, and I knew exactly what I wanted to do with my life, no question. It still baffles me a little bit as to why the lightning bolt hit me, but it did."

Once Petty was firmly entrenched in the Gainesville music scene, Los Angeles became even more of a draw to him, as it was the place where fellow local musicians with substantial talent had gone to find their fortunes. The 1960s and early 1970s Gainesville scene, which revolved around the University of Florida, proved to be remarkably fertile. Stephen Stills may have taken a roundabout way to get there, but both Buffalo Springfield and Crosby, Stills & Nash were formed in Los Angeles. Bernie Leadon had become a member of the Flying Burrito Brothers and a founding member of the Eagles in Los Angeles. Even Tom Leadon, two years' Petty's junior and a one-time member of Mudcrutch, had made it to Los Angeles and was playing in Linda Ronstadt's band. These musicians spent years cutting their teeth in Gainesville and were now writing and performing hit records. It was all Petty wanted, and he knew that to do it he too would have to go to Los Angeles.

Ironically—but not surprisingly considering the well-documented crooked history of the entertainment industry and the music industry in particular—Los Angeles record labels became both the key to Petty's musical dreams and one of his biggest obstacles. He had several well-known major battles with the music industry, some of which became first-paragraph mentions in his obituaries. Famously, he declared bankruptcy to get out of his first record contract, later went to battle with his label when they wanted to release his 1981 album *Hard Promises* with a premium price tag, and even released a single to radio about how disappointing radio had become under expanding corporate ownership. He was an agent of change that fought against rising concert-ticket prices and lamented the direction of MTV, a channel whose popularity he helped develop with his imaginative music videos. But he also had other pet peeves with the industry that clearly bothered a man whose public image seemed to be laid-back and carefree—the same supposedly laid-back man who declared, "Call me a punk and I'll cut you." Whatever the public thought of Petty based on the image he portrayed on stage, in music videos, and in interviews, those who knew him best never considered him "laid-back." As he confessed in *Conversations with Tom Petty*, "My kids have this huge laugh about me. I just spent some time with them, and they were laughing about my image. They said, 'The world pictures you as this laid-back, laconic kind of person, and actually you're the most intense, neurotic person we've ever met.' [*Laughs*] And that's kind of true. You're not always what people picture you as."

One of those peeves that Petty certainly wasn't laid-back about was a long-running dispute he had with the *Los Angeles Times* for not ranking the Heartbreakers highly on a 1988 list titled, "L.A.'s Greatest Rock 'n' Roll Band—Who Is It?"

In Petty's recollection, which he shared in an interview with the *Los Angeles Times* in 2014, the newspaper had erroneously claimed that the Heartbreakers were ineligible because the band had formed in Florida. He took particular umbrage with the list because the lead singer of the band ranked number one, Jim Morrison of the Doors, was also from Florida. In Petty's estimation, points were being unfairly deducted from his band. However, Petty's recollection wasn't entirely accurate. The Heartbreakers were indeed included on that 1988 list, but the band had been ranked eighth, between Little Feat and Love.

While Petty and nearly all of the original Heartbreakers hailed from Florida (the exception being bassist Ron Blair, a Navy brat born in San Diego, who later lived in Gainesville), the Heartbreakers did not form until 1976 at the Village recording studio in West Los Angeles. And though Petty and the Heartbreakers' pianist Benmont Tench and guitarist Mike Campbell had also played in Mudcrutch in Florida, in Petty's estimation the Heartbreakers was a separate band entirely from Mudcrutch, and, thus, a child of the Los Angeles music scene. But the Heartbreakers understood that their lack of Van Halen flash may have been held against them in the late '70s and early '80s Los Angeles music scene. As Tench carped to *BAM* magazine back in 1978, "You're only an 'L.A. band' if you go and hang out on the Strip a lot and make a big deal of pointing out to people that you hang out on the Strip a lot. We're not into that."

Petty certainly considered the Heartbreakers' place in music firmly within the California rock tradition. "I think maybe if we were gone, God forbid, there would be a different take on us," he said in a 2006 interview with *Rolling Stone*. "Because this group is really the last link to that whole California thing—to the Byrds, Buffalo Springfield and that whole era of music that came along. This is probably the last thing that attaches to that." In the same period, he spoke about the unfairness in *Conversations*, adding, "We loved the Byrds and we loved the Beach Boys, and Buffalo Springfield and The Burrito Brothers. And we kind of felt we belonged here [in L.A.]. And we always have, though we're still never referred to as an 'L.A. band.' We're always referred to as a Southern band. But the truth is every bit of music we've ever made was in L.A. We've been in L.A. for over thirty years. We're a Los Angeles band." By that time, there were few people left who would argue against Petty's assessment.

In 2010, Petty expressed his disappointment directly to the *Los Angeles Times* that his group was often left out of these assessments. "I think we're really Californians, I've been in California longer than I was in Florida. Certainly where you grow up is always going to be deeply embedded in your soul. I don't know, but sometimes it kind of hurts my feelings that we're not included in discussions of Southern California music. The Heartbreakers formed here. We really are an L.A. band."

While the Los Angeles media and some rock critics might have initially excluded Petty and the Heartbreakers from the Southern California rock pantheon, area fans embraced Petty as a Los Angeles icon.

CHAPTER I

"THERE'S SOMETHING HAPPENING HERE"

The modern recording history of Los Angeles began in 1942 with the founding of Capitol Records by songwriters Johnny Mercer and Buddy DeSylva, along with Glenn Wallichs, owner of famed record-store chain Wallichs Music City, whose flagship store was in Hollywood. Capitol's original offices were located upstairs in the Wallichs Music City building. While recording studios and small record labels had existed in Los Angeles prior to Capitol Records, the company headquarters, which remains an iconic part of the Hollywood skyline, came to symbolize the shift of the music industry's base from New York City to Los Angeles.

Each of the three men entered the partnership with considerable success. While Mercer had yet to pen "In the Cool, Cool, Cool of the Evening," "Moon River," or "Summer Wind," and had not yet won the first of his four Academy Awards for Best Original Song, by that time he was already an established songwriter who had moved from New York City to Hollywood the previous decade to write songs for RKO Studios. His credits include what could be considered the anthem of Tinseltown, "Hooray for Hollywood," which appeared in the 1937 Warner Bros. film *Hollywood Hotel*.

Buddy DeSylva, fifteen years Mercer's senior, had also been a celebrated New York City songwriter who had worked with iconic figures like Al Jolson, George Gershwin, and Lew Brown, before heading to Hollywood to produce films. At the time of the founding of Capitol Records, he was an executive producer at Paramount Pictures.

Wallichs' music store was known for popularizing several record-store innovations, such as sealing records in cellophane, placing records in waist-high bins that made browsing them easier for customers, and listening booths. On the retail level, Wallichs understood how to sell records better than just about anyone else in the United States.

By the 1940s, Hollywood had long been the home of the film industry, and in spite of the popularity of popular music in film since Al Jolson introduced the sound era in 1927's *The Jazz Singer*, there were no major record labels based in Los Angeles. With their backgrounds, Mercer, DeSylva, and Wallichs recognized the potential that a major record company could have in the entertainment capital of the world. Capitol Records ended up a runaway success and the three men's gambit paid off. By 1955, Capitol Records was one of the industry's heavyweights and was acquired by British record company EMI for $8.5 million. Shortly thereafter, EMI began construction on the Capitol Records building in Hollywood that would later be dubbed the "Sound Capitol of the World" because of the famed studio's prominence in popular music. The circular building and its 151-foot spire became an instantly recognizable landmark of Hollywood.

Similar to how the film industry gradually moved much of its operations from New York City to Los Angeles from 1910 to 1930, the 1940s and 1950s saw a rapid increase in record labels of all sizes planting roots in Los Angeles. Many of the labels had corporate ties to the major film studios. American Decca Records, which bought into Universal Pictures in 1945, took full control of Universal Pictures in 1952, creating a powerhouse media company. (Decca and MCA would merge in 1962 to create an even larger company.) MGM would establish MGM Records in 1946, and Disney established Disney Music Group in 1956. United Artists would establish its own United Artists Records in

1957. Warner Bros. Records was established in Burbank in 1958, and 20th Century Fox Records was established the same year. The rapid expansion didn't stop there. Even Motown, a label distinctly associated with Detroit, would move much of its operations to Los Angeles by 1972. In addition to these conglomerates, the Los Angeles landscape became dotted with dozens of independent record labels and recording studios. The proliferation of labels, studios, and performance spaces led to young musicians heading to Los Angeles to make it. By the mid-1960s, Los Angeles had birthed a music scene that would produce famous groups like the Byrds, The Mamas and the Papas, the Doors, and Buffalo Springfield, as well as a burgeoning club scene in the area of what became known as the Sunset Strip in Hollywood (later West Hollywood) that would host decades of rock stars on its stages. All of these venues soon learned that by catering to popular musicians' every need—on-stage, off-stage, or in-studio—they could count on repeat business from repeat clientele.

In late 1966, the Sunset Strip area became subject to strict regulations, including a 10:00 p.m. curfew on the clubs, after locals complained that the district had been a haven for youth drinking, drug use, loitering, and noise. To protest the curfew, organizers called for a rally at Pandora's Box, a popular club located at the corner of Sunset Boulevard and Crescent Heights Boulevard that was owned by KRLA disc jockey (and later *Shindig!* host) Jimmy O'Neill, for the evening of Saturday, November 12, 1966. Pandora's Box had become the prime target for locals, even though it did not serve alcohol on its premises. That initial protest, which reportedly attracted about one thousand demonstrators, kicked off several weeks of unrest in the area that resulted in dozens of arrests and were later dubbed the Sunset Strip riots. In the aftermath of the first few weeks of almost nightly demonstrations, the Los Angeles City Council purchased Pandora's Box with the intention of closing and demolishing it, which it did the following year.

In those weeks, the demonstrations had already begun to be mythologized in the media. Buffalo Springfield recorded "For What

It's Worth (Stop, Hey What's That Sound)" in early December 1966 as a narrative of the demonstations, and it was released before the end of the year. Stills performed the song for the first time publicly on Christmas Day 1966 on the stage of the reopened Pandora's Box during its final night of operations. "For What It's Worth" would soon become a Top 10 hit and a counterculture anthem of the late '60s. Showing their understanding of Southern California music history, the Heartbreakers regularly covered the song during their 1987 US tour, and Petty performed it alongside members of Buffalo Springfield after his speech inducting the band into the Rock and Roll Hall of Fame in 1997.

March 1967 saw the release of *Riot on Sunset Strip*, a low-budget exploitation movie released by B-movie distributor American International Pictures, featuring the title song performed by Los Angeles garage-band legends the Standells, best known for their hit "Dirty Water" (which the Heartbreakers would also cover a handful of times decades later). Though significantly embellished, the film did help add to the idea of Hollywood being a haven for counterculture musicians. In fact, *Riot on Sunset Strip* was one of the first of several low-budget exploitation films released in the late '60s to depict hippie culture.

Yet even those who contributed to the myth of the Sunset Strip riots admitted that the name was a result of media hype, with Stephen Stills telling the *Los Angeles Times* in 2007, "Riot is a ridiculous name. It was a funeral for Pandora's Box. But it looked like a revolution." Indeed, it became clear that the Sunset Strip riots became just one of the growing number of youth counterculture protest movements that would go hand in hand with pop-music culture for the rest of the decade.

The soon-to-be-iconic Rainbow Bar and Grill opened in April 1972, and the Roxy Theatre opened in September 1973, as the Los Angeles music scene in the early '70s shifted from the famous "Laurel Canyon Sound" and psychedelic rock of the Byrds, Buffalo Springfield, the Doors, and Love, as represented by Pandora's Box and the Whisky a

Go Go, and gave way to singer-songwriters like Neil Diamond, James Taylor, Carly Simon, Joni Mitchell, and Randy Newman, who all helped establish the Los Angeles club Troubadour as one of the country's premiere music venues. Though many of those musicians were very much in the same tradition as, and contemporaries of, the Byrds and Crosby, Stills & Nash, by the mid-'70s, much of what represented the late '60s in California rock was gone or had moved on in the wake of the Manson family murders in Southern California and the disastrous Altamont Speedway Free Festival in Northern California, both in the latter half of 1969. Buffalo Springfield, the Doors, the Byrds, and The Mamas and the Papas had broken up due to deaths or infighting. Crosby, Stills, Nash & Young were on hiatus after touring arenas and stadiums in 1974, while the Eagles had their first number one album with 1974's *One of These Nights*, and were well on their way to becoming rock 'n' roll powerhouses with the addition of Joe Walsh and the releases of *Their Greatest Hits (1971–1975)* and *Hotel California*. Even the Beach Boys, who served as influential predecessors to the entire Los Angeles scene, were rapidly establishing their position as America's favorite nostalgia band with the 1974 release of the *Endless Summer* compilation and its 1975 follow-up, *Spirit of America*. The vocal-driven, folk-psychedelic rock combination that had marked the era had all but vanished, leaving Elektra/Asylum Records artists like Jackson Browne, Linda Ronstadt, and Warren Zevon as the remaining products of the movement.

* * * * *

This was the world that Petty, Roberts, and McAllister entered when they arrived in Los Angeles in 1974 with Mudcrutch's demo in hand. They had left Gainesville with a list of addresses for record companies taken out of *Rolling Stone*. The band—at the time consisting of Petty, Campbell, Tench, Roberts (guitars/vocals), and Randall Marsh (drums)—having reached their limit in Gainesville, made the decision to head west. Petty first attempted to land a deal with Georgia-based Capricorn Records, home to the Allman Brothers Band. "I remember hanging around the studio with the Marshall Tucker Band who were making their first record and invited us in—and we sat around all day and waited for someone to listen to our tape," he told *Mojo* in 1999. "And the answer was, 'It's too British.' So we decided then we were going to California. Florida wasn't the place for us. We'd done everything we could do there. We had a huge following. We could do a thousand people. But it wasn't going anywhere."

Petty elaborated on the decision when discussing the period in *Conversations*: "We realized we were just on a merry-go-round, that we would just keep playing the same bars and the same thing and not really get anywhere. So that's when California came into the picture. Because Bernie [Leadon] had gone to California and had a lot of success, and started the Eagles, and he would come home now and then. We'd talk to him. And then Tom Leadon, when he left [Mudcrutch], he got a job with Linda Ronstadt playing bass. And that was before she was really happening. But he was going on tour with Linda Ronstadt. We were really impressed, like, 'Wow, you got a gig.' Then he got in some group that actually had a hit single, in some band named Silver. A completely forgettable single, but it was a hit. That did it. Okay, we're going to California. That's the way it is. We're going to L.A. Where the Byrds are. Because the South had become completely inundated with the Allman Brothers. The Allman Brothers had gotten big, and every group had become an imitation of that. Literally everybody but us was an imitation of the Allman Brothers. And they were playing really long songs, and jamming. And we hated it. We liked the Allman Brothers, but we hated all the imitations. We thought it was stupid." The often soft-spoken Campbell put it much more succinctly when speaking to *BAM* magazine in 1978: "L.A. is opportunity. It's where we went to do what we wanted to do but couldn't do in Florida."

Prior to leaving, Mudcrutch had sent their demo—which was recorded on a two-track in the Tench family living room—to various record labels and received just one response, from Playboy Records' Pete Welding. Welding was a jazz and blues historian who had worked for various record labels throughout the years, often producing albums for obscure artists. "He was really respected in the jazz field, and he was A&R for Playboy. He rejected us, but he was nice enough to send us a song-by-song analysis of why he was rejecting us, and what could be better, and what we should work on," Petty said in *Conversations*. "So I took this to be really encouraging. And we drove out to see Pete Welding in L.A."

The trio set out for what Petty called "the greatest trip of my life," and arrived in the city he'd been dreaming about since before he knew he wanted to be a musician. His first impression confirmed those deeply established feelings. Petty continued speaking about the journey in *Conversations*, recalling, "We drove in to Hollywood. And then it seemed really easy to me, because we went down Sunset Boulevard, and in those days, there were record companies everywhere! Everywhere you looked, there was a record company. There was MGM Records, and of course, there was Capitol. I just thought, 'Well, all we've got to do is go in to every one, and we'll get a deal.' And we fell in love with L.A. within an hour of being there. We just thought this is heaven. We said, 'Look—everywhere there's people making a living playing music. This is the place.'"

Armed with equal parts determination and naivety, Petty followed through with his direct plan of attack. Arriving at Playboy Records, they found out that Welding was no longer with the label, and the A&R man there wasn't interested after listening to a few seconds of the demo (the short-lived label would fold in 1978). But going from label to label did lead to results—MGM Records offered them the opportunity to record a single, which was a start, but something akin to a consolation prize for a band hoping to make an album.

Aside from the story of meeting Elvis, Petty's life doesn't lend as well to the mythologizing aspect of American rock (sometimes self-induced, but oftentimes crafted by rock journalists looking for an iconic hook for a profile they're writing). However, what happened next runs a close second to meeting Elvis in the Tom Petty and the Heartbreakers creation story. The trio knew that there had to be more record labels in Los Angeles than what *Rolling Stone* had listed, and while eating at

"THERE'S SOMETHING HAPPENING HERE"

a diner on Sunset Boulevard, Petty stepped out to find a phone booth to look up record labels in the phone book. After finding a booth, Petty discovered that a list of twenty record labels (complete with phone numbers and addresses) had been dropped on the ground.

While finding a list of record company addresses at the exact moment one is looking for it seems like a gift from the rock 'n' roll gods, Petty recognized the downside: that someone else, and perhaps even hundreds of other hopefuls, were on the same quixotic mission he was. One of the companies on the list was Shelter Records, which was located in a nondescript bungalow in a rough section of East Hollywood. In 1978, *BAM* magazine described the building as resembling "the Symbionese Liberation Army 'safe house' where Field Marshall Clinque and his soldiers were barbequed by L.A.'s crack S.W.A.T. team a few years ago. Certainly, the house has little in common with the plush but sterile corporate digs that house most record labels in L.A., but it definitely has its own charm." *CREEM*'s Stephen Demorest saw the shabby nature of Shelter's offices as what set the label apart, when writing about the building in a profile of Petty in the August 1978 issue, remarking, "Shelter Records may have the coolest offices in America, a ramshackle wooden house nestled under a grove of tall trees set well back from Hollywood Boulevard. There's a genuinely rural flavor about it, a substantial earthiness which contrasts the surrounding city of electric lights and sky, Los Angeles, the mirage in the desert. Shelter is not just 'casual,' which is now a designer's term for expensive clothes— it's totally loose." After dropping off a tape at Shelter, the group moved on to the next label.

Even better than the single offer from MGM, the trio received an offer from London Records for a one-album recording contract. London, which was owned by the British arm of Decca Records (American Decca being a wholly separate company after a split), was known to Mudcrutch as the original American label of the Rolling Stones. The only condition was that London wanted the band to earn its own money during writing and recording of the album by playing cover gigs, which Mudcrutch had already been doing for years. Nonetheless,

17

Petty, Roberts, and McAllister had accomplished their mission. Now all that remained was to return home conquering heroes and come back to LA with the entire band.

While still in Hollywood, the trio took one night to indulge themselves in the scene and realized they were entering a world where playing to hundreds in Gainesville meant absolutely nothing. The group made one stop for pleasure, visiting the Whisky a Go Go, the famed West Hollywood club that had kickstarted the rock 'n' roll scene in Los Angeles and popularized go-go dancing, with Johnny Rivers, Otis Redding, the Byrds, Buffalo Springfield, Janis Joplin, Led Zeppelin, Love, the Mothers of Invention, the Doors, Them, and the Stooges all having graced the stage. In an interview for *Petty: The Biography*, Roberts remembers, "We were kids from Florida. This was another world. We went to the Whisky because we'd always heard about the club. We go in, get a little booth. Holy shit! And it's rocking. Then I hear a voice near us that sounds familiar. I listen for a few minutes, and then, finally, I have to get up and look over this little divider between the booths. It was Ringo Starr, Harry Nilsson, and Jesse Ed Davis. It was the only night we went out in Hollywood. And if that happens, I mean, do you think we wanted to go back to Gainesville to do anything more than pack our stuff?" As it turned out, less than four years later, Petty would be performing on the Whisky's stage with a band that didn't include Roberts.

Appropriately, band legend has it that Mudcrutch left Florida for Los Angeles on April Fool's Day, 1974. But plans changed. Though Mudcrutch had the intention of leaving Florida to record an album for London, a phone call led to an abrupt shift in destination. Denny Cordell, the Argentinean-born English producer behind the biggest hits of the Moody Blues, Procol Harum, and Joe Cocker, and co-owner of Shelter Records with famed pianist and songwriter Leon Russell, called after listening to the demo dropped off at the Shelter office in Hollywood and suggested that before committing to London, the Mudcrutch caravan make a detour to Tulsa, Oklahoma, where Oklahoma-born Russell had built a studio in an old church. Cordell would meet the group there and they could feel each other out. The proposal worked—shortly after meeting Cordell in a Tulsa diner, Mudcrutch agreed to sign with Shelter and continued on to Los Angeles to prepare for recording.

Of course, what felt like a dream at first would turn sour years later. Or, as Petty said during a live broadcast of his *Buried Treasure* radio show in 2011, "I came to L.A. and got a record deal the first week—and it took me years to get out of it."

Accompanying Petty on the cross-country drive was his new wife, Jane, whom he married shortly before leaving Florida. She had been Petty's girlfriend for about a year; shortly after arriving in Los Angeles, Tom and Jane learned they were going to become parents. Their first daughter, Adria, was born in November 1974.

Once Mudcrutch arrived in Los Angeles and signed their deal with Shelter, the band was put up in the Hollywood Premiere Motel, a nondescript motel located on Hollywood Boulevard a block east of Western Avenue, which was not far from Shelter's office. The band evenly split the $10,000 advance given to them and spent much of their time hanging around Shelter to absorb the atmosphere. In fact, the band wasn't pushed to start recording right away. Petty told *Billboard* in 2005, "They really nurtured us along for a good year or so before [Cordell] even let us make a record." The band later left the motel and settled into two houses in the San Fernando Valley, north of Hollywood.

A significant part of that "nurturing" involved Cordell introducing Petty to new music, taking him far beyond whatever he could previously find on the radio and in the record stores in Gainesville. "He was my guru," said Petty in the liner notes of *Playback*. "I would go to his house in Malibu every Sunday, and every day when the end of the work day came I would sit in his office and out would come the records. The office was closed and we'd sit there until eight or nine o'clock and he'd play me everything in the world. Just everything. Lloyd Price, reggae stuff, Rolling Stones, everything that had ever turned him on, or me. We'd bring them in. I'm forever indebted to Denny Cordell. Because we couldn't afford that many records. We were so hungry to hear anything.

In Gainesville you could only hear what you owned and we didn't have enough money to have stacks of albums. So running into somebody who had just unlimited access to records was incredible, it was just a bonanza of information."

Future Heartbreakers drummer Stan Lynch had a similar view of Cordell's influence. "He taught me a lot, sometimes in very abstract ways," he told *Modern Drummer* in 2008. "I was still young and I didn't really understand what he meant by 'groove' and 'feel.' I remember asking Denny, 'What does that mean, can you quantify that?' So he tells me he's taking me to a Bob Marley and The Wailers gig, and he flips me the keys to his Ferrari. As we're driving, he's making me haul ass, and he says, 'Stanley, driving a Ferrari fast, that's what a groove feels like.' At the gig, Marley had the place hypnotized. Someone's passing a joint through the balcony and Denny says, 'That's what a feel is.' He was just being helpful in his very '70s way. Saying, 'These are the things that feel incredibly good, that can't be duplicated. You'll know it when you know it.' Sure enough, we went back to the studio and we got two tracks that night. I was so vibed."

Another part of that nurturing involved getting the band into studios to feel themselves out. The first mention of Mudcrutch in *Billboard* appeared on August 31, 1974: "At the Village Recorder in Los Angeles, Mudcrutch is in with Denny Cordell producing and Rick Heenan engineering." The band name wouldn't have meant anything to most readers located outside of Florida at that time, including readers in the band's new hometown. But the Village Recorder was well known as a West Los Angeles recording studio converted from a Masonic temple in the late 1960s. The Village would play an important role in the formation of Tom Petty and the Heartbreakers, but this wasn't quite it yet.

A second mention came in the November 16 edition of *Billboard*, stating that Mudcrutch was recording at Producer's Workshop with Cordell producing and Galen Senogles engineering. Producer's Workshop was another 1960s Los Angeles studio that had started to attract big-name talent in the early 1970s. About the same time

Mudcrutch was recording there, Carly Simon was recording *Hotcakes*, and Ringo Starr was recording *Goodnight Vienna* with a parade of special guests. Mudcrutch's sessions were nowhere near as fruitful.

The change of scenery appeared to do little to help the band with recording, and they returned to Village Recorders to record and mix a single. In a 2016 interview with *Uncut*, Campbell bluntly said, "We weren't any good in a studio. When we got out to California and started really trying to record, either self-consciousness or just incompetence set in and we sounded like hell." Tench agreed. "We didn't sound like us. We sounded better in my parents' living room with a two-track recorder." At one point the band even tried recording covers to take them back to their bar-band roots, but nothing seemed to click.

The sessions did produce a single—the reggae-influenced "Depot Street" backed by the more radio-friendly "Wild Eyes." Cordell, who was fully on board with the reggae craze since before his label released Bob Marley's first American single in 1971, suggested to Petty that he write a reggae song. Cordell thought it was the strongest song from the session and put it out as a single. The idea wasn't so far-fetched: Eric Clapton's cover of Bob Marley's "I Shot the Sheriff" went to the top of the US charts in 1974.

The single didn't receive significant airplay, didn't sell, didn't chart, and didn't amount to anything outside of a short review in the February 15, 1975, edition of *Billboard* in its "First Time Around" column for "new artists deserving of exposure." The review calls the song a "good reggae cut that fits in with the current commercial standards as well. Closest thing to actual reggae to have a chance to be a major AM hit to come along in some time." That forecast was wildly off the mark. Just months after the euphoric high from signing a contract, Mudcrutch emerged from the studio feeling woefully unprepared and, worse, having nothing but a dud single to show for it.

All the while, Mudcrutch had been lying low in the burgeoning Los Angeles rock scene that would soon launch groups like Van Halen and the Runaways to national success. By the mid-'70s, the live Los Angeles rock scene had roared back with a completely different sound than what had graced the club stages only three or four years prior. Several rock bands that had developed followings but didn't have albums were regularly playing both the Whisky and the Starwood, including the Runaways and Van Halen, who had played at both venues several times before the release of their debut albums. The Sunset Strip scene had been heating back up with punk and new-wave bands, many of them being played on Pasadena-based FM station KROQ, which relaunched in August 1976 with Rodney Bingenheimer as the Sunday night disc jockey. In spite of its massive success and huge influence, KROQ was operating on a shoestring budget in early 1976 after it relaunched following a two-year absence from the radio dial, in a desperate attempt by its owner, concert promoter Ken Roberts, to retain the station's license. Roberts was only in an ownership position as a consequence of previous station ownership not being able to pay him for a Sly and the Family Stone concert at the Los Angeles Coliseum the station had sponsored. Roberts later bought out the other owners and embraced the punk and new-wave format, and by 1978 famed KROQ program director Rick Carroll continued to emphasize upcoming artists while mixing enough Top 40 music into the rotation to make the station appealing to audiences all over Los Angeles. Being based at the heart of the music industry only made airplay on KROQ all the more valuable to emerging artists.

Bingenheimer soon became known for breaking many bands—even playing bands' demos on the air—making his show, *Rodney on the ROQ*, a must-listen program for music fans in the area. The station soon became the dominant rock station in Los Angeles for punk and new-wave music. But the growth of that scene had little impact on Petty at the time, since his music didn't fit into either of those categories.

Furthermore, Mudcrutch was nowhere to be seen on Los Angeles club stages. Another blow hit the band when Danny Roberts announced he was leaving the band and returning to Florida shortly after Mudcrutch performed at the 1974 Shelter Records Christmas party. Stories regarding the reasoning behind Roberts's departure conflict depending on who tells the story, but the basic truth is that the man whose van

Petty rode in on the fateful cross-country trip was no longer part of the group.

To replace Roberts on bass and vocals, Mudcrutch recruited Charlie Souza, who, at two years older than Petty, had been a veteran of the regionally popular mid-1960s Tampa-area rock band the Tropics. The Tropics had appeared on *American Bandstand* and seemed to have just missed the opportunity of reaching national fame when the music of the '60s counterculture rendered them relics before they really had their chance. Souza, who had returned to playing bars in Florida with a new band, seized the opportunity. In a 2016 interview with *Uncut*, Souza recalled his initial impression of the current state of Mudcrutch, remembering, "Tom picked me up at LAX. He was waiting for me at that gate, just him. I got in his little Opel sports car, threw my bass in the back, and we started riding up the 405 and down into the Valley. That was an experience. We bonded and he wanted me in the band. Eventually, I found myself over at Shelter Records on Sunset Boulevard looking up at the Hollywood sign, thinking to myself, 'Well, this is it. I'm on top of the world now.'" Unfortunately, that moment was arguably the height of Souza's short-lived experience with Mudcrutch.

By that time, the band had stopped wasting Shelter's money on studio sessions that weren't producing results. Petty had been asked by Shelter to housesit for Leon Russell and, in return, Mudcrutch could use the studio at his house. According to Souza, the sessions at Russell's Encino home (and a brief return to the studio in Tulsa) were "a period of four or five months where nothing was really happening and we just kept recording stuff. I would listen to what Tom would play on the piano and sing, then I'd put a bass part on it." The sessions weren't a total loss. One song the band recorded was the original demo of "Don't Do Me Like That," a song the future Heartbreakers in the room didn't know would become that band's first Top 10 hit before the end of the decade. Petty had written it on a piano at Alley Studios (rendered as "All3y" on the sign) located on Lankershim Boulevard in North Hollywood. "I didn't have a piano," Petty remembered in *Conversations*. "But in my head I could hear that rhythm. The piano playing that right hand part: 'Ding

ding ding ding ding.' It was only about eight bucks an hour. It wasn't much money to rent the studio, but it was the loneliest feeling, walking in there by myself, sitting there, and playing the piano." Though Petty described Alley as "kind of dingy," the studio has a celebrated history as a rehearsal space for dozens of artists, including the Eagles, the Red Hot Chili Peppers, the Black Crowes, Jackson Browne, Stone Temple Pilots, and many others. Among the many signatures that adorn the brick walls of the space is that of "Thomas Petty."

Petty also wrote and recorded "Hometown Blues" at Russell's house, which ended up on the first Heartbreakers record with Randall Marsh on drums, Charlie Souza on saxophone, and legendary Booker T. & the M.G.'s Donald "Duck" Dunn playing bass.

Those bright spots, however, weren't enough to keep the enterprise going. Cordell called Petty to his office to tell him he was cutting his losses and dropping the band. Still, Cordell saw potential in Petty and decided to keep him under a $6,000-a-year Shelter contract as a solo artist. Petty managed to talk Cordell into retaining Campbell as well, but it was left to Petty to relay the bad news to the rest of the band.

In the aftermath, the Pettys moved to the Winona Motel on Hollywood Boulevard, just three blocks east of the Hollywood Premiere, which forced Tom and Jane to make a major life change. He recalled, "By then I'd had a kid, a baby. I actually used to put Adria in a drawer. I'd pull out a drawer and she slept in it. And then I was so busted that Adria and Jane went back to Florida, for a while, and I was out here on my own."

Before Petty could get into the studio to record his solo album, he received a call that would result in another phase of his rock 'n' roll education. "The phone rings and it's Leon. He said, 'Do you feel like writing?' And I said, 'Yeah, Buddy, I'm ready right now!' He came over to the Winona in a Rolls Royce. I got in the car thinking, 'Whoa, shit!' as we were driving through town."

Leon Russell was planning on creating an album which had a different producer for every track. He offered Petty the opportunity to cowrite some songs for the album, in addition to being something of a gofer to help in the process of lining up the producers. In *Petty: The Biography*, Petty remembered, "Leon says to me, 'What do you think of Brian Wilson?' I'm like, "Yeah, that'd be pretty good.' I simply don't know what to make of this. Leon looks at me and says, 'Then let's go see him.' And with that we pile into the Rolls-Royce and head for Brian's Bel Air house. And then there we are, and there he is, and holy shit!" Wilson was just the beginning of this journey for Petty. "So Leon says, 'How about George Harrison?' That's the way it went," he continued, pointing out that Harrison already had a song for Russell to work on—along with friends Ringo Starr and session drummer Jim Keltner. "We went to Sound City, and Ringo, Keltner, and Leon played," remembers Petty. "Then we went back that night to Leon's, just hanging out. They were all cool guys, and I was awestruck. It just wasn't real. How could that be real?" Russell also started working with Terry Melcher, the musician and producer who had produced the biggest hits for the Byrds. Russell and Melcher recorded their collaboration at Gold Star Studios, the famed studio one mile south of the Capitol Records Building, where dozens of classic records—including many of those by Phil Spector—had been recorded. Petty was able to observe first-hand dozens of Los Angeles' finest studio musicians recording parts for Russell's tracks. For a musician whose band fell apart after the group's inability to find its sound in a studio, it was a masterclass of unparalleled value.

Petty recalled one of those valuable lessons during his 2017 MusiCares Person of the Year acceptance speech when he shared a memorable moment at Russell's home with Russell, Harrison, Starr, and Keltner. Petty said, "They didn't need any words, but those cats were so cool, you know. And I found myself, after the session when we were hanging out, I found myself slipping my sunglasses on. Leon said, 'What the hell are you doing with the dark glasses, man?' I said, 'It feels cool, you know, like Jimmy Keltner—he's got his on.' [Russell said] 'Wearing sunglasses at night is an honor you earn.'"

Though Mudcrutch being dropped from Shelter was a major blow, these experiences with Russell had a much more enlightening effect on

Petty. In *Petty: The Biography*, he recalled, "Musically, I was feeling kind of like I was without a home. But here I was, meeting some of the Beatles, the Byrds' producer, Brian Wilson. I had to wonder what was going on. Like, what am I doing here? And I started thinking, 'Well, I must have been put here for a reason. This must be what I'm supposed to be doing. Somehow.' Through that whole period, I never ended up writing anything with Leon. Nothing. I just watched these legends come in and out of the picture. They talked to me, told me things. I got to watch them in recording studios. I don't think Leon really knew what he wanted to do next, but he was great to me. I learned a lot from him. I saw a lot of things that maybe you shouldn't do, and some things you should. Cautionary tales were in every other room I passed through." However, in a 1995 interview with *Musician* magazine, Petty explained that he ended up uncredited on the songwriting he did with Russell, explaining, "The way it worked was, I would write a song called 'Satisfy Yourself.' Leon would rewrite it as 'I Wanna Satisfy You' and I'd get no credit.... But I could never feel bad about Leon—it was a great learning experience" (a song titled "Satisfy You" appears on Russell's 1976 LP *Wedding Album*, with Russell having sole writing credit).

While Petty was meeting with rock royalty, he had moved to the Encino Travelodge on Ventura Boulevard to be closer to Russell's home, just two blocks from US Highway 101. When he wasn't working with Russell, Cordell was putting Petty in the studio—mainly Warner Bros. Recording Studio in Burbank—to work on his solo album with session greats like multi-instrumentalist Al Kooper and legendary drummer Jim Keltner, but Petty was unhappy with how those recording sessions were proceeding. In an interview with *Rolling Stone* in 2009, Petty recalled, "I had really good musicians...great players. But I felt weird, like 'This ain't what I wanna do. This could be anything. I want to be in a band.'" Those sessions produced "Since You Said You Loved Me" and an early version of "Louisiana Rain," both of which were included on the Heartbreakers' *Playback* box set.

While Petty was working on his solo album, Benmont Tench, who had been playing in a Los Angeles soul cover band after the dissolution of Mudcrutch, was able to use some gratis studio time at Village Recorder. Tench reached out to more or less everyone from the Gainesville scene that was in Los Angeles and available, including Petty and Campbell, to work on tracks for a potential solo album. Of the gathering, Ron Blair said to *Rolling Stone* in 2014, "We were all living in Hollywood, and I was playing in three or four bands, like everyone else. Stan [Lynch] called me up one day and said, 'Do you want to do this session for me with Benmont [Tench]?' Tom just showed up to watch or something, and I guess it struck him that we were a good bunch of players. Not long after that, he asked us to do a session for him."

Petty saw the session differently when he arrived—he finally saw the band that he had been looking for. "I walked in the Village Recorder one day and the Heartbreakers were playing," Petty recalled in *Conversations*. "Benmont had put them all together. And it instantly hit me that, man, you know this is home. This is where I should be. And I quickly did my pitch about talking them into going in with me. [Laughs] Well, my pitch was, 'I've got a record deal, and so you know you could go all the way around the search for record labels, [or] just come with me.' And they all knew me and I think that they quickly decided to go in with me." Randall Marsh, who was present at the session, was not included in the initial lineup, but guitarist Jeff Jourard was. Jourard appears in some very early publicity photos of the Heartbreakers and, according to the website of Jourard's brother Marty, "Tom Petty and Nightro" performed a one-off gig at the Van Nuys Recreation Center on March 19, 1976, with Jourard (what the group played during that performance or how they were received by the audience has been otherwise lost to history). Jourard would stick around with the group long enough to record guitar for several songs on the Heartbreakers' debut album—including "Strangered in the Night," the last song Petty recorded during his solo sessions. But by the time the bulk of the recording of the debut began, the now-renamed Heartbreakers (with the name reportedly courtesy of Cordell, who didn't like Petty's suggestion of "Tom Petty and the King Bees") were a five-piece of Petty,

Campbell, Tench, Lynch, and Blair. Though Petty considered himself a band-orientated person, keeping his name up front was important for two reasons: first, it was his recording contract; and second, at least his name would be out there if this band also failed to catch on.

Also joining up with the Heartbreakers around this time was Alan "Bugs" Weidel, a veteran roadie who had previously worked with one of Lynch's former bands. He joined the Heartbreakers as a roadie and a gofer, and in time, he became Petty's confidant and right-hand man.

While Petty was off with Russell and forming the Heartbreakers, Cordell had built Shelter Studio in the building adjacent to the Shelter Records office. It certainly was not a studio of the caliber that Mudcrutch had been working in. In an interview with Petty that appeared in the October 19, 1978, issue of *Rolling Stone*, the studio is described as "an abandoned Armenian nightclub way down on Hollywood Boulevard. The only view of life outside the single red bulb-lit studio is through a porthole, out of which one can see a gay porno theater. While recording, the group marked time by waiting for the 'Gibbon Woman,' an elderly woman who passed by every day at the same time and shrieked like a banshee."

Most of the tracks for the Heartbreakers' debut album were recorded at Shelter Studio over fifteen days in the summer of 1976. The band recorded "Fooled Again (I Don't Like It)" at Warner Bros. Studios in Burbank, while "Mystery Man" was recorded at A&M Studio in Hollywood, which was formerly Charlie Chaplin Studios. The famed comedian had built the English cottage-style complex in 1917 after achieving international fame in his comedy shorts, and filmed several of his classic films there, including *The Kid* (1921), *The Gold Rush* (1925), *The Circus* (1928), *City Lights* (1931), and *Modern Times* (1936). Chaplin sold the studio in the early 1950s when he left the United States, after which it passed through several owners, including comedian Red Skelton, who dubbed it "Skelton Studios." In 1966, it was purchased by A&M Records, a record label established four years prior by musician and businessman Herb Alpert and partner Jerry Moss. A&M converted several of the lot buildings into recording studios. Today the studio serves as the headquarters of the Jim Henson Company, founded by the famed creator of the Muppets, and the gates are topped by a statue of Kermit the Frog dressed as Charlie Chaplin's Tramp. The recording studios remain, now dubbed the Henson Recording Studios.

The recording of "Mystery Man" represented how much Petty, Campbell, and Tench had grown as studio musicians. The song was recorded live in a single session. In a 2014 interview with *Rolling Stone*, Blair remembered, "We set up, and we all played the songs just to get the sounds, and at the end of the take, the producer, Denny Cordell, went, 'Fucking ace!' We were like, 'What? We just cut it? It was that easy and quick?' It's kind of like Keith Richards' theory of catching musicians when they don't know they're working. You get some good stuff providing you are rolling tape."

The sessions at Shelter Studio included what would eventually become one of the Heartbreakers' signature anthems, "American Girl." The song was recorded, appropriately enough, on America's Bicentennial—July 4, 1976. Though many rumors about the subject of the song have been debunked over the years (including the oft-repeated story that it was about a female student who had committed suicide at the University of Florida), Petty revealed in *Conversations* that it was largely written about the traffic outside his apartment window. He said, "I was living in an apartment where I was right by the freeway. And the cars would go by. In Encino, near Leon's house. And I remember thinking that that sounded like the ocean to me. That was my ocean. My Malibu. Where I heard the waves crash, but it was just the cars going by. I think that must have inspired the lyric. I know it was in the bicentennial year. When there were a lot of American things going on. Super red, white, and blue things going on."

The other major Heartbreakers anthem from the album, "Breakdown," resulted from a short hiatus the Heartbreakers took so Petty could write more material. In 2014, Petty told *Performing Songwriter*, "I wrote it on the piano. I still have that piano. I bought it [Laughs]. Many years later, it's sitting in my living room."

When he brought it to the band, they had trouble getting a handle on the song. It took Shelter labelmate Dwight Twilley—who was recording with his band at the same time—to notice when genius had struck. Petty remembered in *Conversations*, "Somewhere near the end, [Mike] played that lick.... And it was quite late, it was eleven or twelve at night, and Dwight Twilley came in, and when that lick went by, he goes, 'That's the lick! Oh, man, that's the lick!'" That lick became the riff the song was built around, eventually resulting in the Heartbreakers' first American hit. To add to the Twilley connection, Dwight Twilley Band drummer/vocalist Phil Seymour sang backing vocals on the track.

Compared to Mudcrutch, the Heartbreakers were studio savants. The process of writing and recording came much more naturally to the band. Petty said to *Billboard* in 2006, "We were really excited in those days. We weren't afraid to try anything, I'll say that. I hear those records now and I can't hardly believe that we did them, but we somehow did. The songs came really effortlessly and the tracks were all played live. It was a joy, really. We were really proud of it when we got it done."

Though Petty was no longer a solo artist, the newly formed Heartbreakers were clearly established as his backing band. Petty's name was up front; his was the only photo on the front cover of the debut album; and his was the only name in nearly all the writing credits. Whereas the Mudcrutch demo had songwriting contributions from several members, Petty shared writing credit on *Tom Petty and the Heartbreakers* on only one song, the opening track "Rockin' Around (With You)," which was cowritten by Campbell. The nine other songs were solely credited to Petty, many having been written during his brief solo period.

Billboard was one of the few major publications to review the Heartbreakers' debut upon its November 9, 1976, release. In the December 4 edition it was listed under "Recommended LPs," which stated, "Petty, another punk rock, black leather jacketed off shoot, delivers an assortment of sullen ballads and uptempo shriekers. This LP gains impact on its second spin. Petty's laid back vocals become rather infectious." So, like Petty's first review in *Billboard* of "Depot Street," it was positive.

Unfortunately, the other thing the two releases had in common is that neither sold very well. By February 1977, the album had sold only 6,500 copies.

After a brief, largely unsuccessful East Coast tour, the Heartbreakers played their first performances in Los Angeles, opening four shows for Blondie at the Whisky a Go Go in February 1977. Petty explained to *Billboard* in 2005 that the combination of the two bands touring behind their debut releases (*Blondie* had been released a month after *Tom Petty and the Heartbreakers*) built a word-of-mouth audience over the four nights. "Really, by the end of that week it just exploded. There were lines around the block." Petty's labelmates Phil Seymour and Dwight Twilley joined the Heartbreakers during one show to perform backing vocals on "Strangered in the Night," as Twilley had done on the album.

More significantly, the Heartbreakers were building buzz with people who had the capability to tell Los Angeles just how damn good they were. Jon Scott, who was the vice president of album promotion at ABC Records, which was now distributing Shelter's releases, heard the Heartbreakers' debut album and, despite the fact that it was months old and that the first single had gone nowhere, felt the album still had potential. Coincidentally, Scott was working promotions for MCA when Mudcrutch released "Depot Street" and was responsible for getting that single some of the only airplay it ever received. Now several years later, Scott convinced Charlie Kendall, the DJ at Los Angeles rock station KWST, to not only take another listen to the album but to accompany him to one of the Whisky performances with Blondie.

In an interview with *Yahoo!* shortly after Petty's death, Scott explained that he went backstage to tell the Heartbreakers the good news—that Kendall was impressed enough with the performance that he was adding "Breakdown" to KWST's rotation. The band, however, frustrated with ABC for lack of promotion over the past several months, blew him off, with Lynch in particular ranting about the label's nonexistent support.

Naturally, the story would change when "Breakdown" hit the radio and, soon after, the Billboard chart. Petty would ultimately credit Scott for breaking the Heartbreakers. Four decades later, he even gave Scott an onstage shoutout at the Hollywood Bowl at what would end up being the Heartbreakers' final concert, saying, "He went to the radio stations with a vengeance and brought that sucker onto the charts. And it wasn't easy. We're forever grateful."

Los Angeles Times Music Editor Robert Hilburn attended the first night at the Whisky and two weeks later included "Anything That's Rock 'n' Roll" in the tenth spot on his "Alternative Top 10" list in his column two weeks later. He remarked that the band was "a bit stiff in its Whisky debut, but Petty writes solid rock 'n' roll songs and sings them with the passion of a truly compulsive rocker" (Petty later said in a *Rolling Stone* profile that he was sick for one of the shows). A month later, after Byrds frontman Roger McGuinn's solo album *Thunderbyrd* was released with a cover of "American Girl" on it, Hilburn titled his column "Petty & the Heartbreakers Merit a Second Hearing," and devoted the first part of it to praising the band's overlooked album. Hilburn wrote, "I've seen the band live, heard how well Petty's material lends itself to interpretation (Roger McGuinn's version of 'American Girl') and listened to the album several more times. Like the best of Rolling Stones, Petty's music gains with repeated playing. What appeared to be slightly off-center and fragmented has become a strikingly seductive, expertly woven rock 'n' roll mosaic. It's the strongest dose of pure, mainstream rock by an American band since Aerosmith's *Rocks*." Hilburn, who had become the chief pop music critic of the *Los Angeles Times* in 1970, provided some much-needed good press to the Heartbreakers precisely when they required it. Between the airplay arranged by Scott and Hilburn's praise—with much more of that to come from the influential critic—the Heartbreakers were finally getting noticed in their adopted hometown.

More significantly to Petty personally, however, was the meeting with McGuinn that resulted in the former Byrd covering "American Girl." In a 1989 interview with *Q*, Petty recalled, "Somebody had played him the song and he immediately sent for me. He was rehearsing with his band (Thunderbyrd at the time) in some studio in LA and I had to go and see him and it was like being summoned to the headmaster's office. I thought I was in for a real tongue-lashing about stealing his sound and stuff. I was really nervous...and then he said, 'You know, I heard this song called 'American Girl' and when I heard it I thought it was me. And then I thought, but I don't remember recording this...' And I said, 'Yeah, well, I'm sorry about that...sir.' And he said, 'No, I just wanted to tell you that I think it's a really good song and I'd like to record it.' I was thrilled. 'Yes, sir, well, you have my blessing!' He was such a good fellow to us. He recorded it and got us a good deal of attention by recording it."

By the time the Heartbreakers returned to the Whisky for two shows on April 26 and 27, the group was now headlining. In the April 26 edition of the *Los Angeles Times*, Hilburn published an overwhelmingly positive review of Petty's opening slot performance for Bob Seger two nights earlier at the Winterland Arena in San Francisco, remarking that "after 10 years in rock 'n' roll bars and back streets, Petty, 24, could be on the threshold of something big. His growing radio airplay, strong concert response and glowing reviews make him a hot new property in a field whose vitality depends on finding new attractions." Aside from shaving two years off Petty's age (two to three years were typically knocked off Petty's age in most early press about him), the review also included excerpts of an interview Hilburn did with Petty at an International House of Pancakes in Los Angeles.

Back Door Man's Thom Gardner was in the audience for one of the Heartbreakers' opening slots for Blondie at the Whisky and also for one of their headlining performances in April. He would write about both shows later in the famous "Call me a punk and I'll fucking cut you" profile of Petty in the November/December 1977 issue, remarking, "Opening a bill for Blondie in Los Angeles at the Whisky is a rough job. Blondie brings in about the strangest audience of all the professional new wavers, also the most dedicated (except maybe the Ramones'). When Petty hit the stage it was silent. A typical Whisky hipper-than-thou crowd. But Petty had them screaming for more by the end of the show. When he returned to headline a few weeks later, he had matured considerably as a performer. No longer as nervous and unsure as he once was, he commanded the stage and showed signs of the swagger that he now employs full-time." Then, in defiance of Petty's "Call me a punk..." line that subtitled the piece, Gardner facetiously added, "Some might even call it punk."

Likewise, in *Sounds*, Barbara Charone heaped similar praise on the Heartbreakers' Whisky performances, writing, "Although their debut album contains excellent slices of the best rock 'n' roll to erupt in the Seventies, the band truly must be seen live to be fully appreciated. This is an old fashioned, classic band in the truest sense. In short, they are magnificent." Her review concluded, "Tom Petty and The Heartbreakers may at times sound like numerous Sixties bands but in the end they remain pure and unique. Undoubtedly one of the best new bands around. And they're not bad looking either."

Other outlets were certainly noticing the growing buzz and weighing in on the months-old album. The *Valley News and Green Sheet*, a free paper in the San Fernando Valley, reviewed the album in its April 29, 1977, edition, calling it a "promising work, engaging in its uncluttered, no frills approach to pop and rock styles," and lavishing praise on "American Girl" in particular.

Afterwards, the Heartbreakers embarked on what would turn out to be an extremely successful seven-week tour of the UK (with a few performances on the European mainland in France, Germany, the Netherlands, and Sweden), where both "Anything That's Rock 'n' Roll" and "American Girl" charted in the UK Top 40, and where the Heartbreakers went from opening for Nils Lofgren to headlining their own shows and appearing on television and magazine covers. While that was thrilling for the band, returning home to relative obscurity was disheartening. As Petty told *Billboard* in 2005, "By the time we left England, we were a headlining band, and then we flew home and we got off the plane, and you're nothing again."

Truth be told, the Heartbreakers weren't exactly "nothing" when they returned from the UK after their last gig there on June 25. In his

May 28 column in the *Los Angeles Times*, Hilburn called "American Girl" "easily the best American rock debut single of the year," even though it was actually the second single from the album. KROQ, the popular Pasadena-based radio station that catered to the punk and new-wave fans, picked up the single. The strong reviews and Hilburn's frequent mentions of the band in his column were having a significant impact on their growing popularity in Los Angeles.

Other major outlets were now writing about the Heartbreakers, too. Petty received a short profile with interview excerpts in the June 30 issue of *Rolling Stone*, which also included praise for the Heartbreakers' April Whisky performances. Then the July 9 issue of *Billboard* featured a positive review of the April 27 Whisky show that began, "Rock is gaining new life through such as Petty & the Heartbreakers," and remarked, "The band does not require stage gimmickry for its presentation, depending instead on instrumental ability and its own enthusiasm for the rock idiom to keep the audience dancing." While positive, the prose seems like the kind of review Petty referred to in his *Rolling Stone* interview from the month before when he complained about the music press going over the heads of fans, remarking, "It's so jivey. I found myself looking things up in the dictionary a lot just to see what the guy's saying. And shit, if I'm doing that, who knows what in the hell the guy's talking about? Who is he writing this to?"

By his July 17 column, Hilburn was now calling *Tom Petty and the Heartbreakers* "my favorite American rock album of the year," saying that the group has "a purity...that combines the shadowy, late-night compulsion of the Rolling Stones' *Exile on Main St.* with a classic American immediacy that goes back to Elvis and Eddie Cochran.... A sensational new arrival." The Heartbreakers were back at the Whisky on August 12 and August 13. Continuing his string of praise, Hilburn wrote in his column the following week, "Tom Petty's return to the Whisky last weekend left little doubt that he is potentially the most exciting American rock discovery so far in 1977. He is a first-rate songwriter, strong vocalist and he's developing that all-important persona on stage," and also remarked, "His return to the Whisky after the English tour was dampened somewhat Friday by the typically stiff 'industry' audience that crowds clubs to scout hot new acts. But things were much improved Saturday when he showed flashes of the rock 'n' roll brilliance that was only hinted at opening night."

Just days after these Whisky shows, Petty's first musical influence, Elvis Presley, died. In the linear notes of *Playback*, Petty reflected on what happened that day when he heard the news and how, despite the sadness, it was an important day for his career. "I was home in L.A. Very weird day, because it was also one of the first times I heard myself on the radio. I'm listening to KROQ and I hear that Elvis died. KROQ, if you believe this, didn't have any Elvis records! The disc jockey said, 'Our Elvis library is locked. While we're getting it open we're going to play some artists that Elvis inspired.' And then on comes ME. And I thought, 'Well, this is wrong, get him on as quick as possible!'" Because KROQ played new wave and punk bands (and reaped the benefits of the expanding audience for those genres), it shouldn't have been a complete surprise that the station didn't have Elvis records on hand to play on air. Petty reflected on that day and on hearing his music instead of Elvis' on the radio in more detail in a 1977 interview with *Back Door Man*, remarking, "It was just getting more surreal all the time...*Melody Maker* is on the phone wanting to know what I think. I really don't know, it's one of the strangest things that ever happened to me." Then he added an insightful afterthought, "This generation needs its own rock bands."

CHAPTER 2

THANK GOD FOR CALIFORNIA

Almost exactly a month after their latest shows at the Whisky, the Heartbreakers were opening for the English prog-rock band Be-bop Deluxe on September 14 and 15 at the Santa Monica Civic Auditorium, a three-thousand-capacity, multi-use venue that had already hosted countless concerts since opening in 1958, including the famed T.A.M.I. show that featured the Rolling Stones, James Brown, the Beach Boys, the Supremes, Chuck Berry, and several other groups. It also hosted several Academy Awards ceremonies in the 1960s, and was where comedian George Carlin debuted his groundbreaking "Seven Words You Can Never Say on Television" routine. Though many of the seating areas of the venue were closed for public events in 2013 because of safety concerns regarding the aging structure, the Civic Auditorium remains in periodic use for conventions and other events.

Hilburn's *Los Angeles Times* review of the first concert panned the headliners, but once again heaped praise on the Heartbreakers, saying Be-bop Deluxe was "underscored by the vitality and drive of Tom Petty & the Heartbreakers. Though the group's local concert hall debut was severely hampered by a faulty sound mix that obliterated the vocals, Petty is a rocker with a stronger sense of vision and passion.

In an age of imitation and pose in rock, Petty delivers the goods solidly and believably.... He's still the most promising rock arrival of '77." According to *Billboard*, the two concerts drew a combined audience of 5,723 and grossed $48,000. The Heartbreakers returned to the Santa Monica Civic Auditorium on November 7 to open for another prog-rock band, Nektar.

Petty then made his first national TV appearance on the short-lived CBS Saturday morning variety series *Wacko* in October 1977, backing Shelter labelmate Dwight Twilley's performance to mime four songs with Petty "playing" bass. The Dwight Twilley Band had no permanent bassist at the time, so Petty stepped in, perhaps as a thank-you for Twilley's input on "Breakdown." The performances were shot in Los Angeles and were spread out over four episodes of the series. It wasn't the most glamorous television appearance for Petty—who often appears to be unsure of what he's supposed to be miming to in the footage—but it would be the first of many in his career.

More significantly, Petty appeared in his first movie role when he filmed a cameo as himself in the movie *FM*, which was later released in April 1978. The film is about a popular Los Angeles FM station whose manager is ordered by his bosses to devote more airtime to commercials—particularly commercials promoting the US Army. Supporting the station manager's position against the decree, the DJs barricade themselves within the station and air rock music commercial-free while preaching the injustice of it all to their listeners. An uncomfortable-looking Petty appears early in the film in a quick interview with DJs about the Heartbreakers' touring schedule, with the Heartbreakers' "Breakdown" playing in the background. "Breakdown" is also featured on the film's soundtrack album, making it the first time a Heartbreakers' song appeared on a film soundtrack. Involved in the production of the movie was Eagles' manager Irving Azoff, already a major force in artist management and, from 1983 to 1989, chairman of Petty's record label.

Petty was rather dismissive of the process when he spoke about filming the part in the as-yet-unreleased movie to the *Cleveland Scene* in December 1977. "Well, I had to be there on the set at 6:45 a.m. to start shooting every day; I didn't leave until 6 p.m. It's a lot like making a record in a way—the routine of doing something over and over again to get it right. They had to get the sound and the lights just right, too. I'm glad it's over." He was even more dismissive when he was interviewed about it in the August 18, 1978, issue of *Dark Star* after the film was a flop, saying, "I wanted to be in it because I thought it was gonna be exposing the truth about FM radio; I think Azoff thought that too. The band weren't into it very much, we certainly never went into it as a Heartbreakers project. I just said, 'I'm gonna go down and see how they make movies,' and I went down twice for twelve hours and did a five minute scene. I just do one of those interviews where I'm meant to be on the road; I come in looking really burned and talk to this guy and chick. It ain't very interesting to tell you the truth, I wouldn't advise going to see it. It's just a beach-party radio movie. We don't really have anything to do with it."

Nonetheless, the film's soundtrack album went platinum, and likely served as an introduction for many to the Heartbreakers just weeks before the release of the band's second album. Another song off the first album, "Strangered in the Night," was featured on the soundtrack for the critically derided John Travolta and Lily Tomlin box-office bomb *Moment by Moment*, which was also released in 1978. Though the Heartbreakers weren't having much luck with outside media in the late '70s, these flops still prepared Petty to embrace television in the next phase of his career.

Yet, even with all the growing Los Angeles area recognition, the Heartbreakers hadn't broken through on the charts, and certain radio stations in Los Angeles, including KMET, one of the most popular FM rock stations in the area, weren't playing their songs. Jon Scott booked a live recording of the Heartbreakers performing at Capitol Records Studio on November 11 that would air on KWST. Scott invited KMET staff to the performance, and the band's short set—including "Breakdown," a song from their next album, "Listen to Her Heart," a cover of the Animals' "Don't Bring Me Down," and their popular take on the Isley Brothers' "Shout"—was well received by the audience. Two tracks from the Capitol Studios performance, "Anything That's Rock 'n' Roll" and "Breakdown," were included on the deluxe edition of the 2018 box set *An American Treasure*. The KMET representatives were impressed. Within days, the station was playing "Breakdown," which finally entered the Billboard Hot 100 in November 1977, peaking at #40 in February 1978. The following month, *Tom Petty and the Heartbreakers* peaked at #55 on the album charts. A year after its release, the album and single were finally selling. It would still take another ten years for the album to be certified gold by the RIAA, but the Heartbreakers could now take pride in a successful record and single.

Of course, the Heartbreakers weren't simply waiting around for "Breakdown" to finally become a hit. During breaks in the extensive touring schedule throughout 1977, the band was in Shelter Studios working on its follow-up album.

In the months after the Heartbreakers formed, released their debut, and struggled to gain traction with it, Shelter Records had been undergoing radical changes. Shortly after Russell and Petty stopped working together on Russell's ambitious producer project, Russell and Cordell had business disagreements and split, with Cordell remaining as the head of Shelter. Even before that, Shelter's US distribution rights had bounced among various companies: first Capitol, then MCA Records, then ABC Records, and then splitting the roster between ABC and Arista (the Heartbreakers were retained on ABC). All the while, Shelter was not bringing in enough money to remain solvent. Shelter may have been putting out quality records by artists like the Heartbreakers, J.J. Cale, and the Dwight Twilley Band, but they certainly weren't selling in significant numbers. In the midst of recording his second album, Petty renegotiated his Shelter contract to better financial terms for himself and to include the other Heartbreakers. According to the court filings in MCA's 1979 lawsuit against Petty, Petty's contract was upped from $50,000 per album to a $250,000 advance against royalties, with increases based on number of albums sold. Petty would receive a $350,000 advance for a third album, half due at the beginning of recording and the other half when the album was submitted to the label. The contract also had the option for a $400,000 advance for a fourth album.

The Heartbreakers' second album, *You're Gonna Get It*, was largely recorded over three months at Shelter Studio, which Petty coproduced with Cordell and Noah Shark, who had engineered the first album. The Heartbreakers had already been performing two songs from the upcoming album during their 1977 performances, "I Need to Know" and "Listen to Her Heart," and perhaps that was an influence on releasing them as the album's two singles.

"Listen to Her Heart" was played during the band's performance at Capitol Studios for KWST, so it had already been broadcast before the studio version had been released. The mid-tempo, catchy tune features the singer telling another man that he isn't going to take away the singer's girl (the lyric had been inspired by Jane attending a party at Ike Turner's house, which resulted in Turner locking the guests in the house so they couldn't leave). It attracted some controversy from distributors because the second line included the word "cocaine" as something the other man was using to lure the girl away. Petty was asked to change it to "champagne," but he refused (he later recounted that he didn't change the lyric because cocaine is a lot more expensive than champagne).

Another song on the album is the first Heartbreakers tune released with references to California, a Petty/Campbell groove titled "Hurt": "Thank God for California / Thank God I'm going home" in the first verse; the second verse refers to a flight back to Los Angeles. After just three years living in the Golden State, Petty was declaring it home. Campbell's contribution to the song came when Petty brought the song into the studio after shooting *FM*.

The other Petty/Campbell cowritten song on the album, "Baby's a Rock 'n' Roller," features some sampled audio throughout the track. Petty told *Dark Star* in August 1978, "Denny Cordell, our producer, and Jim Lenahan went down Hollywood Boulevard with a cassette deck, turned it on and walked down. It's an interesting street to walk down in the middle of the night, slightly dangerous. They went into a Penny Arcade and the first noise they recorded was one of those guns in a booth that shoots rockets and we liked that so we put that in front of the track. There's a lot of street noise running throughout."

Since *You're Gonna Get It* was recorded with a more cohesive group with a stronger idea of its direction, Petty told *Dark Star* in August 1978, "I think it's a California album, but not in the Linda Ronstadt sense; it's an East Hollywood record, it's the other side of Western Avenue, so it's different. We've been in California quite a while and it's really nice now, it's great for us to play there."

Nearly all reviewers declared *You're Gonna Get It* as a superior album compared to the Heartbreakers' debut. Previewing the album in April 1978, *BAM* magazine writer Blair Jackson said Petty's songs "are charged with the sort of thunderous urgency and manic energy that has always characterized the best rock 'n' roll. These songs are a quick, glorious nitrous oxide high—they take you up with a rush, vibrate every pore of your body, and leave you tingling when they're gone." Jackson also declared, "If this album doesn't sell a million copies, there will be sufficient cause to worry about the health of this country." *You're Gonna Get It* became the Heartbreakers' first gold record, becoming certified on July 7, 1978. The album also peaked at #23 on the Billboard Top 200 in August 1978. Selling five hundred thousand instead of a million copies in the first two months didn't trigger a national health check, but it did establish that the Heartbreakers were well on their way to rock stardom.

"I Need to Know" also topped Robert Hilburn's "Alternate Top 10" in the May 20, 1978, edition of the *Los Angeles Times*. While the Heartbreakers' sophomore album sold better than their debut album, the two singles did not chart as high as "Breakdown" did. "I Need to Know" just missed the Top 40 when it peaked at #41 on the Billboard Hot 100 in August 1978, while "Listen to Her Heart" peaked at #59 in October 1978. Of course, placing two singles in the Hot 100 was nothing to complain about, and momentum was definitely building for the Heartbreakers in Los Angeles and elsewhere.

The Heartbreakers rehearsed for their upcoming tour at SIR Rehearsal Studios on Sunset Boulevard in Hollywood, and on May 7 recorded their national television debut for NBC's popular music program *The Midnight Special* at NBC Studios in Burbank. The band played three songs, "American Girl," "I Need to Know," and "Listen to Her Heart." The appearance aired on NBC on June 2. Following that performance, the Heartbreakers played three warm-up shows at Southern California colleges: San Diego State University (May 11); University of California, Davis (May 13); and University of California, Riverside (May 14). Those performances built up to the Heartbreakers' first headlining appearance at the Santa Monica Civic Auditorium on June 5 after opening for other bands there the previous year.

In a Hilburn-penned preview of the concert in the June 4, 1978, edition of the *Los Angeles Times*, ABC Records President Steve Diener was effusive in his praise of the new album's performance, saying, "The interest is phenomenal. The reaction is the kind you normally expect only for an artist who has been around five years and has a dozen gold albums. The record is an event. I feel something building here that is like an eruption."

Three days later in his review of the concert, Hilburn declared, "Tom Petty's going to be a superstar in rock," noting that the sold-out audience "erupted with a shrieking cheering ovation normally reserved for rock's most established figures." Based on how Petty went from opening for Blondie at the Whisky in February 1977 to headlining the Santa Monica Civic Auditorium in June 1978, Hilburn even predicted that the Heartbreakers would be playing the much-larger Inglewood Forum by early 1979. Hilburn was off by a year—the Heartbreakers would headline the Forum in January 1980.

Before the full tour kicked off, Petty took one day off to attend Bob Dylan's concert at the Universal Amphitheater on June 7, 1978, with Bugs Weidel. The Universal Amphitheater was located in Universal City, the home of Universal Studios, just north of Hollywood. It was the final show of Dylan's seven-night stand at the venue between the Australian and European legs of his 1978 World Tour, by far Dylan's most ambitious tour up to then. Petty had no idea that Dylan even knew who he was, and thus was surprised by what happened at the concert. "We left the Shelter studio, and we went to drive to the Universal Amphitheater, had a flat tire, and both of us got out on the road trying to change the tire. So we were just covered with grease and dirt. And we got to the Universal Amphitheater and we found our seats, and the show had just begun. And then midway through the show, Bob introduced the celebrities in the audience, which was kind of unusual for Bob. It was like, 'Joni Mitchell's here,' and there'd be applause. And then suddenly he said, 'Tom Petty's here.' And there was applause. And that was the first time it really hit me that people knew who we were. Because I'd only made two records then. Then a guy came up to us while we were sitting in our seats, and said, 'Bob would like you to come backstage.' So we went backstage, and had a brief conversation. Nothing of any substance, because we didn't know each other. But I met Bob." Audio from the concert reveals Dylan announced Petty in between introductions of Joni Mitchell and Raquel Welch, saying, "And Tom Petty is here. He's a new rising star. Rock 'n' roll! I'd like to say hello to him, too." This was the beginning of a long association the Heartbreakers would have with Dylan. Dylan enlisted Tench to play keyboards on his 1981 album *Shot of Love*, the first of many times members of the Heartbreakers would collaborate with Dylan. The Heartbreakers themselves would also perform at the Universal Amphitheater just thirteen months later, with many more appearances in the following years.

The Heartbreakers played several other West Coast dates, including their first Canadian show in Vancouver, before a quick return to England to appear on the *Old Grey Whistle Test* and perform at the Knebworth Festival. The band's full US tour started immediately afterward, with the Heartbreakers oscillating between headliner and opener, depending on the market.

After the tour wrapped, Petty had an infamous rock-star moment in October in what he later claimed was his first-ever visit to the Troubadour, the famed West Hollywood nightclub where many top acts—in particular, Elton John, whose first US concert was there, and Neil Young and James Taylor, who played their first solo concerts there—had performed as they were coming up. The Troubadour initially opened in 1957 as a coffeehouse venue for singer-songwriters. The nucleus of the Byrds formed after Roger McGuinn (then going by "Jim"), Gene Clark, and David Crosby met while performing regularly at the nightclub's open-mic nights. Similarly, the nucleus of the Eagles formed when Don Henley and Glenn Frey met there in 1970. By the '60s, comedy had also been featured at the venue—it was the site of one of Lenny Bruce's several arrests for obscenity, in this case for using the word "schmuck." Richard Pryor recorded his self-titled debut album there in 1968. By the '70s, rock acts were welcome on the stage, and by the end of the '70s, that included new-wave bands. One of the most popular and buzzworthy bands on the Sunset Strip at the end of 1978 was the Knack, who later became known for their 1979 number-one hit "My Sharona." The Knack played regularly at the Troubadour in the fall of 1978, and several special guests, including the Doors' Ray Manzarek, joined the band onstage for encores.

Petty was asked onstage while attending one of the band's gigs. The only problem was that Petty was heavily intoxicated. According to *Petty: The Biography*, "Handed a guitar, [Petty] plugged into an amp, turning the volume all the way down on the guitar before he brought the volume on the amplifier all the way up. Then he waited for his moment, watching as the Knack kicked off the song. A minute or so in, Doug Feiger gave Petty the sign, letting him know it was time to solo. And that was when Petty turned the guitar volume to ten, filling the room with feedback before hitting one power chord that if not musical was nonetheless a message. He then stumbled out from the stage, his cord coming unplugged, onto a row of tabletops in front of the stage, kicking people's drinks into their laps...the next day a review of the show featured the headline 'Tom Petty Digs the Knack!'" At Mudcrutch's April 2008 gigs at the Troubadour, Petty told the story onstage and revealed that the next day his management company received a bill for $480 from the club to cover the damage. Continuing the story, he added that the following night, he had dinner with Bruce Springsteen, who said that the Knack had asked him to come down to the Troubadour and jam with them. Petty remarked, "I said, 'Whatever you do, Bruce, don't go on the tables.'"

The Heartbreakers played three gigs in California to close out 1978— Redding (December 29), an infamous concert in San Francisco, where Petty was pulled offstage by enthusiastic fans during a performance of "Shout" (December 30), and a sold-out New Year's Eve concert at the Santa Monica Civic Auditorium. The entire Santa Monica show was recorded and released as part of the deluxe edition of the Heartbreakers' 2009 box set *The Live Anthology*. As a live document, it presents one of the most energetic live performances by the band ever committed to tape, with the group clearly celebrating the huge successes they had achieved over the past year. To celebrate the occasion, the Heartbreakers welcomed Phil Seymour and 1950s rock legend Del Shannon on stage to perform Shannon's number-one hit "Runaway."

By 1978, Shannon hadn't had a Top 10 hit since "Keep Searchin' (We'll Follow the Sun)" in 1964. Shannon had spent much of the 1970s touring increasingly smaller venues and battling alcoholism. Petty met Shannon in 1978, shortly after Shannon had gotten sober. Shannon said in a 1989 interview with the *Los Angeles Times* that he told Petty he was going to record a country record in Nashville. He recalled Petty responding, "Hell, you can do country stuff when you're 60. You're a rocker, man." Shannon said to Petty, if that were the case, perhaps Petty would be interested in producing an album for him. Petty said in the *Runnin' Down a Dream* documentary, "I was very interested. I had never produced a record for anyone except for us, so I took the job. I thought it would be fun, and it was." The Petty-produced *Drop Down and Get Me*, which featured contributions from all the Heartbreakers, was released in 1981 and peaked at #123 on the Billboard 200, also producing Shannon's first Top 40 hit since 1965, with a cover of "Sea of Love."

The year 1978 had been a banner one for the Heartbreakers and for Petty personally. The Pettys rented a house in Sherman Oaks, the town next to Encino where the Pettys had housesat for Leon Russell. Petty also spent his first royalty check in typical rock-star fashion, telling *Rolling Stone* in 1999, "Got a royalty check for $6,000 when we had our first hit record, and walked in and spent it all on a Camaro. Didn't have a dime left. A '78; had an 8-track." That was the car Petty picked Bruce Springsteen up in when Springsteen cold-called Petty one night to hang out. According to *Petty: The Biography*, "Petty picked him up at the Sunset Marquis. They went down Sunset Boulevard to the water, stopping at Tower Records on the way, picking up half a dozen eight-tracks. They drove until they'd listened to every song on every one of them. The Stones' *12 x 5* was among the tapes. When 'Congratulations' came on, Springsteen raised his arms to the heavens and said, 'You can take me now!' Petty loved that. He liked knowing another man out there who went to the same church." West Hollywood's Sunset Marquis Hotel had been a favorite spot for rock stars almost since it opened in 1963, and it would briefly serve as Petty's home in 1986.

While that encounter with Springsteen might have seemed to place Petty on the level of rock 'n' roll royalty and on the cusp of breaking through to the next level, what happened on the way to that "next level" brought Petty to the most notable legal battle of his career, and also delivered one of the best albums he would ever record.

CHAPTER 3

CENTURY CITY'S GOT EVERYTHING COVERED

When speaking to Gary Sperrazza of *Trouser Press* in late 1978, Petty shared his somewhat grandiose initial plans for the Heartbreakers' third album. "The new album will have a very different feel to it, just like the first two differ from one another," Petty said. "I'm going to try and make the third a double album that sells for a dollar more than a single LP. We're going to record it with a mobile unit—not a live album as such, but new songs recorded onstage in a lot of different locations because there are these little places that we really love to play in. And then we're going to incorporate regular studio stuff along with the live stuff. I'd like the third LP to cover the band in every position—in a club, in a concert hall, in a studio—so that people will get a good idea of just what the group is capable of. So far, I think both of our albums only give a limited picture."

None of those plans came to fruition, except for the album showing what the group was capable of—in fact the sessions would be as far from being "live in the studio" as anything the Heartbreakers had yet done. On January 13, 1979, *Billboard* announced that Jimmy Iovine was producing the next Heartbreakers album at Sound City Studios. Brooklyn-born Iovine was something of a music-producing wunderkind, having engineered albums by John Lennon, Harry Nilsson, and Bruce Springsteen, as well as Meat Loaf's *Bat Out of Hell*, by the time he was twenty-five years old. Iovine was recommended to Petty because of his production of Patti Smith's Top 20 hit "Because the Night." Cordell, facing business challenges with Shelter, agreed to step back from the production seat. Petty and Iovine had a meeting to feel each other out. In 2006, Iovine recalled to *Billboard* that first meeting with Petty: "The first two songs he played me were 'Refugee' and 'Here Comes My Girl.' That doesn't happen every day." Iovine was floored, and Petty fed off of his reaction. In a June 3, 1979, profile of Iovine in the *Los Angeles Times*, Iovine praised working with Petty, saying, "Tom really understands the dynamics of rock 'n' roll. His band's great too. I feel like I'm working with the Stones." Petty was equally impressed with Iovine's understanding of what he was looking for with his sound, saying, "Most of the time I'll say this should sound like a Sun record or a Stax single or like the echo in 'Walking in the Rain.' Jimmy always knows exactly what I'm talking about."

The business affairs that had previously preoccupied Cordell came to a head in early 1979. On March 4, ABC Records was acquired by MCA Records, which meant that the Heartbreakers' past and future releases would now be distributed by MCA. However, in the deal Petty's management renegotiated during the making of *You're Gonna Get It*, Petty was given the right to "consult and cooperate in the process of selecting another record company to distribute [Petty's] recordings" if the distribution deal between Shelter and ABC ever ended. Petty wasn't happy that he had no say in the control of his music as a result of the acquisition and believed that he should be considered a free agent by the terms of his contract.

On March 12, Petty's management informed MCA that his contract was non-assignable and that Petty would be looking for a new label. An article in the March 18, 1979, *Los Angeles Times* quoted Petty's co-manager Tony Dimitriades as saying, "We don't consider ourselves affiliated with MCA because there is no provision in our contract for our transfer to MCA. We're not affiliated with any company. We're talking to various people." The English-born Dimitriades, who managed Petty for virtually his entire career, had first become acquainted with Petty when he initially approached Denny Cordell to see if Dwight Twilley had management. Since he already did, Cordell recommended that Dimitriades take on Petty as a client instead.

Petty told his side of the story to Robert Hilburn in the *Los Angeles Times*, explaining, "I've got nothing personally against MCA—except they tried to buy me without asking. When we negotiated the deal with ABC, we put in a clause that they couldn't sell the contract without my consent. I don't think the fact that you've got $35 million means you should be able to buy my business or my music or my life. So I decided to fight to the wall even though it's important to have another record out there now...I just hope I can get out there and participate in it again. The only thing I want from a record company is assurances that they believe in my music and will give it a real shot."

Shortly afterward, Petty was sued by MCA, who accused him of breaching his contract and demanded that he fulfill the obligations set forth in his original Shelter-ABC contract for MCA, now that MCA had purchased ABC Records. He was also sued by Shelter, who alleged that Petty had recorded an album, for which it had given him an advance, that he was now withholding from the label. Petty did record an album—that much was true. But what entity, if any, had the legal right to release that record was another question entirely. In May, the *Los Angeles Times* revealed that reports that Petty had signed a deal with Epic Records were false, in light of the temporary restraining order that MCA had acquired that prevented Petty from signing with any other record company until the courts resolved the matter. Years later, Petty elaborated on the frustration in *Petty: The Biography*: "I was at the Troubadour one night, and a guy walked up to me who, I guess, was fairly high up at Columbia Records and he comes up to me and says, 'Hey, we'll give you a million bucks an album right now if you sign.' At the time, that was a lot of money. I was reeling. I called the office the next day and told them about it, because the guy had given me his card. They said, 'Yeah, we know. We're having a lot of those discussions with people.' So in a way, it was frustrating to me. We had a deal where we got almost nothing...and there's this buzz going on. But it gave me more energy for the fight for something better."

In response to the lawsuits and being required to borrow money from his comanager Elliot Roberts to finance the recording of his album, Petty filed for Chapter 11 bankruptcy, detailing that he was over half a million dollars in debt against $56,845 in assets. The David and Goliath story of Petty declaring bankruptcy in the midst of two lawsuits with record labels is ripe for mythologizing, and it's no surprise that Petty received overly glowing coverage in the media—both at the time and for the rest of his career—for standing up for himself and then releasing his breakthrough album.

Decades later, more details about that period of time in Petty's life came out in *Petty: The Biography* that cast much more light on Petty's bankruptcy filing, portraying it as more of a legal bluff than anything else, a way to pressure Shelter to nullify Petty's contract. As Dimitriades recounted, "If you're insolvent, and there's no likelihood that the terms of your existing contracts will allow you to get out of your insolvency, then the court has the right to readjust all of your contracts and deals, and you can make a fresh start. And *that* is what we were after when we filed for Chapter 11. Obviously, the record companies didn't want to see us win this kind of case—it would mean a precedent would be established that could have far-reaching effects." (The book also referred to the bankruptcy filing and courtroom proceedings as an "elaborate farce," and Petty himself is quoted calling it "a sham in some ways...but I was going to win with it.") Petty and his management team had figured that the entire recording industry didn't want to see Petty's team win the case with a plan that would essentially serve as a "get out" legal maneuver for any artist who wanted to get out of a recording contract, so Cordell settled. Cordell told *Rolling Stone* at the time, "I didn't fancy the way things were going. It was better to settle and get out than let Petty successfully prove bankruptcy." Had Cordell allowed Petty to create a precedent in this fashion, it's likely that the next phase of his career in the music industry would've been over before it even had a chance to start—what label would've wanted to work with the guy responsible for creating a path for artists to get out of their recording contracts?

* * * * *

While the legal issues were going on, the Heartbreakers were finishing recording with Iovine at Sound City Studios. Of all the recording studios that dot the landscape of Los Angeles, none holds a more significant position in the history of the Heartbreakers than Sound City, located among warehouses and industrial buildings in Van Nuys in the San Fernando Valley.

Opened in 1969, Sound City quickly became one of the most-booked studios in the region, despite its dingy appearance, with artists like Neil Young (*After the Gold Rush*), the Grateful Dead (*Terrapin Station*), and Fleetwood Mac (self-titled 1975 album) recording there in its early years, and bands like Nirvana (*Nevermind*), Rage Against the Machine (self-titled), Tool (*Undertow*), the Black Crowes (*Amorica*), Red Hot Chili Peppers (*One Hot Minute*), and Weezer (*Pinkerton*) recording there in the 1990s. Its popularity with major recording artists stemmed in part from its celebrated sound. Founders Tom Skeeter and Joe Gottfried purchased a Neve 8028 Console, one of only four in existence, giving the studio a unique analog sound that could not be achieved elsewhere.

Tom Petty and the Heartbreakers made the studio a frequent home for their recording sessions. As one of the most prolific and successful artists who had recorded there, Petty was interviewed for Nirvana drummer (and one-time temporary Heartbreaker) Dave Grohl's 2013 documentary about the studio, *Sound City*. Petty remembered that Iovine was skeptical of the studio, saying, "When we showed up with Jimmy at Sound City, he was just horrified. Just horrified. Like, 'What is this place?' The first thing he said to me was, 'I don't know if we could make a record in here.' I said, 'I think you'll be surprised.'"

Some recording was also done in Cherokee Studios, a Hollywood recording studio that opened in the early '70s in the former home of MGM Records. Prior to Petty recording there, David Bowie recorded *Station to Station*, and Harry Nilsson recorded *Flash Harry*. The album's liner notes also state "some additional recording" was done at Goodnight LA Studios, another Van Nuys studio where Stevie Nicks recorded tracks for her 1981 solo debut album *Bella Donna*, which Iovine also produced.

The Heartbreakers dug out two old tracks to rerecord for the new album, which would be titled *Damn the Torpedoes*. First was an old Mudcrutch demo that Petty had once offered to Peter Wolf of the J. Geils Band, "Don't Do Me Like That." Another oldie was "Louisiana Rain," which had been recorded during Petty's brief period as a solo artist, and had been recorded by Bonnie Tyler for her 1979 album *Diamond Cut* and released as a single that failed to chart.

The ballad features a reference to an "all-night beanery," perhaps a reference to Barney's Beanery, a bar founded in 1920 whose original location moved from Berkeley to Santa Monica Boulevard (Route 66) in 1927. It got its name for serving cheap food, including beans, a staple during the Great Depression, and that name soon followed its opening in what would later become West Hollywood. A long-time celebrity hangout through the end of the '90s, Barney's is also infamous for a sign that the owner hung up that said "FAGOTS—STAY OUT" (including the misspelling), which, surprisingly, wasn't permanently removed until 1985. By then, the West Hollywood area had long been established as one of the biggest gay communities in the United States. Petty would've undoubtedly been aware of the popular late-night spot during the time that he was writing the song.

Petty released some of the pent-up steam from the ongoing lawsuits by penning a song titled "Century City" after the Los Angeles neighborhood to which he regularly traveled in order to meet with his lawyers. Century City had been built on part of the 20th Century Fox movie backlot in the mid-'60s, which gave the commercial area its name. Fox had sold part of its lot to finance the studio after losses suffered from Elizabeth Taylor's *Cleopatra*, which went so over-budget—in the process becoming the most expensive movie ever made up to that point—that it somehow managed to still run millions of dollars in the red despite also being the highest-grossing movie of 1963.

The up-tempo "Century City" features a singer pleading with his lover to run off with him to the "modern world" of the titular city. Petty remembered in *Conversations*, "It's kind of an acre of skyscrapers, a really modern-looking place. It's full of lawyers. And they take you up to big glass conference rooms. Just *completely a million* miles away from where I was at the time. I dreaded going there." Petty framed the song in the context of a romance, telling the *Los Angeles Times*, "I wouldn't want to write a song that is just about a lawsuit. Kids don't want to go to court or even hear about courts. Besides, my favorite songs are the ones that mean more than one thing. That's what is so good about Bob Dylan songs. You can fit them into a lot of different situations." That reasoning is probably why Petty ended up not releasing a song he later penned titled "Reptiles" ("about what scumsuckers lawyers are," he told *Musician*).

In March, the Universal Amphitheater announced that the Heartbreakers would perform on July 28. Within days, a second show was added for July 29 due to demand, with both concerts selling out. Given that they hadn't played live since the New Year's Eve show in Santa Monica, the Heartbreakers decided to embark on a short California tour leading up to those dates, which was dubbed the Lawsuit Tour. This moniker appeared on the concert t-shirts sold at the shows. The Lawsuit Tour ending at the Universal Amphitheater was particularly appropriate because at the time the venue was owned by MCA. In fact, at one point, MCA attempted to block Petty from performing those two shows, as well as the rest of the tour, because of the ongoing legal action against him. In June 1981, Petty told *Melody Maker*, "The other side were saying, 'unless he can stand here in court and show us some security for him being allowed to make this much money, he can't go.' And the judge says, well what have you got to say? An' I said there is no security in rock 'n' roll, and the whole courtroom just burst into laughter and the judge laughed and he said you can go on the road." After that, MCA relented.

Petty explained to the *Los Angeles Times* that the short tour came about because he was told, "'You can't just do two shows. You've got to have some break-in dates.' So I said we'll book a tour. Then they said you can't tour without a new album. How would we promote it? But I knew the kids would be waiting. Besides, we could promote the lawsuit. That's when we decided to call it the lawsuit tour. We'll tell the kids what's going on and why we haven't been around." To make the message behind the tour even more apparent, the Heartbreakers covered Bobby Fuller's "I Fought the Law" during the shows. The brief Lawsuit Tour clearly developed a deeper connection between Petty and his audience, and the press could see that, with the *Hollywood Reporter* declaring in its review of the shows, "Tom Petty appears to be on a collision course with major rock stardom."

In early October, Petty agreed to an arrangement to remain with MCA under its new subsidiary label Backstreet Records after settling out of court with Shelter. The label would be run by Danny Bramson, the executive vice president of the Universal Amphitheater. ABC's J.J. Cale also joined the new label. Bramson agreed to all of Petty's management's terms, including hiring Jon Scott, who had broken "Breakdown," and a new record contract worth a reported $3 million. The release of *Damn the Torpedoes* was rushed for October 19, with the Heartbreakers' national tour to begin after a performance on *Saturday Night Live* on November 10.

Years later, Petty reflected on the 1976 deal he had signed with Cordell that eventually led him into court and declaring bankruptcy. He chalked it up to youthful ignorance, but was able to see the positives that came from his early experiences in the music industry. He explained to *Billboard* in 2005, "We didn't think it was bad, because we all got new amplifiers and we had a house with a pool and somebody paying the bills. It wasn't a bad deal until we started to sell a lot of records. So it was really kind of the price of an education. You know, some days it really pisses me off, but it's probably fair in the long run.

Because [Cordell] really did save our lives in a lot of respects. Had we made a record the minute we hit town, it probably would have come and gone, and we would have been back playing clubs in Gainesville."

Not surprisingly, Hilburn continued to support Petty by giving *Damn the Torpedoes* extremely high praise, calling it "the most passionate American rock album since Bruce Springsteen's *Darkness on the Edge of Town*," and saying, "The scorching rock collection is being received so well by radio stations that it was added to more playlists in its first week than even the Led Zeppelin album [*In Through the Out Door*]." He also called the album "music with vitality and purpose."

Sales of the album reflected the critical praise. *Damn the Torpedoes* peaked at #2 on the Billboard 200 in early February, and by the end of February 1980 it was certified platinum by the RIAA (*Damn the Torpedoes* would eventually be certified triple-platinum in 2015). The first single, "Don't Do Me Like That," became the Heartbreakers' first Top 10 single, peaking at #10. *Damn the Torpedoes* produced another Top 20 single when "Refugee" peaked at #15. "Here Comes My Girl" was also a hit, peaking at #59.

Of course, as with many artists who shift from obscurity to the top of the charts, the Heartbreakers received some cold shoulders as a result of their success. Petty didn't understand it, and remarked in *Petty: The Biography*, "I remember one of the most heartbreaking things was going to the Whisky right after *Damn the Torpedoes* had come out. Everybody treated us different, almost like we were sellouts or something. There was that vibe. We had a hit. A hit. It was as if they were couching it as this integrity versus popularity thing. But I wanted to have hits. That was the point. Jerry Lee Lewis had hits. I didn't want to not get the music out there."

The Damn the Torpedoes Tour made its way across the United States to the Los Angeles area for a January 20, 1980, concert at the Forum (a planned concert the night before at the University of California, Santa Barbara, was postponed until January 27 because Petty had a sore throat). The 17,500-capacity Forum, which opened as a state-of-the-art facility in 1967 in Inglewood, has been one of the premiere entertainment venues in the Los Angeles area, having hosted both the Los Angeles Lakers and the Los Angeles Kings from its opening until 1999 (the arena was built by businessman Jack Kent Cooke, who owned both teams). In the '60s and '70s, it became the premiere rock arena for major acts in Los Angeles, including artists such as Elvis Presley, the Rolling Stones, Led Zeppelin, Cream, Deep Purple, the Eagles, and Bob Dylan (whose live album *Before the Flood* was mostly recorded there).

Hilburn's review of the show in the *Los Angeles Times*—in the column where he had once predicted that the Heartbreakers would headline the Forum—was, as per usual when it came to his words on the Heartbreakers, ecstatic. Referencing Super Bowl XIV, held earlier that day just about twenty miles north at the Rose Bowl in Pasadena—in which the Los Angeles Rams lost to the Pittsburgh Steelers—Hilburn wrote, "From the enthusiasm in the arena, you'd have thought that the Rams had *won* the Super Bowl. Petty's a vital enough figure in rock to deserve the cheers wherever he plays, but the Forum show was special." Hilburn labeled Petty, "the most important rock attraction to emerge from Los Angeles in years." Though he wrote more about Petty than about the concert, what Hilburn did write about the performance was all glowing.

In *Sounds*, Sylvie Simmons also noted the festive atmosphere of the concert, writing, "The sound is pretty bad in this big barn of a place, but the music is loud and penetrating, and, what the hell, this is no mere gig, it's a celebration. The prodigal son has returned to MCA; the hometown (adopted) boy has come home, and there's the cover of *Rolling Stone*, blurbs in *The Times*, coveted club dates and top bill at the Forum, the trappings of Big In The USA. Sure beats lawsuits."

The following night, the Heartbreakers played a surprise show at the Whisky a Go Go. After the show, reflecting on how far the Heartbreakers had come since their first appearances at the Whisky, Petty said to *Melody Maker*, "My life has changed in the three years since we first played the Whisky, when we opened for Blondie. It seems like an eternity ago. I was watching the news recently and they were talking to these kids who waited hours to get in, and most of them said, 'Wow,

Tom Petty and the Heartbreakers have got so big in such a short time.' I guess to them it was a short time, but to me it's been ages. The lawsuit alone seemed like ten years."

The Heartbreakers then wrapped up the first US leg of the tour with a sold-out make-up date at the University of Santa Barbara in the Robertson Gymnasium. Afterwards, Petty went to a specialist to investigate his throat issues and was diagnosed with tonsillitis. In fact, in the one thousandth issue of *Rolling Stone*, Petty remembered seeing the first-ever *Rolling Stone* cover he appeared on, which was the issue dated February 21, 1980. He said, "I was convalescing at a Santa Monica hospital after having my tonsils removed. A visitor came in and threw it on the bed. I felt I had arrived." Appropriately enough, the cover story opened with an account of Petty first noticing his vocal issues during the Heartbreakers' November 13 concert in Philadelphia.

After tour legs in England in March and Japan and Australia in April and May, the Heartbreakers returned to Los Angeles to work on Del Shannon's *Drop Down and Get Me*, with Petty producing. Before embarking on the second US leg of the Damn the Torpedoes Tour, the Heartbreakers appeared on the June 6, 1980, episode of *Fridays*, the ABC-TV live Los Angeles-based sketch comedy show patterned after the New York-based *Saturday Night Live*. Curiously, the Heartbreakers played an album track from *Damn the Torpedoes*, "Shadow of a Doubt (A Complex Kid)," instead of one of the singles. The second song they played was "American Girl." After the tour wrapped on July 18 in Florida, the Heartbreakers returned to Los Angeles to finish work on Shannon's album and begin production on the next Heartbreakers album, which the *Los Angeles Times* revealed was under the working title of *Benmont Tench's Revenge*.

With the success of *Damn the Torpedoes*, Petty admitted that he had to ignore the pressure to deliver another strong album or simply try to copy the sound of the previous album. He told the *New York Times* in May 1981, "I had to constantly talk myself out of wondering whether people would accept this or that and so did our producer, Jimmy Iovine. But we weren't interested in making *Torpedoes Two*."

During the production of the Heartbreakers' fourth album at Sound City and Cherokee Studios in late 1980, the band received word that John Lennon had been shot and killed in New York City. In *Conversations*, Petty recalled the moment when he found out. "I was in Cherokee Studios...And Ringo was working next door that week. The talk right around that time was John was coming to sing on Ringo's album. So we were kind of jazzed up, thinking that we'd get to meet John. A call came. It seemed like the early evening. A call came and said John had been shot. We just thought it was nonsense. And then a call came right back in about fifteen minutes that said that John's dead. So we stopped work." As a tribute to Lennon, the original pressing of the album has "WE LOVE YOU J.L." etched in the runout.

During recording, Fleetwood Mac singer Stevie Nicks, who was then in a relationship with Iovine, contributed vocals to two songs, "Insider" and "You Can Still Change Your Mind." In *Petty: The Biography*, Nicks explained that Iovine was concerned about introducing them because he thought Petty would be annoyed that Iovine had started work on Nicks's first solo album before finishing work on his album (which would be titled *Hard Promises*, taken from a lyric in the song "Insider"). She recalled, "Jimmy didn't even want to mention me to Tom because he thought Tom would think, 'Oh great, now you're all involved with Stevie Nicks, which means you're not going to be focused on this new record we're doing, which is *not done yet!* And Jimmy was right, knowing Tom, that *is* what he would think. So Jimmy had this house in Sherman Oaks, and I was pretty much living there, but whenever Tom would come over, just to hang with Jimmy and talk about where they were at and what they wanted to do next, I would hide in the bedroom downstairs."

During the production of both albums, Iovine asked Petty if he would write a song for Nicks's album, *Bella Donna*. Petty ended up giving Nicks a finished song he cowrote with Campbell, "Stop Draggin' My Heart Around," that wasn't going to be used on *Hard Promises*. Nicks and two female backup singers overdubbed most of the vocals, and "Stop Draggin' My Heart Around" became a Nicks/Petty duet. Jane

Petty also inspired another hit on Nicks's album, "Edge of Seventeen," when Nicks misunderstood Jane saying that she first met Petty "at the age of seventeen" and thought that the misheard phrase would make an excellent song title. Petty, Campbell, Tench, and Lynch also played on other songs on *Bella Donna*.

The Heartbreakers filmed four performance-based music videos for the album, plus a video for "Stop Draggin' My Heart Around," in two days in March 1981, in Los Angeles. All were directed by Jim Lenahan, a one-time Mudcrutch member who was responsible for the lighting design of the Heartbreakers tours. The four album videos were for "The Waiting," which features the Heartbreakers performing on a paint-splattered stage (and Tench and Lynch memorably switching instruments in the final moments); "A Woman in Love (But It's Not Me)," shot in black-and-white with slow-motion and spotlight effects; "Insider," shot in a studio setting with Petty and Stevie Nicks singing a duet, which was virtually repeated for the "Stop Draggin' My Heart Around" video; and "Letting You Go," which Petty later called "hard to watch" in an interview with Lisa Robinson. The video features the Heartbreakers performing the song on what looks like a variety show stage as several cameramen get intrusive with the cameras (Tench in particular appears to be annoyed about how close the cameras get to him and kicks one away). At the end of the video, the cameras appear to dance to the song. Petty continued, "It was a little out of character for us, you know, we did get a few laughs out of it, but that's why the cameras are dancing and everything, because we said, 'ah, you know, let's make it funny if we have to do this.' We're really just musicians. We're not even personalities you know or anything other than we see ourselves as anything but just musicians so it's really hard for us to be like actors or whatever that is when you lip-sync songs."

While the *Hard Promises* videos show little evidence that the Heartbreakers would create celebrated, award-winning videos later in their career, the video for "A Woman in Love (But It's Not Me)" showed the most promise. In a 2013 interview with the website Video-static.com, Lenahan recalled the experience shooting that video with cinematographer Daniel Pearl (who was the cinematographer of the original *Texas Chain Saw Massacre* and would go on to shoot award-winning music videos for the Police, Guns N' Roses, U2, and Meat Loaf), and storyboarding the video at Pearl's house while *Texas Chain Saw Massacre* director Tobe Hooper was present. Lenahan explained, "I was describing what we were going to do to Hooper, and he goes, 'Ah, sounds like film noir. Why are you doing that like film noir?' I didn't know what film noir was. And I said, 'Well, the song, as you listen to the music, is real dynamic and parts of it are very down, very quiet and other parts of it are very up. The chords are very up and bright and loud and all the verses are way down, real quiet.' And so that's what I said, this black and white in the shades of gray, and that's the way we're going to shoot it." That artistic quality seems prescient in hindsight, considering the video was shot just months before the launch of MTV, a network that in a few short years would make Petty an even bigger star.

* * * * *

After resolving their issues over his contract, Petty and MCA butted heads over a different issue with *Hard Promises*, something that Petty was continually asked about in nearly every interview for the rest of his career: the sticker price of the upcoming album.

MCA had recently started listing certain albums with "superstar pricing" at $9.98, which was a dollar more than the standard retail price of a new album at the time. Previously, Steely Dan objected to MCA using the higher price on their album *Gaucho*, released in November 1980, but eventually gave up the fight. After the success of *Damn the Torpedoes*, MCA also wanted to charge $9.98 for *Hard Promises*. The *Los Angeles Times* reported that Petty threatened "to delay finishing the album for as long as a year before giving into a dollar price hike." The *Times* also reported that influential DJs at rock stations across the country backed Petty, threatening to boycott MCA artists if the Petty album was released at $9.98. On March 8, the *Los Angeles Times* reported that MCA agreed to keep the album at $8.98 after Petty even threatened to name the album *$8.98*.

Other outlets jumped on the story, supporting Petty as the ultimate man of the people in rock 'n' roll. *Rolling Stone* put a photo of Petty tearing a dollar in half on the cover of its March 19 issue. In *Conversations with Tom Petty*, he revealed that he heard from other artists that the bad publicity that MCA got kept record prices down across the board. "Mick Jagger told me, at the time, that it held down the price of their record. They were going to do it to them, and then I came out on the cover of the *Rolling Stone* tearing a dollar in half. And he said they actually threw that down on the table in a meeting. And they said, 'No way we can do it. No way we can bring the price up.'"

Though less taxing than the legal battle Petty fought the previous year, Petty expressed to *Billboard* in 2005 that it affected him in other ways as an artist. He said, "I didn't worry about my career ending, but there were days where I felt pretty beat up by it all and just pretty tired, because they didn't make it easy for me. And coming right off the last lawsuit, it was the last thing I wanted to get involved in. When it was over, we didn't really celebrate, we were just exhausted. I lost all interest in the record business and never wanted to do anything except hand in a record again. To this day, I don't have any interest in it."

In all, 1.5 million copies of *Hard Promises* were shipped to stores for the album's May 5 release. The album was listed as the Spotlight album in the *Billboard* "Top Album Picks" page on May 16, 1981, which said, "This LP bristles with passion, something that the competition never manages to convey with the exception of a few artists. This is what rock 'n' roll should be—convincing, emotion laden vocals, blazing instrumentals, melody and above all a true sense and command of the rock language." The *Los Angeles Times* called it "better crafted and ultimately more satisfying than *Damn the Torpedoes*. Petty asked for the audience's trust in his first two albums, won it with his third, and demonstrates here that he still deserves it."

The first single from the album, "The Waiting," peaked at #19 on the Billboard Hot 100 in June 1981, but the second single "A Woman in Love (It's Not Me)," was less successful and peaked at #79 in August 1981. Petty felt both singles would've done much better if he hadn't been competing with himself. His duet with Nicks, "Stop Draggin' My Heart Around," was released in July and peaked at #3 in September 1981, which was Petty's highest-charting single in his entire career. However, despite Petty's affection for Iovine and Nicks, the fact that "Stop Draggin' My Heart Around" was released as a single by Nicks's label in July while the two *Hard Promises* singles were on the charts bothered him. Brian Hart, who worked as an assistant engineer at Sound City during the time Petty recorded there in the early '80s and had worked on "Stop Draggin' My Heart Around," told the *Los Angeles Times* in 2017, "I was still working with Petty during this period, and I can say this: Tom, who had yet to notch a top five single at that point in his career, was not happy that Stevie was getting all the credit for the song." During the shooting of the *Hard Promises* music videos, the Heartbreakers and Nicks recorded a video for "Stop Draggin' My Heart Around," which consisted of the Heartbreakers and Nicks performing the song in studio, although it had mainly been recorded by Iovine dubbing Nicks on an unused Heartbreakers track. It also featured Ron Blair on bass even though Donald "Duck" Dunn played on the recording.

Hard Promises peaked at #5 on the album chart in July and was certified platinum in August. The album was a success, but not as successful as *Damn the Torpedoes*.

The start of the Hard Promises Tour was delayed for two weeks when Petty injured himself in pre-tour workouts, but the Forum dates scheduled for June 28 and 30 were not affected. In a profile of the tour by Robert Hilburn that appeared in the *Los Angeles Times*, Petty said, "Sometimes I feel like I'm just stepping back on the same carousel when I go on the road. You jump up grab a horse and go round and round. By the time we stopped touring last year, we had been out for nine months and we were all a little nuts. We needed to get away from it for a while."

The tour made its way to Los Angeles in late June. First Petty appeared on *Rockline*, a new syndicated interview show hosted by veteran Los Angeles KMET disc jockey B. Mitchel Reed from Sunset

Sound Recorders. Sunset Sound, where the Heartbreakers would later record, was established on Sunset Boulevard in Hollywood in the late '50s by Salvador "Tutti" Camarata, a musician and record executive who founded the studio after he was hired by Walt Disney to be the head of the company's new record label, Disneyland Records. Camarata established Sunset Studio independently of the Walt Disney Company (according to the Sunset Sound website, when Camarata proposed the idea of opening a Disney-owned recording studio to Walt Disney, the legendary entrepreneur remarked, "Why would I want to own a studio? I'd rather be a client"), and left Disney to run the studio full-time in 1960. Nonetheless, true to Walt Disney's word, the company ended up becoming a significant client for Sunset Sound, and the soundtracks of several iconic Disney films like *Mary Poppins* and *101 Dalmatians* were recorded there. Of course, Sunset Sound didn't just record Disney's family-friendly fare. Several of the most iconic albums of the '60s and '70s, including the Beach Boys' *Pet Sounds*, the Rolling Stones' *Beggars Banquet* and *Exile on Main St.*, Led Zeppelin's *Led Zeppelin II* and untitled fourth album, and Van Halen's self-titled debut album, were recorded in part or mixed at the studio.

Petty's *Rockline* interview took place on June 22, with the Heartbreakers returning to the road for concerts in Las Vegas (June 24), Reno (June 25), and Daly City (June 26). The Heartbreakers then played three dates at the Forum on June 28, 29 and 30, with the band introduced by none other than Lakers legend Kareem Abdul-Jabbar, who, in addition to playing for the Lakers in the Forum, copromoted concerts at the venue. The Heartbreakers were also joined by Stevie Nicks on "Insider" and for a cover of the Searchers' "Needles and Pins." Unfortunately, Petty himself marred the first concert when he invited fans to come too close to the stage, which resulted in a twenty-minute delay after hundreds of fans rushed the stage. The *Los Angeles Times* reported, "First the bouquets came bouncing on stage—then came the girls. By the end of the evening, a half-dozen young rockettes had vaulted onto the stage, all eager to give Petty bearhugs." *Billboard* explained, "As the onrush poured out into the aisles, blocking them, the fire marshal cut the lights, took over the p.a. system, warning all that they return immediately to their seats. Petty then got back on mike and apologized, saying he never anticipated such a stampede." In 2010, Petty told *USA Today*, "The fire marshals were very upset at how out of control the crowd was and wanted to cancel the next two nights. We really had to do a song and dance for the fire department."

Nonetheless, Robert Hilburn's review of the first show in the *Los Angeles Times* was extremely positive, saying, "Petty and the Heartbreakers played with such boldness and flair that they seemed to be expanding artistically before your eyes—already injecting striking new tones in songs," while praising Petty for his cool-headed handling of the security issue of the fans rushing the stage. The review of the same concert in *Billboard*, however, was negative, saying the performance "lacked the kind of emotional intensity that separates great shows from the routine. Petty lacked that intangible element that makes a performer rise above his peers. Unlike Springsteen, who gives his all for hours, Petty seemed to go merely through the motions for 90 minutes. Listening to his catalog at home would have sufficed." A letter-writer to the *Los Angeles Times* expressed similar feelings to *Billboard*'s take, calling it "one of the most lackluster, unenergetic performances I have ever seen. To put it bluntly, he was boring." Nevertheless, the concerts were extremely successful. According to *Billboard*, the three Forum concerts drew a combined 46,810 and grossed $564,390. "Needles and Pins" and "Insider" on the Heartbreakers' 1985 live album *Pack Up the Plantation: Live!* and several tracks on the 2009 live compilation *The Live Anthology* were recorded at these concerts.

In August, the *Los Angeles Times* announced that the Heartbreakers would be one of the first bands to perform at the brand-new Irvine Meadows Amphitheater, with two concerts on September 18 and 19. The sixteen-thousand-capacity outdoor venue was a popular stop for concert tours coming through Orange County before it closed in 2016 and was demolished to build apartment buildings. Both Petty shows were sellouts. The Heartbreakers were joined by Nicks at both concerts to perform "Insider" and "Stop Draggin' My Heart Around."

During the Hard Promises Tour, a major development in the music industry occurred: the launch of MTV. The Heartbreakers were part of the MTV revolution almost from the very beginning—the video for "Stop Draggin' My Heart Around" was the twenty-fifth video played on the channel when it launched on August 1, and it aired four times that day. Needing more content for its rotation, the network soon added the music videos the Heartbreakers shot for the *Hard Promises* album and two performance videos that the band shot for *Damn the Torpedoes*—"Refugee" and "Here Comes My Girl," which, according to Petty in the book *I Want My MTV: The Uncensored Story of the Music Video Revolution*, the band had recorded so they wouldn't have to appear on the *Merv Griffin Show*, not expecting that the recordings would ever be aired again. The fact that these old recordings were now shown multiple times a day inspired Petty to think of music videos more in the sense of a permanent artistic statement.

After the Hard Promises Tour wrapped with a homecoming performance in Gainesville on October 8, Tench joined Stevie Nicks for her tour supporting *Bella Donna*. On December 10, Petty made a guest appearance on stage at the Reseda Country Club for a few songs during Del Shannon's performance (Petty was spotted at the Reseda Country Club again in February 1982 in the crowd for a James Brown concert and in June 1982 for an Emmylou Harris concert). The Reseda Country Club was one of the most celebrated rock clubs in Los Angeles history, from its opening in 1979, with its name coming from its original intention of being a country-music club, until it became a church in 1999. Shortly before it became a church, the Country Club was prominently featured in Paul Thomas Anderson's 1997 film *Boogie Nights* as the Hot Traxx Disco. Shannon's *Drop Down and Get Me* was released at the end of the year, and Petty earned praise in the *Los Angeles Times* review of the album for his production: "Producer Tom Petty and his band, the Heartbreakers, stay in the background, but their touches add fire to what could be an overly lush record."

Meanwhile, the Heartbreakers had their first personnel change when Ron Blair left the group after the tour. Blair explained in *Petty:*

The Biography, "I don't know if every band goes through it but things had gotten tension filled. I remember early on, at something like our second gig, our road manager telling me never to wear my Levi's shirt, like we shouldn't appear to be southern. Wearing cowboy shirts with snaps or growing beards: these were a no-no. Later on, we were back in L.A. in the studio, and, hey, I was growing a beard! It wasn't what we were supposed to be doing. Was I trying to be the sticky wheel? I don't know what it was I was doing. Maybe I was trying to distance myself. It was just an odd period for the band. And I wasn't digging it." Blair ended up leaving the music business for several years, explaining to *Rolling Stone* in 2014 what he did in the meantime: "My wife's family manufactured swimwear, and they had this great little store in Hermosa Beach. I was real sick of the music business, just jaded. So we ran a store, and I realized you can get jaded in any business. Even people at this little store could have monstrous egos. Every situation has its ups and downs."

CHAPTER 4

"I WAS AMAZED AT
JUST HOW BAD MTV WAS."

To replace Blair, Petty recruited Howie Epstein, who he met while producing Shannon's album. Though Epstein had spent much of his early career as a guitarist, he had played bass with John Hiatt before joining Shannon's backing band. What most impressed Petty about Epstein in the *Drop Down and Get Me* sessions were his high harmony vocals, which Petty thought could add depth to the Heartbreakers, especially live.

Work on the follow-up to *Hard Promises* began at the end of 1981, with Iovine again at the helm. The album was primarily recorded at the Record Plant in Los Angeles, a popular recording studio known for its relaxed atmosphere, where Fleetwood Mac had recently recorded *Mirage* and where the Eagles had recorded *On the Border* and much of *Hotel California*. One of the songs on the album, the Petty/Campbell composition "Between Two Worlds" was recorded at RCA Studios on Sunset Boulevard. In *Conversations*, Petty pointed out, likely with a measure of pride, "That was where [the Stones] cut 'Satisfaction.'"

Additional recording was done at Wally Heider Recording and Crystal Studios, both in Hollywood.

Overdubs for the album were recorded at Rumbo Studios in Canoga Park, which was owned by Daryl Dragon of Captain & Tennille. In 1990, Dragon spoke about the studio to the *Orlando Sentinel*, saying, "Because it was way out in the West (San Fernando) Valley, it was considered a vacation area back in the late '70s. I didn't like the direction Hollywood was going. I was scared to go out in the parking lot (at some studios there) late at night. The bands needed a place to record where there weren't a lot of groupies around. Rumbo is a nice, loose place with not a lot of pressure."

In April, Petty appeared as a guest lecturer at UCLA to speak about the music business. He spoke about the new album he was recording, and said if he didn't get it right, "I'll just go back to Florida." It was an idea that Petty flirted with for recording his next album, but he ended up never leaving Southern California on a permanent basis.

Prior to the release of the album, the band kept busy in Los Angeles over the summer of 1982. On June 6, 1982, Petty appeared at the Rose Bowl for the Peace Sunday concert, organized by Graham Nash and various activists and religious leaders to promote world peace. The Rose Bowl, one of the most hallowed stadiums in all of American sports, opened in 1922, and is best known for the annual Rose Bowl Game, the oldest bowl game in college football, held annually on New Year's Day. At the time of the concert, the stadium could seat over one hundred thousand people. Prior to Peace Sunday, few bands had ever performed at the Rose Bowl, perhaps due to its immense size. In August 1965, Los Angeles radio station KFWB (founded by Sam Warner, one of the Warner Bros.), which at the time was facing stiff competition in the pop music market, held a concert at the Rose Bowl headlined by Herman's Hermits and featuring the Turtles, the Lovin' Spoonful, and the Bobby Fuller Four, that charged just one dollar per ticket and drew 38,000 people. Another concert occurred in September 1968 featuring nine acts, including Joan Baez (who also performed at Peace Sunday), the Byrds, Big Brother and the Holding Company, and the Mothers of

Invention. Peace Sunday organizers claimed the benefit was attended by just under eighty thousand and raised about $400,000 for nuclear disarmament groups. However *Billboard* reported that the concert had a sellout crowd of 66,224 attendees.

Peace Sunday also featured Bob Dylan, Stevie Wonder, and Crosby, Stills & Nash (who had recently reunited to record the *Daylight Again* album), among others. Petty appeared unadvertised as part of a trio with Jackson Browne and Gary U.S. Bonds, who performed two Buddy Holly songs, "Well…All Right" and "Not Fade Away." The review of the concert in the *Los Angeles Times* said, "By the time that trio had swung into Buddy Holly's 'Not Fade Away' shortly before 11 p.m., hundreds of fans were bouncing up and down on the field with such vigor that it looked from high in the stands that they were on a trampoline."

In July, it was announced that the Heartbreakers would perform at the US Festival that would be held Labor Day weekend at Glen Helen Regional Park in San Bernardino. Other acts announced included Fleetwood Mac, the Police, Pat Benatar, and Talking Heads. The concert was financed by Apple, Inc. co-founder Steve Wozniak, and would also feature exhibits that demonstrated new technology. The US Festival was promoted by iconic concert promoter Bill Graham, who launched shows at San Francisco's Filmore, which later became the venue the Heartbreakers performed at more than any other venue. The festival production team was required to make numerous improvements to the grounds in order to host the festival, including building a temporary off-ramp from the highway and a stage for the performers. The festival boasted that it would have the largest sound system ever built for a concert.

Wozniak had come up with the idea after almost losing his life in a plane crash, telling the *San Bernardino County Sun*, "I heard a few great songs in a row on the radio, and I just got to thinking that it's about time someone did a big festival and got lots of groups together. I know it was ludicrous to think of me doing it. But I met some people who could actually pull off the logistics of the thing. My motivation was fearless. I decided to go for it. The time was right." Regarding the technology demonstrations, Wozniak added, "There's no way to make a computer fair splendid for a quarter million people. Most people will be coming for the music." In fact, the dual concept ended up causing some confusion about the festival. One of the organizers, Peter Ellis, told the paper that the idea behind the festival was to celebrate "the role technology is going to play in the eighties. It's that simple. I can say it in about a sentence. But boy, I'm sure having a hard time communicating it with people."

Reportedly, the festival cost $12.5 million. The Heartbreakers headlined the second day, September 4. The festival was considered a success by Wozniak and the production team, although it lost money and there were numerous medical problems having to do with the hundred-plus degree weather. There were also numerous drug overdoses. When asked about the festival two years later by *CREEM*, Petty responded, "For that much money I'll play anywhere! I'd be a fool not to do it. But I wouldn't want to do it every day. I like having some hint of intimacy."

Later that month, Petty and Tench appeared onstage during a Plimsouls concert at the Whisky a Go Go, marking what was the final night of the Whisky for several years (it would reopen in 1986, with much of the interior removed). Petty and Tench performed "Route 66," Sir Douglas Quintet's "She's About a Mover," and Gary U.S. Bonds's "New Orleans."

Long After Dark was released on November 2. The original release date was later in the month, but the retail date was moved forward after Los Angeles radio station KIQQ-FM announced it would begin airing songs from the album on November 2. Robert Hilburn gave the album a positive review in the *Los Angeles Times*, praising the lyrics in particular. He wrote, "Though most of the collection's lively, engaging songs deal with the search for romance, it's more rewarding to view the lyrics as statements about maintaining integrity in the pursuit of your dreams, whether they involve career or relationships."

Long After Dark peaked at #9 on the Billboard 200 in January 1983, and was certified gold by the RIAA that same month. The first single,

"You Got Lucky," peaked at #20 on the Billboard Hot 100 in January. A second single, "Straight into Darkness," failed to chart. The third single, "Change of Heart," peaked at #21.

"You Got Lucky" also marked the Heartbreakers' first music video following the creation of MTV, and was their first attempt at narrative in the burgeoning form. It features a minute-long intro in which the Heartbreakers arrive in futuristic vehicles to a large tent in a desert wasteland like something out of the 1979 Australian dystopian movie *Mad Max*, which Petty later stated had inspired the video. The tent is a kind of storage space for technology from the '80s, including televisions and arcade games. The video was shot at the Vasquez Rocks in Santa Clarita, a landscape formation on the US National Register of Historic Places commonly used as a location in film and television productions including classics like *Dracula* (1931), *The Ten Commandments* (1956), the original *Star Trek* television series, and *Blazing Saddles* (1978).

"By the time we got to 'You Got Lucky,' we were well ahead of the game, because we'd done a lot of videos," Petty explained in *Conversations*. "And 'You Got Lucky' was really a groundbreaking video. It really changed everything. No one had ever—even Michael Jackson—done a prelude to the video. A bit of business before the song started.... And we never lip-sync or anything in that video. That was the idea. We were sick of lip-synching. And we were going to make a film and not sing in it. But, boy, did it explode. It really did change the way the videos went. There were a lot of imitations after that. A lot of bands out in the desert.... And talk about famous. [Laughs] That's when everybody knew who you were. Like, you know, grandmas knew who you were. 'Cause you're on TV all day long, you know? [Laughs]... MTV was this incredible promotional device. It was really great for promoting your songs. It was really exciting. There was this whole new thing happening, and we were right in the front of it.... And we made really good videos. We tried to be inventive there, too. It was a lot of fun. I always liked films, and I liked being on the set." Regarding the minute-long intro, Petty later claimed in an interview for *I Want My MTV*, "Michael Jackson called us, saying what an incredible idea that was." Of course, Jackson would go on to create some of the most creative music videos in MTV's history, and parts of his 1993 music video for "Black or White" were also shot at the Vasquez Rocks.

Petty explained to the *Desert Sun* in 2009 that, at that time, it was easy to make a music video that stood out. "It wasn't hard to make something better than everyone else....I was amazed at just how bad MTV was....Terrible videos and terrible songs, and most people made them almost all the same....I thought let's just get out of the box here and do something different."

The Long After Dark Tour rehearsals took place at Universal Studios' soundstage four. The tour started in Europe, with the US leg starting on January 22, 1983, in Phoenix, Arizona. When the Heartbreakers finally came to Los Angeles for three nights at the Universal Amphitheatre that would end the tour, the band ran into numerous issues. The first concert was supposed to be on April 17 but was pushed back to April 19 because Petty was having vocal issues. Nick Lowe was scheduled to open the show, but an injury to one of Lowe's band members forced him to cancel (the Plimsouls filled in at the last minute). It was the band's first performance in the venue after a two-year renovation, which included adding a roof and a thousand additional seats.

During that concert, technical issues required the Heartbreakers to leave the stage for a few minutes. Nonetheless, Robert Hilburn's review in the *Los Angeles Times* was full of praise. He wrote, "Tuesday's fast-paced show was, on balance, the most uplifting local appearance yet by the man whose earlier concerts had already ranked him, along with Bruce Springsteen and Bob Seger, as one of the most rewarding post-'60s figures in mainstream American rock." The Heartbreakers performed at Universal Amphitheatre on April 21 and 25, with a concert at San Diego's Jack Murphy Stadium sandwiched in between those two shows on April 23.

Attending one of the concerts was Ron Blair. In *Petty: The Biography*, he said, "I remember sitting there at the Universal Amphitheatre... must have been a year or two later. I'm watching the band play, sitting next to Jimmy Iovine. And Jimmy's going, 'Ron, what's it like, man?'

To me, his question felt like, 'What's it like, you being a loser now?' I just wanted to hit him. Maybe it's what I was hearing more than what he was saying. I was like, 'Jimmy, it's fine. These guys were my friends. These guys will still be my friends. Just let me enjoy the fucking show.'"

The April 25 tour finale featured the Heartbreakers playing two special songs—first, the Byrds' "Ballad of Easy Rider," which was announced as a salute to the road crew, and then the Valentinos' "It's All Over Now." The *Los Angeles Times* reported that "If the show didn't set a house attendance record, it certainly earned one for the most bouquets of roses ever thrown on stage in one night. In a scene that looked like something out of an old Beatles film, Petty braved wave after wave of maddened teen-age girls, who eluded security guards and charged the stage, throwing their arms around Petty's neck like drowning swimmers grabbing a life preserver."

Though the Long After Dark Tour was over, the Heartbreakers scheduled a handful of California dates surrounding the band's head-lining performances at the two-day Mountain Aire Festival in Angels Camp, California, located east of San Francisco. On May 6, the *Los Angeles Times* announced that the Heartbreakers would play June 10 at the Irvine Meadows Amphitheatre. On May 14, the *Times* announced that a second date was added for June 11. The *Los Angeles Times* reported that at the second Irvine show, the Heartbreakers performed covers of "Little Bit O' Soul" and Gram Parsons's "I Can't Dance," but called Petty's performance "less than inspiring.... Petty's performance didn't become genuinely impassioned until the final half hour.... Had Petty exhibited the emotion throughout the show that he did in the final portion, he could have closed his tour with a thoroughly triumphant night, rather than one that was memorable only in part." The June 11 concert was recorded, and the performance of "Rockin' Around (With You)" was included on the Heartbreakers' 1985 live album *Pack Up the Plantation: Live!*, while the 2009 live compilation *The Live Anthology* featured "Refugee," "Surrender," and the Dave Clark Five cover "Any Way You Want It" from the same concert.

Almost immediately after this short tour ended, Tench went back on the road again as part of Stevie Nicks's band on her tour to support her second solo album, *The Wild Heart*. The album includes another duet between Nicks and Petty, "I Will Run to You," which featured the Heartbreakers backing them. Tench also played on two other tracks on the album. Lynch went on a short tour with guitarist and producer extraordinaire T-Bone Burnett (Lynch had previously played drums on Burnett's 1983 album *Proof Through the Night*). In the meantime, Petty began building a studio in his home in Encino to record the next Heartbreakers album. He told the *New York Times* in 1985, "After that last tour, I just wanted to push the chair away from the table for a while. It had been recording, then touring, more recording, more touring, for something like seven years, and I just felt *burnt*. So there was a year when I wrote some songs but mostly just hung around, while the guys in the band were busy doing other things. Then I took another four months or so to build a studio in my house. It's always taken us a long time to make records, and sometimes it's hard to let your mind flow freely when you know it's costing $200 an hour, and you have to leave at midnight because somebody else has the studio booked." While building a home studio to record the next Heartbreakers' album might have been a good idea in theory, it ended up causing significant turmoil in both Petty's professional and personal lives.

After three albums with Jimmy Iovine as coproducer, Petty decided to move in another direction with his next album. The shift in Petty's thinking came after he submitted an unused song from the *Hard Promises* sessions, "The Best of Everything," to the Band's Robbie Robertson, when asked if he was interested in contributing a song to the soundtrack of Martin Scorsese's film *The King of Comedy*, which was released in the US in February 1983. Though MCA ultimately refused to allow the song on the soundtrack because it was released by rival Warner Bros. Records, Robertson did extensive overdubbing on the track at Village Recorders without Petty's input—in fact, Robertson didn't even allow Petty into the room when he stopped by the studio. Petty was a huge fan of Robertson's added horns and backing vocals, and it inspired him to move the Heartbreakers' next album in a similar, more sonically lush, direction. "It made me realize there was a lot more we could do with our sound," Petty told the *Los Angeles Times* in 1985. "It was still basically a Heartbreakers track, but it didn't sound anything like the Heartbreakers. It had a real liberating effect on me and, I think, the band."

Speaking with the *New York Times* in 1985, Petty talked about why he wanted to move the Heartbreakers' sound in another direction. "You keep hearing the same drum sound, the same guitar sound, the same high-voiced singing on so many bands' albums," Petty said. "I was beginning to feel that people were expecting more of our sound from us, and I didn't want people to like us just for one particular sound, wanted them to like us for being us. So I figured it was time to move on, to take some risks and come up with something new."

While writing the first songs for the band's next album, Petty was significantly influenced by his Southern upbringing. In fact, during the Long After Dark Tour, Petty even considered recording the album in Florida, remarking to *CREEM* in 1984, "I wasn't going to leave, but I wanted to go back and make a record in the South, just to get away from Hollywood. But it turned out to be such an incredible expense to take a year in a hotel that we could never really work it out."

One of the first songs that Petty wrote for this new album was "Rebels," an anthemic ode to the multi-generational Southern rebellious streak that surrounded Petty in his youth. He began to envision the upcoming album, *Southern Accents*, as a concept album about the South, but the songs began to drift from that concept after Petty met musician-producer Dave Stewart.

Stewart was one-half of the new-wave band Eurythmics, which had a #1 hit in the US with "Sweet Dreams (Are Made of This)" in 1983. After coproducing or producing all of the Eurythmics work, Stewart was interested in producing for other artists as well. In *Conversations*, Petty recalled how quickly the two of them hit it off. "We hooked up at a studio in Hollywood. Sunset Sound. I went down there and we hung out, and we got along really well. Quickly. And it was his first trip into L.A. and he was going to stay awhile.... We were getting into that and going all over town. And lots of people were coming around. And Dave liked it so much that he bought a house just a block or two away. In Encino." Petty and Stewart spent a lot of time together, with Petty remembering in *Petty: The Biography*, "Dave put on the best parties in the eighties. Somehow, there were always midgets involved. At one, Timothy Leary reached out to me with a hit of acid, and when I declined, he said, 'More for the rest of us,' and put it on his tongue. I had to escape Dave's house that night. I locked the bathroom door and went out through the window, since my house was only a block away. I knew Dave wouldn't want me to leave. Dave could just keep going, and he wanted us all with him."

After Petty and Stewart had gotten acquainted, the two of them met with Jimmy Iovine and Stevie Nicks at Sunset Sound to try working up ideas for Nicks's next solo album. Nicks left to get some sleep, and when she returned Petty and Stewart had created a demo for a song that floored her so much that she refused to take it away from Petty.

That song was "Don't Come Around Here No More," the title based on what Stewart later claimed was a phrase he had heard Nicks say to her on-again, off-again boyfriend Joe Walsh of the Eagles. It was unlike anything that Petty had ever written for the Heartbreakers, but not just because it was cowritten by Stewart. The song would go on to include synthesizers played by Campbell, Tench, and Stewart, electric sitar by Stewart, "Bugs" Weidel on piano, a cellist, and three female backing vocalists that were borrowed from Nicks's recording session. "Stevie [Nicks] had booked the time. And the girls that sing with her had turned up for the session, but Stevie had canceled the session," Petty explained in *Conversations*. "So the girls were still there. Dave said, 'Let's get them out here and see what they can do.' And then they did that great bit. [Sings "Ah ah ah ooh ooh."] And then there's a girl named Stephanie who we brought in to sing that really high, wailing thing at the end. [Laughs] She was having a little trouble finding her thing. And Dave actually ran into the room in his underpants as she was singing that bit. And that actually worked, and she went up into that register and did that note, and then burst out laughing. But he was that kind of guy. He figured, well, this will get her jazzed up."

"Don't Come Around Here No More" was one of the best songs the Heartbreakers had ever recorded, but aside from the Southern-style phrasing of the title, it didn't fit the Southern concept album idea that Petty had in mind. Songs like "Southern Accents," "Rebels," and the B-side "Trailer" all lyrically or instrumentally reflect Southern rock or country music influences. Yet on the other hand, the three songs cowritten with Dave Stewart that ended up on the final album were the closest the Heartbreakers had ever sounded to new wave. This unlikely marriage of styles makes *Southern Accents* an inconsistent listening experience, and even though "Don't Come Around Here No More" was a huge success, Petty would later lament that it pushed songs that adhered to the original concept, like "Trailer," off the album.

The album's identity crisis also reflects the long, arduous, and tumultuous process that the Heartbreakers went through to create it. Much of the recording took place at Petty's new home studio, dubbed Gone Gator One, with sessions carrying on at all hours of the day and night. In addition, the crumbling of his marriage coupled with cocaine use led to chaotic recording sessions.

During the prolonged recording of *Southern Accents* and Petty's personal ordeals, the other Heartbreakers turned their attentions to session work for other prominent artists throughout a number of Los Angeles-area recording studios. Most notably, Campbell, Tench, and Lynch all contributed to the sessions for Don Henley's second solo album, 1984's *Building the Perfect Beast*. While Tench had previously played on Henley's first solo album, 1982's *I Can't Stand Still*, on this album each of the Heartbreakers received cowriting credits on songs, with Tench cowriting "Not Enough Love in the World" (which hit #34 on the Billboard Hot 100) and "Sunset Grill" (#22); Lynch cowriting "Drivin' With Your Eyes Closed;" and Campbell cowriting the #5 hit "The Boys of Summer," the album's lead single. Campbell originally brought "The Boys of Summer" to Petty for the Heartbreakers, but Petty didn't see much potential in the song (Campbell received only one cowriting credit on *Southern Accents*, the non-single "Dogs on the Run," after receiving four cowriting credits on the previous album). Stewart also borrowed Campbell, Tench, and Lynch to play on the recording sessions for the Eurythmics' 1985 album *Be Yourself Tonight* (most notably, the trio plays on the Top 20 hit "Sisters Are Doin' It for Themselves," a duet between Annie Lennox and Aretha Franklin that also appeared on Franklin's 1985 album *Who's Zoomin' Who?*). Campbell, Tench, and Epstein all appear on multiple tracks on Bob Dylan's 1985 album *Empire Burlesque*.

Tench was in high demand as one of the best organists in the industry, playing and cowriting songs for rock artists (Stevie Nicks, U2), country artists (Lone Justice, Rosanne Cash), and even playing keyboards on the Ramones song "Howling at the Moon (Sha-La-La)" from the punk band's 1984 album *Too Tough to Die* (the song was produced by Stewart). Tench explained to *Glide Magazine* in 2014 how his role as a session player grew: "By great fortune, Jimmy Iovine had produced a couple of records of ours and he was going into the studio to record one song with Bob Dylan and asked me to come. I met some of the other players and they passed my name around, and he also asked me to work with Stevie Nicks and I met a whole other crew of players and producers. And they started suggesting me. So since I had time and I knew I can learn by doing this and bring it back to the Heartbreakers, whatever I've learned, I started playing more sessions...if I have time on my hands and some friends are making a record or somebody I admire is making a record and they would like me to play, and I have the time, then why not. Plus, it's a great deal of fun." Unfortunately for Petty, the Heartbreakers had even more downtime away from their main gig after the bandleader injured himself. In mid-October 1984, Petty pulverized the bones in his left hand after punching a wall in his house. Repairing the damage required a four-hour operation at Los Angeles' Cedars-Sinai Medical Center that involved inserting two pins into Petty's hand. There have been conflicting stories over the years on exactly what prompted Petty to do something so foolish. In December 1984, Petty told *Rolling Stone* that it came after listening to

Robertson's production on "The Best of Everything," again, saying, "It was so fucking good I couldn't believe it," and happened out of Petty's frustration of being unable to match the bar that he felt Robertson had set for what the album could sound like. Campbell said in *Petty: The Biography* that it happened the same day that he brought in the mix of his collaboration with Henley, "The Boys of Summer," which would become a Top 10 hit in a matter of weeks. Another account has Petty punching the wall after growing increasingly frustrated with his issues mixing "Rebels" to his satisfaction. Regardless of the impulse behind the action, it was seriously questioned if Petty would ever be able to play guitar again. He told *Mojo* in 1999, "The hand thing was sort of embarrassing when I look back, because I broke it in a fit of temper, and temper is not good. And I think the temper was fueled by drugs and alcohol. It was a dumb thing; as dumb as being a football hooligan. I was pissed off, frustrated and I really, really, really, really broke my hand. I pulverized every bone in it. It was just powder." When asked in *Conversations* if cocaine affected his songwriting in this period, Petty quipped, "No. I think it affected my breaking my hand." That humor carried over to the band—Petty told the *Los Angeles Times*, "The band also tried to keep it real light. They'd joke about how I'd have to take less money if I was just the singer."

By February, Petty was able to move his hand well enough to play guitar. Though Petty eventually recovered, after his surgery he realized that he had been in over his head trying to finish the album. He turned to Jimmy Iovine for help, who recommended that Petty finish the album in a studio. The album was finished at Village Recorder.

Despite all the chaos surrounding the production of *Southern Accents*, when it was released on March 26, 1985, it marked a sales rebound for the Heartbreakers. The first single, "Don't Come Around Here No More," peaked at #13 in May. The two follow-up singles, "Make It Better (Forget About Me)" and "Rebels," were less successful on the Billboard 100 but were both Top 20 hits on the Album Rock Tracks chart. *Southern Accents* was certified gold in May and then platinum in September. The album was released by MCA after the record company folded Backstreet Records into the main company when Irving Azoff, the manager of the Eagles, became chairman of the label. Though Petty officially became an MCA Records recording artist, something he had fought so hard against six years earlier, this time he did not fight it.

Referring to the album's five producers (Campbell, Iovine, Petty, Robertson, and Stewart), the *Billboard* review remarked, "A certain amount of stylistic and sonic continuity seems to have been sacrificed through an excess of chefs in the kitchen," but praised Robertson's production on the "The Best of Everything" in particular and also gave the Heartbreakers credit for how diverse the songs were on the album. Robert Hilburn, in his review in the *Los Angeles Times*, gave the Heartbreakers his typical high praise, particularly to the album's differences in tone and style to previous work, remarking that *Southern Accents* "is a sometimes affectionate, occasionally disheartened commentary on the stifling bonds of tradition that often inhibit social mobility in the South. [Petty] is especially concerned with the way that tradition discourages the youthful aspiration that has always interested him as a writer."

Adding to the success of "Don't Come Around Here No More" was the now-classic music video, which depicts a twisted version of *Alice in Wonderland*. The concept of the video originated from a remark made by Stewart, while the band was recording the song, regarding his sitar contribution. In a 1989 interview with *Q*, Petty explained, "Dave said, 'You know, I picture myself with a hookah on top of a big mushroom,' and I said, 'Yeah, Dave, I can see you sitting on a mushroom with a hookah, too,' and from there I stumbled into this concept for a video, making this bizarre *Alice In Wonderland* thing. It cost an enormous amount of money and it was exhausting but it was, er, interesting, I guess."

The video was directed by Jeff Stein, who had previously directed videos for the Cars, the Jacksons, and Hall & Oates, and would later direct the Southern Accents Tour concert video, *Pack Up the Plantation: Live!* It was filmed at SIR Rehearsal Studios on Sunset Boulevard in Hollywood. In one of the trippy video's most memorable images—and arguably one of the most memorable images of any '80s music video—Petty portrays the Mad Hatter.

In the book *I Want My MTV*, Petty remembered, "Jeff Stein...really caught on to our idea and took it forward. When I saw the set, I went, 'Oh man, we killed it.' We didn't use any special effects. Everything that's big was big, and everything that's small was small. It was a two-day shoot, and each day was fourteen hours, *way* into the night. Even for musicians, those were challenging hours. But we knew while we were doing it how shit-hot it was." The weekend video shoot was particularly grueling for the actress playing Alice, Wish Foley, who spent much of the second day in a pool of cold water to film the teacup scene. Later that year, the video was awarded Best Special Effects in a Video at the second annual MTV Video Music Awards, an ironic turn of events considering the "effects" were, as Petty noted, actually life-sized props.

In a particularly grotesque moment, Alice is turned into a cake and all of the Heartbreakers slice her up. In an interview with *Billboard* in 2005, Petty said that there was backlash from women's rights groups, remembering, "[MTV] actually made me edit out a scene of my face when we were cutting her up. They said it was just too lascivious. It was just a shot of me grinning, and they were like, 'Well, you can do it, but you can't enjoy it that much.'"

Another video was shot for "Make It Better (Forget About Me)" featuring the Heartbreakers invading the brain of a woman (also played by Wish Foley) and performing the song inside her head until she shakes the band out of her ear.

The Heartbreakers again rehearsed for their tour at Universal Studios. On this tour, the Heartbreakers would be backed by three horn players, dubbed the Soul Lips Horns, and two female background singers, dubbed the Rebelettes. The tour also featured one of the Heartbreakers' first major tour sponsors, Levi's jeans, something Petty had been reluctant to allow previously. The set design for the tour included an antebellum mansion as a backdrop, nicknamed "Tara West" after the estate in *Gone With the Wind*, and imagery of the Confederate flag. In his Rhythm & Blues column in *Billboard*, acclaimed rock journalist Nelson George reported that a New York organization named the Black Rock Coalition sent Petty's management a letter criticizing his use of the Confederate flag as well as the title of Petty's live album that was released after the tour, *Pack Up the Plantation: Live!* Petty would apologize for using the Confederate flag as part of his stage design years later ("I wish I had given it more thought," he told *Rolling Stone* in 2015. "It was a downright stupid thing to do").

The Heartbreakers' Southern Accents Tour kicked off on June 6, 1985, in St. Louis and included a short performance at Live Aid in Philadelphia on July 13. Humorously, a Petty fan wrote to the *Los Angeles Times* to complain about the overlong sideburns Petty was sporting at Live Aid and said she would donate one hundred dollars to the cause if he shaved them. Jane Petty saw the letter and offered to match the donation. Tom Petty obliged and the $200 was donated to Live Aid.

On tour, the Heartbreakers played almost all of the songs from *Southern Accents* as part of the standard setlist, with the exception of "Mary's New Car." The tour ended with various dates in Southern California at the Forum (August 1), Universal Amphitheater (August 4), the Pacific Amphitheater in Costa Mesa (August 5), the Wiltern Theatre (August 6 and 7), and the Sports Arena in San Diego (August 9), followed by three one-off dates, including the Mulholland Tomorrow Benefit at the Universal Amphitheater (September 17). At the Forum concert, Dave Stewart joined the band to perform "Don't Come Around Here No More" and "Little Bit O' Soul."

Robert Hilburn's review of the Forum concert in the *Los Angeles Times* was uncharacteristically critical of the Heartbreakers, calling it as "schizophrenic" as the *Southern Accents* album, saying that Petty's older songs dominated the show, "which gave the show a definite 'oldies' feel at times." He called the additional backing musicians "window dressing." The review ended with Hilburn stating, "Petty is still a strong talent but that he needs to listen more to his heart," a plea referencing the Heartbreakers' 1978 single that flew in the face of the band's changing sound.

The August 5 concert was held at the Pacific Amphitheatre in Costa Mesa in Orange County, a venue that opened in the summer of 1983 at the site of the OC Fair & Event Center. The original capacity was nearly nineteen thousand, but it was eventually scaled back by over ten thousand seats because of frequent noise complaints from the surrounding neighborhoods, and has since been used only for concerts affiliated with the annual OC Fair.

Much of the Heartbreakers' 1985 *Pack Up the Plantation: Live!* album was recorded at the August 7 performance at the Wiltern Theatre. The Wiltern Theatre (its name a portmanteau of the intersecting streets where it is located, Wilshire Boulevard and Western Avenue) was built in 1931 as part of the Pellissier Building, an art-deco office building in Los Angeles. It had undergone a significant renovation in the early '80s, after plans to demolish the building were halted and the building was added to the National Register of Historic Places. The Heartbreakers were among the first rock bands to play the renovated venue, and with a capacity of around two thousand, it offered the most intimate Heartbreakers concert in Southern California since the surprise show at the Whisky in 1980. The concerts were also shot for a film release by Jeff Stein, utilizing nine Panavision 35mm cameras.

On September 17, the Heartbreakers participated in a benefit concert at the Universal Amphitheater to support Mulholland Tomorrow and the William O. Douglas Outdoor Classroom, organizations devoted to, according to the *Los Angeles Times*, "combat[ing] housing development in the Santa Monica Mountains." The concert also featured Linda Ronstadt, Stevie Nicks, Jackson Browne, and headliner Don Henley. Tickets cost $125, and the Heartbreakers played a half-hour set to the celebrity-studded crowd, many of whom attended an after-party hosted by Jack Nicholson and Warren Beatty. The *Los Angeles Times* called it "the most consistently superb onslaught of pop ever to grace a Los Angeles benefit, with more smartly played, fun, invigorating and morally charged music packed into four hours than all of Live Aid's 16." The same article called Petty's set the "most playful, mixing raucous oldies with lesser-played originals." At the benefit, Petty also joined Nicks onstage to perform "Stop Draggin' My Heart Around." In an interview with the *Wall Street Journal* about the cause, Henley said, "We aren't doing this just to protect my view. Mulholland belongs to everybody. Besides, I don't even have a view." The Heartbreakers and Henley also performed at the inaugural Farm Aid benefit concert in Illinois just five days later.

That benefit would have profound implications for the Heartbreakers and the next phase of their career, as they would go from one of the top rock acts to serving as the backing band for one of the most iconic figures in popular music—and would wind up an even better band for doing it.

CHAPTER 5

THE BEACH WAS BURNIN'

In addition to playing their own set at Farm Aid, the Heartbreakers served as the backing band for Bob Dylan, who had inspired Farm Aid after controversially remarking on stage at Live Aid that he hoped some money that was raised could go to American farmers who were facing economic struggles. After the performance at Farm Aid, conversations between Petty and Dylan led to the idea that the Heartbreakers would open for Dylan and then perform as his backing band for Dylan's True Confessions Tour, which started on February 5, 1986, in New Zealand and was initially booked just for New Zealand, Australia, and Japan.

In *Petty: The Biography*, Petty explained how the rehearsals for the tour reinvigorated the band. He said, "They were long rehearsals—five hours sometimes, where we played a hundred songs in a night. We played so many songs every night—it was really inspiring. 'Cause Bob was excited—everybody was excited. We were just havin' a great time. And then, when we started realizing how to drive that thing, we really started getting excited." The rehearsals also prepared the Heartbreakers to be ready for anything, since Dylan frequently called out songs to perform on the fly or began playing his classics in radically different arrangements.

In April, it was announced that the tour would come to the US, and on April 22 the *Los Angeles Times* reported that "more than 800 fans" had lined up at the Pacific Amphitheatre box office to buy tickets for Dylan and the Heartbreakers' June 16 concert (a second show was added June 17 in response to demand, with both shows selling out). Dylan and Petty held a press conference in Los Angeles to announce the tour, with *Rolling Stone* reporting, "Both looked bored; neither had much to say. When asked how the tour came about, Dylan said, 'We just felt like it.' Asked what it was that brought them together, Petty said, 'Money.'"

Temporarily separated from Jane (which Petty hinted at in a 1987 interview with *Rolling Stone* when he said, "It wasn't the best period of my life"), Petty had moved into the Sunset Marquis Hotel. While there, he and Dylan wrote lyrics to a song that Campbell had written, "Jammin' Me," which ended up the lead single on the Heartbreakers' next album. The lyrics consist of the singer shouting out things in the news that have been overloading him, everything from "acid rain" to "Iranian torture." "We wrote it with just an acoustic," Petty later explained to *CREEM*, "Bob and I just sat there—somebody'd start a line and somebody'd finish a line." Dylan included celebrities on the list, specifically naming Academy Award-winning actress Vanessa Redgrave and former *Saturday Night Live* cast members Eddie Murphy and Joe Piscopo. "That was all Bob, that verse about Eddie Murphy," Petty later said in *Conversations*. "Which embarrassed me a little bit because I remember seeing Eddie Murphy on TV really pissed off about it. And I had nothing against Eddie Murphy or Vanessa Redgrave." Several months later, the Heartbreakers shot a music video for "Jammin' Me" that reflects the message of the song, with the band surrounded by newspaper clippings, flickering TV channels, infomercial excerpts, images of war and destruction in an onslaught of media edited together in a rapid montage.

During those sessions, Petty and Dylan also cowrote "Got My Mind Made Up," which appeared on Dylan's 1986 album *Knocked Out Loaded*. Dylan released *Knocked Out Loaded* on July 14, during the US tour, which featured the Heartbreakers performing on "Got My Mind Made Up." It was recorded in June 1986 at Sound City between gigs of the US leg of the True Confessions Tour.

This collaboration followed the initial recordings for the Heartbreakers' follow-up album to *Southern Accents* at Sound City, although the original intention was to use the studio time to record more with Dylan. Petty later told *CREEM*, "Then it turned out [Dylan] wasn't gonna be ready at that time. And so we had about three songs—I had one or two and I think Campbell had one. And we said, 'Well, let's just go in and try these songs out.' We wound up stayin' there a month at least, right up until we left again (to tour with Dylan)."

The sessions proved fruitful, with the Heartbreakers ultimately recording about thirty songs—and even after cutting out the lesser-quality songs, it yielded enough material for a double album (with a number of the unused tracks later finding a home on the Heartbreakers' 1995 box set *Playback*). The way the band worked with Dylan on tour influenced the recording sessions. Petty told *Rolling Stone* in 1987, "The only rule of the sessions was the tape had to roll from the time the first guy got there until the last guy was gone." Petty elaborated further to *CREEM*, saying, "The tape was rolling like 15 minutes before we'd get there because this ain't the kind of people that can do it again—it's gonna happen once. Some of these songs might've been 15 minutes long originally, and I wound up editing them down to the best three minutes, where it was groovy. That's why almost everything on the album fades." Work on the album was put on hold when the Heartbreakers joined Dylan on the US leg of the True Confessions Tour.

The first Los Angeles-area appearance of Dylan and the Heartbreakers came on June 6 at the Forum at Amnesty International's sold-out A Conspiracy of Hope benefit. Though the benefit was actually a six-city tour featuring U2, Sting, and Bryan Adams as headliners, Dylan and the Heartbreakers performed as a "surprise act" at the Forum show and played three songs, including the live debut of "Band of the Hand," a song they recorded together in Australia for the 1986 crime film *Band of the Hand*. Robert Hilburn's review of the concert in the *Los Angeles Times* said they performed in "blistering down 'n' dirty rock fashion that made their U.S. tour...shape up as something special indeed."

The Dylan and Heartbreakers tour generated significant buzz not only because of the unique pairing, but also because it would be Dylan's first concerts in Southern California in over seven years. The *Los Angeles Times* covered the concerts in various ways, like reporting on the varied ages of the audience at the Pacific Amphitheater, including fans of Dylan that had followed his music since the early '60s and teenagers who were seeing Dylan for the first time because of the Heartbreakers. Eleni P. Austin's review of the first show in the *Desert Sun* praised both Dylan and the Heartbreakers, saying, "Dylan mixed old favorites with newer material as well as some obscure songs and interesting cover versions. Placing the classic 'Positively 4th Street' next to the cutting commentary of 'Clean Cut Kid' from his last LP proved that Dylan still deserves the title of rock's premiere songwriter.... The Heartbreakers performed admirably, both in backing Dylan and during their own set. Petty seemed content to stay in the background, supplying rhythm guitar accompaniment during Dylan's set. This group is the best outfit Dylan has had with him since the Band." She also noted, "The crowd responded a bit more wildly during Petty's set." According to *Billboard*, the Pacific Amphitheater shows drew a combined 37,528 and grossed $626,682.

On June 21, the *Los Angeles Times* announced that Dylan and the Heartbreakers would return to the area for another concert, August 3 at the Forum. Robert Hilburn's review of the show in the *Los Angeles Times* noted that the Heartbreakers appeared to have expanded their role over the six weeks since the tour was last in the Los Angeles area. He wrote, "This time, Petty and company were more like co-stars, drawing ovations from the audience with both their endearing, idealistic, expressions ('Straight Into Darkness') and their playful new tunes." The Eurythmics and Al Kooper joined Dylan and the Heartbreakers on stage for the encore of "Knocking on Heaven's Door." Three days later, the True Confessions Tour ended in Paso Robles.

After the tour, the Heartbreakers returned to the studio. Though Petty had contemplated putting out a double album, he ultimately decided on having the Heartbreakers polish enough songs for a single album, focusing on the tracks that seemed to require the least amount of work. "So what got finished the fastest got on the album, pretty much," he explained to *CREEM*. "There was some stuff that we could see was gonna be good, but we were gonna have to study it and figure out how to do it, and nobody felt like doin' that very much. Most nights it was, 'Let's get some more songs going.' Nobody wanted to go back— although we did on a couple of things."

The Heartbreakers were working in the studio on August 31, 1986, when a jet airliner was clipped by a small civilian plane over Cerritos, California, which caused the airliner to crash, killing all sixty-seven passengers on both planes and fifteen people on the ground when the airliner crashed in a neighborhood. On the same day, a riot broke out on Huntington Beach during a surf competition sponsored by Ocean Pacific. The day's events inspired the line, "The beach was burnin' and someone was throwin' rocks / They said an airplane had fallen on my block," in the song "My Life/Your World."

In *Petty: The Biography*, Petty admitted that he felt he had given up on the album before it was ready. He explained, "With that album, though, I kind of stepped out to the back alley for a smoke and didn't come back, just as we were finishing recording. I was ready to hand it off." Petty ended up "handing" the album off to the album's mixing engineer, Mike Shipley, who had previously worked on albums for the Damned, Def Leppard, A Flock of Seagulls, the Cars, Joni Mitchell, and Jimmy Iovine protégés Lone Justice. "It was the first time, the only time, I handed a Heartbreakers record over to someone else to bring it home. I shouldn't have. No one knows a record as well as the people who made it."

Petty kept busy with some extracurricular activities. In October, Petty attended the unveiling of the Everly Brothers' star on the Hollywood Walk of Fame, and remarked, "The Everly Brothers have been an important influence on music. Their harmonies were ground-breaking." On October 5, Petty also appeared on stage at the Elvis Costello and the Attractions concert at the Beverly Theatre, guesting on Costello's hit "(What's So Funny 'Bout) Peace, Love and Understanding," Petty's "American Girl," and the Byrds' "So You Want to Be a Rock 'n' Roll Star." It was the fifth concert of Costello's five-night stand at the Beverly Theatre, a 1,372-capacity venue in Beverly Hills that was a former movie theater used as a music venue in the '80s (the Beverly Theatre was demolished in 2005).

The Heartbreakers' seventh album, *Let Me Up (I've Had Enough)*, was released on April 21, 1987. The album peaked at #20 on the Billboard 200 in June, the lowest-charting Heartbreakers album since *You're Gonna Get It*. The same month it was certified gold. Of the album's four singles, "Jammin' Me" was the only one to chart the Billboard 200, peaking at #18 and #1 on the Top Rock Tracks chart. The three other singles, "Runaway Trains," "All Mixed Up," and "Think About Me," were all Top 40 songs on the Top Rock Tracks chart. Robert Hilburn's review of the album in the *Los Angeles Times* called it "the group's liveliest and most assured work since *Damn the Torpedoes* eight years ago," and said, "the Heartbreakers—perhaps rejuvenated by extensive touring last year with the unpredictable Bob Dylan—bring such energy and spunk to the songs that much of the LP has the fresh, exhilarating feel of a great new band's debut work." The *Billboard* review agreed, calling it "Petty's best album since *Damn the Torpedoes*." Eleni P. Austin's review in the *Desert Sun* was along the same lines, saying, "Tom Petty sounds angry, sad and even a little fed up. And that's great because his dissatisfaction has produced his best album since 1979's *Damn the Torpedoes*.... Tom Petty and the Heartbreakers' *Let Me Up (I've Had Enough)* is an album that combines righteous indignation with blistering instrumentation."

On April 17, the *Los Angeles Times* announced that the Heartbreakers would perform at the Pacific Amphitheatre on June 6. Again, the Heartbreakers rehearsed for the tour at Universal Studios. But another life-changing incident occurred that would again cause turmoil in Petty's personal life.

On May 17, 1987, Petty's home in Encino was destroyed by fire. Tom and Jane Petty escaped with their two daughters, though a housekeeper suffered minor burns. It was a harrowing experience, later revealed to be an act of arson. Petty revealed in *Conversations*, "They found the evidence where someone had cut a hole in the back fence on a hill and had been watching the house. For probably a period of time. And really early one morning they came down and set the house on fire. And it was a wooden house, and it went up really quickly. The whole place, just like a matchbox, it went up really fast.... It really frightened me. They didn't just try to kill me, they tried to wipe out my whole family. And it was a hell of a day. It was my wife's birthday. We were planning an afternoon barbecue. So as the house was burning, guests were arriving." No one was ever arrested for starting the fire. As to any suspects he had in mind, Petty told *Men's Journal* in 2014, "I can't name anyone publicly, but I have some suspicions." While the entire upstairs was destroyed (damage estimated at $800,000), Gone Gator One Studio, where Petty stored his guitars and master recordings, was largely undamaged. Annie Lennox of the Eurythmics brought the Petty family clothes and took them to a hotel.

Not surprisingly, the devastating loss had a significant effect on Petty and affected his songwriting. He explained to *Mojo* in May 1999, "It was so vicious and angry it completely scared all of that out of me. I didn't want to do anything except sing really light, happy music after that. I didn't know this while I was doing it but, in retrospect, I wanted to go to some much tighter place. I was really glad to be alive, like someone who had survived a plane crash. If you've ever had anybody try to kill you, it really makes you re-evaluate everything. They never caught whoever set fire to the place. The funny thing was I kept insisting it was an accident, telling the investigators, 'Who'd want to kill me?' And then 10 people confessed to the police. None of them did it, but they wanted to confess. Fortunately I left on a tour days later, so it was all contained on the road. I think knowing someone was maybe trying to kill me revitalized me. I came out of it in a good spot. It just made me glad to be alive."

Just days later, the Heartbreakers embarked on the Rock 'n' Roll Caravan '87 Tour, which began May 26 in Tucson, Arizona. The Heartbreakers were scheduled to appear June 6 at Pacific Amphitheater and June 8, 9, 11, and 12 at the Universal Amphitheatre. In his review of the Pacific Amphitheater performance in the *Los Angeles Times*, Robert Hilburn focused on Petty's speeches to the audience between songs that focused on social ills like Los Angeles' homelessness and air quality. Hilburn wrote, "This toughened social attitude and more open manner on stage gave the evening a freedom and focus that makes this tour shape up as potentially the Heartbreakers' best in years. Things should get even better as the quintet begins featuring more songs from the new album. (Saturday's lineup offered only three of the new tunes including the raucous single, 'Jammin' Me,' and the melancholy 'It'll All Work Out.')"

Unfortunately, the Heartbreakers' Pacific Amphitheatre concert made the wrong kind of headlines in the *Los Angeles Times*, which reported that the concert exceeded noise ordinances and that, by a judge's order, future concerts would need to be in compliance to reduce noise levels for the surrounding neighborhoods.

After the Rock 'n' Roll Caravan Tour ended on July 26 in Tampa, Florida, the Petty family rented a house on Mullholland Drive (the same house where Stevie Nicks once lived) as their home was being rebuilt. The Heartbreakers went into rehearsals with Bob Dylan at Universal Studios for the Temple In Flames Tour that would go to the Middle East and Europe, from September 5 to October 17.

During the rehearsals, Dylan accompanied Stan Lynch to a Frank Sinatra and Sammy Davis Jr. concert at the Greek Theatre during the Rat Packers' three-night stand in late August. In 1990, Lynch told *Musician*, "We were all playing and I said, 'Look, I gotta bug out early tonight.' And they go, 'Lynch, what's your crisis?' I go, 'I got tickets for Sammy and Frank at the Greek.' The whole band covers their eyes going, 'Oh geez, I can't believe he really said that.' And Dylan looked up at me in all seriousness and said, 'Sammy and Frank? I love those guys.' So Dylan and I went to the Greek. I really didn't know who to look at! I don't mind saying I was a little starstruck by the whole concept that I came from Gainesville to L.A., and now I'm sitting with Bob Dylan watching Sammy Davis and Frank Sinatra." In *Petty: The Biography*, Lynch added, "We get to the Greek Theatre, and he tightens his sweatshirt hood around his face. We make our way to the fourth row. He looks like the Unabomber. But by that point, a few people are realizing that Bob Dylan is there. You can sort of feel the energy. The show starts, and it's fucking great. But I kinda got one eye on Bob, one eye on Sammy. Like, 'How's Bob reacting to this? How's Bob reacting to me loving Sammy so much? What's happening here?' The whole thing is odd, with the people around us reacting to how Bob is reacting to Sammy."

For Petty, working with heroes like Del Shannon and Bob Dylan was only the beginning of what would come in terms of performing with rock 'n' roll legends—and, over the next few years, it would result in lasting friendships and the recording of some of the most memorable songs in his entire career.

CHAPTER 6

WONDER WHAT TOMORROW WILL BRING

George Harrison had not released a new album since 1982's commercially unsuccessful *Gone Troppo* when he approached Electric Light Orchestra multi-instrumentalist Jeff Lynne in late 1986 about collaborating on new music. Lynne, who had self-produced or coproduced most of his own releases and had coproduced two albums for Dave Edmunds (1983's *Information* and 1984's *Riff Raff*), had long been alternately praised and criticized for creating music in the tradition of the Beatles. Depending on the critic's point of view, Lynne is either a brilliant musician who proudly wears his Beatles influences, or little more than a Fab Four copycat whose production work sounds like he learned all the wrong lessons from George Martin. But in Lynne, Harrison had met something of a kindred spirit who understood and appreciated Harrison's musical influences and sensibilities and, perhaps more importantly, his humor. The two collaborated on production of Harrison's comeback album (with Lynne also cowriting three of the album's songs) over the first half of 1987. The result was perhaps Harrison's finest album since 1970's *All Things Must Pass*. Released in November 1987, *Cloud Nine* became one of Harrison's most commercially successful albums and produced his first #1 Billboard hit single since 1973 with "I Got My Mind Set on You."

Though *Cloud Nine* would be the last solo album that Harrison released in his lifetime, the collaboration with Lynne would inspire Harrison's desire to collaborate again—much like Petty, Harrison was comforted by the idea of being in a band.

Shortly after the *Cloud Nine* sessions concluded, George Harrison and Jeff Lynne attended the Dylan and the Heartbreakers concert in Birmingham, England, and the subsequent four-night run at the Wembley Arena in London that ended the Temples in Flames Tour, going backstage to hang with the band after the shows. This is where Petty met Lynne for the first time. Then, by chance, Petty and Lynne met again a month and a half later in Los Angeles. As Petty recalled in *Conversations*, "It was Thanksgiving Day. I was at the house in Beverly Hills, and some people were coming over. And I like to have softball games. And so I was going to have a softball game at the house. But I didn't have enough mitts to play ball. So I was going to drive down to the Sav-On in Beverly Hills and buy a dozen ball mitts so everybody could play ball.... So I'm at the traffic light, and I look over to my left, and there's Jeff Lynne. Who I'd only just recently seen in England. So I honked my horn, and he turned around, and we pulled over. And I said, 'Wow, what are you doing here? And I love that album [George Harrison's *Cloud Nine*]; the album's great.' He said, 'I'm working with Brian Wilson.' And he said, 'Where do you live?' I told him where I lived, and he said, 'That's weird. I live really close to there. So we should get together.'" Lynne's work with Wilson resulted in "Let It Shine," a track on Wilson's 1988 self-titled solo album.

In the *Tom Petty: Going Home* documentary, Lynne remembered the meeting differently, saying, "I was driving in Beverly Hills and this horn kept blowing. And I thought, 'Who the hell's that?' And it was Tom. He was going, 'Pull over. I wanna have a word with ya.' We pulled over and he said, 'Oh, I really like what you did with George's album. Do you fancy doing something together?' I said, 'Oh, that'd be nice, y'know.'" Regardless of how it happened, the two were keen on collaborating on music.

Less than a month later, Petty and Lynne had yet another chance encounter—this time in the Valley—that brought another key figure back into Petty's life for the next few years. Petty remembered in *Conversations*, "I was with my daughter Adria, and we were out Christmas shopping. We had driven over to Studio City, there was this one restaurant there on Ventura called Le Seur, a French restaurant that was a really good restaurant.... It was kind of our special night restaurant. I pulled in the parking lot and we came in. I sat down in my chair, and the waiter came over and he said, 'There's a friend of your's [sic] here and he'd like you to come over to the table.' And that's all he said. I said, 'Oh,' and I got up and walked around—there was kind of this private dining room—and as I walk in, there's George [Harrison]. And he was having lunch with some people from Warner Bros. And Jeff. And as I walked into the room, Jeff was writing my number down for George. And George said, 'How strange, I'd just gotten your number and somebody told me you'd walked into the restaurant at the same time.'"

Harrison would follow Petty and Adria home to the house Petty was renting. According to *Petty: The Biography*, Harrison strummed "Norwegian Wood" on a guitar and joked with Petty by asking him, "You know this one, don't you?" It would mark the beginning of several collaborations between Petty, Harrison, and Lynne over the next several years, and a friendship between Petty and Harrison that would last the rest of Harrison's life.

In the new year, Petty and Lynne got together to work on what was initially planned to be a series of demos. Since Lynne preferred the comfort of a home studio, and Petty's Gone Gator One was out of commission while his house was being rebuilt, they convened at Campbell's home studio in Woodland Hills, which the Heartbreakers had first utilized to record parts for *Let Me Up (I've Had Enough)*. Campbell described his studio to *Musician* in 1990 as, "Just a bedroom with a 24-track Soundtracs board. If you get three guys in there you're bumping elbows. It's real funky, all the wires are everywhere. The main thing is, I try to keep all the wires real short. A lot of studios are designed cosmetically—they run the wires through the walls so you can't see them, but then there's miles of wires between the microphone and the board. I think one reason my studio sounds good is because it's so direct." Petty, Lynne, and Campbell performed most of the instruments during the sessions. To play drums, Petty called in Phil Jones, who had played percussion on *Hard Promises*, *Long After Dark*, and *Southern Accents*, and had toured with the Heartbreakers during the first half of the '80s.

As for how the sessions morphed from recording demos to recording an album, Petty would later tell the *Orange County Register*, "I wasn't in the mood to make a record. I wasn't even thinking about making one. We thought we could do it real fast. I told the Heartbreakers, 'Look, I'm going to make a record' and they weren't planning to do anything at the time. I said I could be done with it in a few months. Of course, I wasn't."

Unsurprisingly, the other Heartbreakers were less than enthused about Petty and Campbell working without them on what became a full record. At the time the album was released, Petty told *BAM*, "They weren't in love with the idea when I told them. They were pissed off at first, to be honest. But they've been pretty big about it." In 2014, Tench spoke to *Rolling Stone* about that period and shed some light on how the Heartbreakers took the news, revealing, "I was pissed off and hurt. I was also worried he'd split up the band because there was conflict within the group at that time. There wouldn't be anybody coming to blows, but Tom and Stan [Lynch] would have disagreements, and Stan would leave the band, or get fired, and then come back less than a week later. Stan was always worried that Tom would go [solo], or just grab Mike and pack up. So when he did that, that's how it felt. I was also pissed by the way I found out about it. We were supposed to make a Heartbreakers record. I called the main guy on our crew about a week before we were supposed to start to ask what time we were coming in. He just said, 'Uh...ummmm.' He hemmed and hawed and finally told me they were making a solo record. Nobody told me...."

So that's one side of the story." However, Tench also understood how the decision helped the band both personally and professionally and copped to some personal responsibility for Petty wanting a break from the Heartbreakers, adding, "The other side of the story is that I was out of my mind on cocaine and alcohol. I was a very high man and deeply troubled with drugs and alcohol, so I thank Jeff Lynne. I had nothing to do...so I got to go to rehab, and it saved my life. Also, hell, I'd been doing session work for years by that time. Why the fuck shouldn't Tom go play with someone else and have fun too?"

As Tench noted, for much of the '80s, all of the Heartbreakers had been working as session players when not recording or touring as a group, with each Heartbreaker having developed an impressive resume of work outside of the group—particularly Tench, who by the end of 1990 had appeared on albums by U2, Elvis Costello, Warren Zevon, the Replacements, Jon Bon Jovi, Hall & Oates, Carlene Carter, and Darlene Love.

Of course, none of them had recorded solo albums, and since Petty was the frontman, his solo album could be construed as the first steps of a breakup far more than any of the Heartbreakers contributing to a Stevie Nicks or Don Henley session.

Of all the Heartbreakers, Lynch appeared to take the news of Petty's solo album most personally. In a 1991 feature in *Rolling Stone*, Lynch said he was summoned to Los Angeles to play on the album only to wait around until a "third party" told him that he wouldn't be playing on it. "At that time I thought, 'Well, fuck me.' I mean, you know, call me up...I thought they were shits who were not even man enough to tell me," he recalled. "But about a year later I realized they were embarrassed. We're old friends. How do you call an old friend and say you don't want him at the wedding?" Afterward, Lynch would relate playing Petty's solo songs on tour to feeling like he was in a cover band, which Petty took as an insult. Of course, like Tench, Lynch wasn't just waiting around for Petty's calls. In addition to working as a session drummer, Lynch performed, coproduced, and cowrote three songs on Don Henley's third solo album, *The End of the Innocence*, including the Top 40 single

"The Last Worthless Evening." (Campbell also appeared on the album, cowriting and performing on another Top 40 single, "The Heart of the Matter.")

Though Campbell was a key player in the solo album sessions, he understood the anger from the other Heartbreakers. In 1989, he told *Newsday*, "Yeah, of course there was some resentment. How would you feel if your wife went out on a European vacation with another guy? But I think having gone through it, everybody realized that it was necessary to keep the band from getting stagnant. We're mature people. We know that being a great band is not being on the same bus hanging out with the same five guys for twenty years. We can grow without having to break up."

Tench and Epstein did appear on the album, with Tench playing piano on "The Apartment Song" and Epstein singing backing vocals on "I Won't Back Down" and "Love is a Long Road." In addition, the Heartbreakers did convene for some sessions when Lynne had to travel back to England for other work. The band recorded at Rumbo Recorders in Canoga Park, with Petty and Campbell producing, and finished two tracks, "Waiting for Tonight" and "Travelin'," both of which featured background vocals by the all-female rock group the Bangles. However, the band was less than thrilled with the latter track—in the liner notes of *Playback* (on which the two tracks finally appeared), Petty recalled, "I thought it might be fun to do a real vocal-oriented number with all of them singing. Most of the band were very perplexed with the direction Mike and I were going—a lot of overdubbing. I don't think that everyone was terribly happy. They were confused. 'What IS this? What are we doing? This is not us!' But I quite liked it, so I just went, 'Well, maybe we should put this off.' I went back to doing what I had been doing." Similar tensions over the band's direction would arise during sessions for the Heartbreakers' next album, as Petty continued to explore Lynne's approach to layered vocals when recording.

In particular, the lyrics of the dark-tinged "Waiting for Tonight" reflect views of Los Angeles, with Petty singing in the opening lines, "I went walking down the Boulevard / Past the skateboards and the beggars." The song itself, which sounds like a lament to a lost love, could very well be an ode from a lonely man to a city where he feels comfortable.

One key thing that Petty and Campbell learned from Lynne was efficiency—while it would previously take the Heartbreakers many sessions to complete a track (particularly when working on *Southern Accents*), on Petty's solo album, it was common for almost an entire song to be completed in a single day.

Lynne and Petty had grown so close as collaborators that Lynne called Petty in for songwriting help while working on tracks at Campbell's studio that would later make up Roy Orbison's posthumous album *Mystery Girl*. Orbison—an iconic star from the early '60s, who placed nineteen songs in the Top 40 between 1960 and 1966—had "gone Hollywood" twenty years prior in what turned out to be a major miscalculation professionally. In the wake of the massive success of his biggest hit, "Oh, Pretty Woman," in 1965, Orbison signed a multimedia deal with MGM to release new music from MGM Records and to appear in several MGM films. Orbison's first MGM album release, *There Is Only One Roy Orbison*, was released just a few weeks later, and the first single—an ode to motorcycling titled "Ride Away"—peaked at #25 on the Billboard chart. Unfortunately, it all went downhill for the Orbison and MGM partnership from that point, in terms of sales. At that point, America was almost entirely enthralled with the music of the British Invasion, and while Orbison was producing records that were artistically among his best work, and continued to chart singles in the UK, he was in the beginning stages of a long career downturn.

The decision of MGM to sign Orbison to a film contract at precisely the time when even Elvis Presley was experiencing a significant downturn at the box office is a curious one, even after the massive success of "Oh, Pretty Woman." The lone film Orbison made as part of his MGM deal, the Western comedy *The Fastest Guitar Alive*, was released in September 1967 to bad reviews and an anemic box office. Orbison stars as Johnny Banner, a Confederate spy who brandishes a guitar that is also a rifle in disguise. As charismatic as Orbison was on stage, no amount of charisma would have saved the movie. While Presley's playful onstage demeanor translated successfully to movie screens, Orbison's much more reserved stage presence and mysterious persona did not translate to a Metrocolor Western comedy, particularly after the success of musician films like *A Hard Day's Night* and *Help!* and while Sergio Leone's Spaghetti Westerns were exposing American audiences to a more visceral depiction of the American West.

Nonetheless, Orbison began experiencing the beginnings of a career resurgence in the mid-'80s after several rock superstars like Bruce Springsteen and Elvis Costello cited him as an influence, in addition to Orbison's relentless touring schedule. In September 1987, a Cinemax television concert special titled *Roy Orbison and Friends: A Black and White Night* was filmed at the famed Cocoanut Grove nightclub at the Ambassador Hotel in Los Angeles featuring Orbison performing his greatest hits. The special was a massive critical and commercial success when it aired in January 1988, and Orbison— with a new Virgin Records contract—was ready to apply his comeback goodwill to recording a new album.

The sessions were the first time Petty worked with Orbison, and he recalled in *Conversations*, "One afternoon the phone rang and it was [Jeff], and he said, 'Hey, Roy Orbison's over here, you've got to come over and help me write a song for him. I need some help.' So I jumped in the car, I had a new Corvette, and we went over to see Jeff and Roy, and we all went out to look at the car, and we raised the hood of the car. And we were such a bunch of musicians, non-mechanics, you know, and we couldn't get the hood back down on the car. [Laughs] And I remember my first meeting with Roy, he's got his head under my hood trying to figure out how to get the hood down."

After the trio figured out how to close the hood, they headed inside and wrote "You Got It," which became an international hit when it was released in January 1989, including reaching #9 on the Billboard charts (making it Orbison's first song to chart in the Top 10 since "Oh, Pretty Woman" hit #1 in 1964). Orbison, Lynne, and Petty recorded the entire song with drummer Phil Jones that same day.

The following day, the trio reconvened, again at Campbell's house, and wrote another song, "California Blue," a buoyant ode to the beauty of the Golden State. This time, Campbell joined in on the recording and played acoustic guitar and mandolin on the track. Lynne would also cowrite and record another song with Orbison, "A Love So Beautiful," which features George Harrison on acoustic guitar. Following these sessions, Campbell would coproduce four other songs on Orbison's album and Campbell, Tench, and Epstein would perform on these and other songs on the album.

By May 1988, reports of Petty and Harrison working with Orbison on his Lynne-produced comeback album in Los Angeles were spreading, as were reports that Petty had secretly recorded a solo album titled *Songs from the Garage* at Campbell's home studio. Speaking with *Billboard* at the time, Tony Dimitriades said that Petty recorded without the Heartbreakers because, "When you've worked with people for eleven years, there are always certain things that don't quite fit into the formula that the band has established for itself. I think it was healthy for [Petty] to do at least one album that got something out of his system." Dimitriades also noted that it was initially only intended to be a set of demos and that Petty was planning to record with the Heartbreakers by the end of the year. However, while Petty's first solo album was completed, the announcements on its release were premature—various circumstances would prevent its release for nearly a year.

In the meantime, in August, Warner Bros. Records announced that Petty, Dylan, Harrison, Lynne, and Orbison had recorded an entire album as a supergroup named the Traveling Wilburys, but the individual musicians said very little about the project publicly prior to the album's October release. Though the Wilburys album was recorded after most of the sessions for Petty's solo album and the sessions for Orbison's *Mystery Girl* album, the Wilburys album would be released first.

The origin of the Traveling Wilburys has since become rock 'n' roll legend. Harrison had conceived of creating a supergroup in 1987 while recording his *Cloud Nine* album with Lynne. The duo decided to dub this hypothetical group "the Wilburys" after Harrison said to Lynne that they'd solve the numerous recording errors during their sessions because "*We'll bury* 'em in the mix."

Of course, Lynne would go on to record with Petty and Orbison the following year. While Harrison was meeting with Warner Bros. Records executives in Los Angeles in early April 1988, he was asked to record a B-side for an upcoming European *Cloud Nine* single release. As the story goes, Harrison asked Lynne to produce the session and then asked Orbison to guest on the track while the trio were having lunch. Harrison suggested that they use "Bob's" home studio in Malibu. Orbison later told *Rolling Stone*, "I didn't know who Bob was. It turned out to be Bob Dylan." The final—and youngest—member of the group, Petty, got involved because Harrison had left his guitar at Petty's house. Years later, Petty remembered in *Conversations*, "[George] came by my house the night before to get his guitar. And he told me what he was going to do, and he asked, 'Would you like to come and play rhythm guitar? Will you come with me?' I said, 'Of course I would. I wouldn't miss that.' So in the morning I remember he came in his car with Jeff and picked me up, and we drove out to Bob's house in Malibu. And the night before he had written the chord pattern, pretty much, to 'Handle with Care.' He wrote it in his room at the Bel-Air Hotel. So when we got there, Bob was there. And George kind of showed us the chord pattern. And then he said, 'It'd be great if we had a part for Roy to sing in the tune.' He didn't want to waste Roy Orbison. So I remember Jeff and George sitting on the grass outside Bob's house and they wrote that middle bit: *[Sings]* 'I'm so tired of being lonely...' They wrote the melody and the chords to that." During the sessions, Dylan manned the barbeque for dinner.

In a 1990 radio interview with Roger Scott, Harrison explained, "I just said to Jeff, 'Hey, Jeff, this is it: the Traveling Wilburys.' And it was like magic. It just happened. You could never have planned it. You know, if we'd tried phoning everybody up and said, 'Hey, we got this idea. Will you do it?' You would've got all these record companies and managers and it would've been impossible. It was so spontaneous. We were doing it before we realized it."

To demonstrate the magic of that specific combination of rock greats and how other players wouldn't have worked in the mix, Campbell revealed in a November 2006 interview with *Vintage Guitar* that he was invited to play the guitar solo on "Handle With Care." "I played a little, but I was really scared, you know, 'cause here's *George Harrison*... (pauses) I just felt very intimidated. I did my best, and I didn't really think it was very good. So finally, I just kinda...George was sitting there—and they were being supportive and all—and I said to him, 'Listen, you should play guitar on this, because it would just feel better if it had your style on it.' So he said, 'Okay, I'll try something.' So he plugged into my amp and played that solo. It was just perfect. And I was so happy because he took the heat off me, you know?" Despite the invitation, Campbell did not play on any of the Wilburys' songs.

When Harrison presented the acoustic-based "Handle with Care" (titled after words Harrison had seen on a cardboard box in Dylan's studio) to Warner Bros., the executives thought that it would be a waste of a great track to use as an afterthought B-side and requested that Harrison and his new group create an entire album. Of course, that was easier said than done—five musicians collaborating on a one-off track in a single day is one thing, but agreeing to record an entire album amongst their busy individual schedules was a major roadblock. While Petty, Harrison, and Lynne were already in (and had been working together for much of the year already), and Dylan was available until the start of the first leg of what would become the Never Ending Tour in June 1988, Orbison, who had a heavy touring schedule, was another story.

On April 9, 1988, Petty, Harrison (with wife Olivia), and Lynne drove to Orbison's concert at the Celebrity Theatre in Anaheim, California. Petty explained to *BAM*, "We ran into Roy's dressing room, threw everybody out and said, 'We want you to be in our band, Roy.' He said, 'That'd be great,' then gave this unbelievable show. The whole time we were watching Roy, we'd punch each other and go, 'He's in our band, too.'" On the way home, Petty, Harrison and Lynne stopped at the Denny's restaurant on Sunset Boulevard, and it resulted in two bits of inspiration—one for the Wilburys and one for Petty's solo album. "We were writing everything we saw," Petty remembered in *Conversations*. "One line I remember that we saw on a billboard was, 'Every day is judgment day.' That later turned up in, 'End of the Line,' the Wilburys' song. We stopped at a restaurant on the way back, and these punky-looking guys recognized us and came over. And I said, 'Where have you been? Where are you playing?' And they said, 'The Zombie Zoo' and out came the pads!" The name became a title for the final song on Petty's solo album. (In a 2017 interview with *Rolling Stone*, Petty said he "hated" the song "Zombie Zoo." "I do not understand how that got on the record. I had better stuff," he said. "What frame of mind produced that?")

Later speaking to the *Los Angeles Times*, Petty said of the seemingly spur-of-the-moment way the band came together, "I think it had to be an accident to happen. We couldn't have planned it and done it. It wouldn't have worked. We were really doing it before we thought about it, almost."

The Wilbury sessions took place in April and May 1988 at Dave Stewart's home studio in Encino while Stewart was out of the country and during a break in Orbison's touring schedule. The sessions were marked by how collaborative and laid-back they were, with the Wilburys penning and recording songs in a matter of hours. Going into more detail, Petty told *BAM*, "There wasn't a whole lot of time for decision making. Camp Wilbury is what I called it, 'cause it was like coming to camp every day. Here we go again. Same bunch. We'd get out our acoustics and the five of us would just sit on the rug and the couch, throw out ideas and start a song off. Everyone would throw something in, and if someone was really on the ball we'd all back off and say, 'OK, you take it.' Then we'd usually go up and cut the backing track and take a break for dinner. We'd all eat around the same table, pass the lyrics around and work on them all through dinner. Then whoever drew the straw would sing it. In nine days, we did five songs and the backing tracks." Joining the Wilburys during the session was Jim Keltner on drums.

Though the songwriting was credited to all five members, Petty was the primary writer of "Last Night" (which he sang lead on) and "Margarita," and had substantial contributions to Dylan's "Tweeter and the Monkey Man," a lengthy parody of Bruce Springsteen's narrative lyric style. In 1989, Petty told *Newsday*, "We'd sit there with a tape deck. Bob would say: 'Tweeter and the...' And I'd say, 'Monkey man!' He'd say, 'Monkey man, hard up for cash...' I'd say, 'stayed up all night,' and someone from across the room would yell 'selling cocaine and hash!' And that's how it was done. It was so...easy! It was easy! The key word we used was fun. It sounds frivolous, but it's true. We really did enjoy that, and having a good time."

The music video for "Handle with Care" was shot with all the Wilburys near Union Station, a historic and significant rail transportation hub in downtown Los Angeles. The band members (plus Keltner on drums) performed facing each other in a circle, with the camera in the middle moving around to show the members individually. In addition, long shots showed the whole group performing together.

Upon the release of *The Traveling Wilburys Vol. 1* in October 1988, the *Los Angeles Times* joined in on the almost universal praise for the album. The review said that the Wilburys created "a strange and irresistible blend of classic voices and styles that's certain to be picked apart by music buffs for years to come" and that the sessions allowed the group to let "their collective hair down with 10 wild, woolly, and witty (but seriously good) collaborations." Santa Clarita's *Newhall Signal* called the album "a 10-song collection that is like a breath of fresh air on a sunny day compared to most other things out there," and remarked that the Petty-sung "Last Night" "may just be the best song on the album." *Vol. 1* peaked at #3 on the Billboard 200 and was eventually certified triple platinum, a massive success for the makeshift quintet working on a tight schedule.

Unsurprisingly, rumors that the Wilburys would tour or, at the very least, play a few shows—likely fueled by wishful thinking—ran rampant in the media, but it never happened. When asked about it by the *Los Angeles Times*, Petty said, "My problem is I would rather be out in the audience, watching these guys, than on stage." Any serious consideration of touring ground to a halt when Orbison died of a heart attack in Tennessee on December 6, shortly before he was scheduled to film a music video in Los Angeles with the Wilburys for "End of the Line." Petty and Lynne attended a memorial for Orbison at the Wiltern Theatre on December 13 that featured performances by Bonnie Raitt, Dave Edmunds, Johnny Rivers, and the Stray Cats. Harrison was ill and could not attend, and the *Los Angeles Times* reported that this prevented "an anticipated appearance of the remaining Traveling Wilburys" (notwithstanding the fact that Dylan was not reported in attendance). Orbison was buried in an unmarked grave at Westwood Memorial Park the following day (regarding the unmarked grave, Orbison's son Alex told Reuters in 2010 after Orbison's star was revealed on the Hollywood Walk of Fame, "It's definitely not intentional. It's not like we don't want people going by there or whatever. It's been put to the backburner so long").

Later that month, the Wilburys filmed the "End of the Line" music video in Los Angeles. It was directed by Willy Smax, who had directed several videos for the Eurythmics. The video depicts the remaining Wilburys and Jim Keltner performing the song while sitting in a circle inside a car on a moving train. When it comes to Orbison's part in the song, the camera pans to a photo of Orbison, followed by shots of the group facing a guitar sitting in a rocking chair.

In the following years, Petty frequently spoke wistfully about his time with the Wilburys, and in 1989 even expressed to the Associated Press that it helped him finally get over the trauma of his housefire. "I felt maybe, in a way, some cosmic way, [the Wilburys] was given to me to compensate for the house.... It was very refreshing, one of the nicest things that's ever happened to me."

CHAPTER 7

GLIDE DOWN OVER MULHOLLAND

With the Wilburys album a critical and commercial success, Petty's attention turned back to *Songs from the Garage*, the album which was now nearly a year old. As to why it hadn't been released yet, the album had faced a surprising snag when Petty initially turned it into his label in 1998: MCA rejected it because they did not believe it had any hit singles. Though hindsight is twenty-twenty, MCA was wrong; three songs on the album would eventually chart in the Top 40—including Petty's second highest-charting single in his career—and two more would also chart in the Hot 100 (a total of seven songs from the album would chart on Billboard's Mainstream Rock chart).

Petty was perplexed by the rejection, telling *Billboard* in 2005, "It's the only time in my life that a record's been rejected. And I was stunned. And I was so high on the record, and I tried to think, 'What did I do wrong?' They said they didn't hear any hits, and there turned out to be, like, four or five hits on the record, some of the biggest ones I ever had.... I just thought, 'It's just stupid. I made this really good record and they don't want it.' But I didn't, like, go to work on another one. I just joined the Wilburys, and this just sat on the back burner." Unsurprisingly, the rejection didn't sit well with Petty, and that pushed him toward his next record deal. He continued, "That was actually when I signed to Warner Bros. We were at [record producer] Mo Ostin's house, [and] the Wilburys played 'Free Fallin'' that night. [Warner Bros. Records President] Lenny Waronker was there and said, 'That song's amazing,' and I said, 'Yeah, it just got refused at my label.' Mo said, 'I'll sign you up and put that out, buddy, I'll sign you up right now,' and I said, 'You got a deal, Mo.'" Not long afterward, Petty would sign with Warner Bros. in a secret deal that wouldn't be publicly announced until 1992.

Perhaps one reason why MCA was unhappy with the album was the humor—with song titles like "Yer So Bad" and "A Mind with a Heart of Its Own," and the lighthearted lyrics in songs like "Runnin' Down a Dream" and "The Apartment Song," it was the most lighthearted set of songs of Petty's career. On why his songwriting went in this direction, Petty explained to *Newsday*, "I think because I so desperately wanted to be taken seriously when I was younger, starting out, the Heartbreakers were a pretty serious outfit. We wanted to be taken seriously because, it was like, 'Oh, they're from California, they can't have anything in their brains.' We said, yeah, we do, we're gonna show you." As for the new tone, Petty told *Rolling Stone* in 1991, "After a lot of years and a lot of booze, I came to the conclusion that all I can do is try to amuse myself, really."

Some of the most significant changes that happened to *Songs from the Garage* in the interim were changing the album's title and packaging after Petty had already shot the cover in Campbell's garage. A meeting with Denny Cordell derailed those plans. "I showed him the cover, and he said, 'Oh no, no, no, this is not right. This is far too good to be called *Songs from the Garage*,'" he remembered in *Conversations*. "And he said, 'Give it a name, man.' [Laughs] 'Give this thing a name.' So I rethought it and came up with *Full Moon Fever*. Which was probably good advice. We just completely jettisoned the cover and redid it." Petty told *Rolling Stone* that the new title was "just a little term I use when I'm doing things and I don't know why. I thought the phrase pretty well fit the circumstances behind this album." The final cover ended up being a simple photo of Petty and the album title made to look like a classic multi-color gig poster.

In addition, the nine-song album clocked in at just twenty-six minutes—what would have been the shortest album in Petty's career. To allay concerns with the length, Petty added three additional songs to the album, including a cover of the Byrds' "I'll Feel a Whole Lot Better," which Petty and Lynne were inspired to record after seeing the Byrds perform on January 7, 1989, at the Majestic Ventura Theater. At that same concert, Petty joined the Byrds—which featured a lineup including Roger McGuinn, David Crosby, and Chris Hillman, who had reunited to strengthen their claim to the band name amid legal disputes with other former Byrds bandmates—on stage to perform "So You Want to Be a Rock 'n' Roll Star."

Remarkably, *Full Moon Fever* was accepted by the new regime at MCA, but the battles with the label didn't end. According to Petty in *Conversations*, MCA was against releasing "Free Fallin'" as the album's third single. He remembered, "'Free Fallin'' was the first time, I think, that I ever had a ballad out for a single. And even then it was the third single from the album. [MCA] didn't want to do it because they didn't think anyone outside of Southern California would relate to it. And I said, 'No, you're wrong, they will.'"

MCA thought the song's lyrics were too specific to the Los Angeles area. In fact, Petty did agree that *Full Moon Fever* was "a very Los Angeles record" as a whole, telling *Spin*, "One of the great things about LA is that you can be all alone in your car—alone and moving fast. It's very therapeutic." There were also concerns that the song didn't sound like a typical Tom Petty track. The *Runnin' Down a Dream* book quoted Denny Cordell saying, "Tom asked if I would listen to something, and I said sure. He put on the album with 'Free Fallin'.' I jumped up and shouted and laughed. It was just great. And he said, 'I'm glad you like it because the record company doesn't want to release it.' He told me that they felt it was inconsistent with his image. I fired off a letter to the president saying he should fire his ass."

Also, according to Petty, "Free Fallin'" began as a joke. He told *Guitar Player* in 1999, "I wrote the first two verses of 'Free Fallin'" just trying to make Jeff Lynne laugh. Later on, I could see that I was writing about the Valley because I had to drive through it every day. A lot of the biggest songs only took minutes to write. It's about waiting for that bolt of lightning." He elaborated more on the writing process and the lyrics to *Musician* magazine in 1990, noting, "I wrote it real fast. I started it off on a keyboard. Bugs, who's a roadie who's been with us since the day we started, bought me this Yamaha keyboard. I said, 'Man, why'd you buy that? It's expensive!' He said, 'If you write one song on it it'll pay for itself.' So he charged it to me and left it there. Jeff Lynne was over one night and I started playing with it...Jeff goes, 'Wait! What was that? Just play the first part over and over.' Okay. I did and Jeff's just sitting there smiling and he says, 'Go on, sing something.' So just to make Jeff smile I sang, 'She's a good girl, loves her mama.' And from there I wrote the first and second verse completely spontaneously. We were smart enough to have a cassette on. So I sang the first couple of verses and Jeff says, 'Go up on the chorus, take your voice up a whole octave—what'll that sound like?' I said, 'I'm freeee...' He said, 'Wo! There's power in that, that's good!'"

Petty wrote the first two verses and the chorus in that session, then wrote the final verse ("I wanna glide down over Mullholland...") that night and brought the finished song to Lynne the next day. Petty, Lynne, Campbell, and drummer Phil Jones recorded the song that day. The final lyrics are filled with references to the San Fernando Valley, and the *Newhall Signal* later called it "probably the first song to pay homage to Reseda and Ventura Boulevard," even if, as many Los Angelenos have since correctly noted, there is no freeway running through Reseda (as the second verse erroneously states). There are several songs that predate "Free Fallin'" that reference the two locales. A reference to Reseda appeared in music as early as the 1968 song "Hair Pie: Bake 1" by Captain Beefheart & His Magic Band, and the Everly Brothers released a song titled "Ventura Boulevard" on their 1968 album *Roots*. In addition, Ventura Boulevard was previously most famously mentioned in the 1982 Top 40 single "Valley Girl" by Frank and Moon Zappa. However, none of those songs have had the success or staying power of Petty's ballad.

Being more specific about the mindset behind the song to *Musician* magazine in 1990, Petty reflected, "I know 'Free Fallin'' was influenced by driving up and down Mulholland Drive, where I was living for a while. I did a lot of driving, and a lot of the album came to me on those drives. We were moving all around town, going from house to house, staying in hotels. It was a funny lifestyle, but in the end it was good creatively. I think that was a way of working out all the stuff with the fire so I wouldn't build up a lot of aggression and anger about it. I think looking back—this could be total bullshit—I completely adopted another stance for the album: 'Look, let's just be happy and try to get something over with a positive vibe *and* some credibility; it's easy to go over the line.'" Despite MCA's initial objections, the song became one of the most beloved—if not *the* most beloved—hit of Petty's career. It reached #7 on the Billboard Hot 100, his third Top 10 single after "Don't Do Me Like That" and "Stop Draggin' My Heart Around."

In the liner notes of *Playback*, Petty revealed the story behind the most curious line of the song—the one about "vampires walking through the valley." Fellow California musician Axl Rose was a huge fan of "Free Fallin'" and one day asked Petty where those lyrics originated from. Petty told him, "When I'm driving I sometimes see these shadowy-looking people just off the sidewalks, around the post office. I always thought of them as vampires for some reason."

What also helped boost the song's popularity was the music video, directed by famed director Julien Temple, who had risen to fame working on various video projects with the Sex Pistols and had filmed music videos for Judas Priest, Neil Young, the Kinks, the Rolling Stones, David Bowie, the Stray Cats, Culture Club, Depeche Mode, and had recently directed the film *Earth Girls are Easy*. The video clip features images of two different generations of an idealized Los Angeles—one in which pastel dress-wearing girls listen to Elvis records at a poolside Sweet Sixteen party, and another where skateboarding teens pull off jumps in a halfpipe while surrounded by the San Fernando Valley's mountain ranges—alternating with shots of Petty singing and playing guitar while riding the escalators in a mall (what many might consider an ultimate symbol of Los Angeles in the '80s). The mall scenes were shot at the Westside Pavilion in Los Angeles. The video also includes the once-popular hot dog stand Future Dogs in Sherman Oaks, which was located along Ventura Boulevard. In 2016, *LA Weekly* selected "Free Fallin'" as the best music video shot in Los Angeles, quite possibly because it shows sides of Los Angeles rarely depicted in other media.

While "Free Fallin'" was held off as the third single off *Full Moon Fever*, the record company chose something they felt was more in line with Petty's defiant songs as the lead single—"I Won't Back Down." This Petty/Lynne composition features Petty stating his intentions to stand up against all odds, no matter what, to a driving beat and stellar slide guitar work by Campbell. George Harrison also played on the recording, contributing acoustic guitar and backing vocals. He also encouraged Petty to change the lyric from "I'm standing on the edge of the world," to "There ain't no easy way out." Famously, the music video, which was shot in England, features a half-Beatles reunion with Harrison and Ringo Starr, who plays drums in the video, although he didn't play on the track. However, it served as something of a preview because Starr would play drums on Petty's next solo album. The video also features Campbell playing Harrison's iconic "Rocky" 1961 Fender Stratocaster that he had used to record many of the late '60s Beatles songs.

Though Petty had some hesitations about releasing the song as a single, it was a major success. "I Won't Back Down" peaked at #12 on the Billboard chart, hit #1 on the Album Rock chart, and became one of Petty's most popular songs. In the *Going Home* documentary, Petty said of the song, "'I Won't Back Down' is one of the most rewarding songs I've written. I still get letters from people or they come up to me on the street and tell me how it's helped them through some kind of crisis in their life. And you know, really to inspire somebody is the highest thing a songwriter can strive for."

The second single from *Full Moon Fever* became another Top 40 hit (peaking at #23, and, like its predecessor, it hit #1 on the Album Rock chart), a perennial Heartbreakers concert encore favorite, and a showcase for Mike Campbell: the driving "Runnin' Down a Dream," which features one of Campbell's best solos as a long outro. In *Conversations*, the singer remembered, "The most incredible thing about that one to me, which to this day amazes me, was the solo at the end. Mike played that. There was no one there but me, Mike, and Jeff. And Mike was engineering....Mike was just sitting there with his head down. And that bit came, and he started to play. And he played that incredible solo. But he looked like a stone statue. He didn't ever blink or move. And he had his back to us."

On April 16, Petty and Harrison attended the Long Beach Grand Prix—an IndyCar Series race that started in 1975, and is the longest-running major street race in North America—as guests of driver Emerson Fittipaldi. While Petty previously had little interest in the sport, Harrison was a fan of auto racing (he had penned an ode to it, "Faster," on his 1979 self-titled album). In *Conversations*, Petty recalled of speaking with Fittipaldi, "We went out after the race, and I said, 'How do you prepare for these races?' Because I watched him. We were backstage, and I watched him getting ready and into his racing suit. I thought, this is heavy shit. This guy is going to be going *really* fast for a long time. And if you fuck up, you're dead.... So I said to him, 'How do you prepare for this?' And he goes, 'What I do is I go through the entire race in my head before I go out there. Because I know the track, and I think it through, and I think what I'm going to do, where I'm going to be, and I see myself doing it.'" Petty would later cite that advice as helping him improve his on-stage performances.

Two days later, the release party for *Full Moon Fever* was held in a unique location—on the *Star Trek Adventure* ride on the Universal Studios lot, which featured a replica of the *Enterprise*. Reportedly attending the party were Harrison, Stevie Nicks, Lindsey Buckingham, the Beastie Boys, and Duff McKagan and Steven Adler of Guns N' Roses. Petty was also interviewed by longtime entertainment critic and former MTV News correspondent Kurt Loder for an album-release radio special.

Despite the great acclaim *Full Moon Fever* would receive over time, initial reviews were not overwhelmingly positive. Cary Darling's review in the *Orange County Register* was generally praiseworthy, calling the album "a lighthearted, often humorous effort with about as much weight as a mild ocean breeze," while concluding, "Those who want something more serious may have to wait for Petty's next effort with the Heartbreakers." In Chris Willman's three-star review in the *Los Angeles Times*, he refers to *Full Moon Fever* as "The *Traveling Wilburys, Volume Two*" (although most of it was recorded prior to the Wilburys' album). Like Darling, Willman noted Petty's humor throughout the album and remarked about how light it is. A more laudatory review appeared in *Orange Coast* magazine, prophetically stating it "could be a favorite for years....The songs are refreshing, the production solid. Along the best tunes are 'Free Fallin',' 'I Won't Back Down,' 'A Face in the Crowd' and 'Alright for Now,'" the first three of which charted on the Billboard Hot 100.

For what it's worth, the lighthearted Petty clearly struck a chord with audiences. *Full Moon Fever* peaked at #3 on the Billboard chart in July and spent seventy-one weeks on the Billboard Top 200. It was eventually certified quintuple platinum. *Full Moon Fever* remains Petty's bestselling non-compilation album.

The *Full Moon Fever* supporting tour, called the Strange Behavior Tour, began on July 5 in Miami and made its way to Southern California for one performance at the Pacific Amphitheater in Costa Mesa on July 27 (with the Replacements opening) and performances on July 29, 30, and 31 at the Universal Amphitheater (with Dion opening). Notably, the tour featured a somewhat elaborate stage design—at least by Heartbreakers standards. The *Los Angeles Times* described it as "the interior of a tent with the air of a massive, stately drawing room, garnished with such furnishings as cattle horns, a suit of armor, a totem pole, a stuffed bear and Egyptian hieroglyphics—all emblems that, one way or another, suggest *classic*." According to *USA*

Today, the set also included a "cigar store Indian," "Zulu war shield," and "weathered trunk."

During the tour, the Heartbreakers typically played five songs from *Full Moon Fever*: "Free Fallin'," "I Won't Back Down," "Yer So Bad," "Feel a Whole Lot Better," and "Runnin' Down a Dream." During the Universal Amphitheater concerts, the Heartbreakers were joined by their 1987 tour openers, the Georgia Satellites, for renditions of that band's biggest hit, "Keep Your Hands to Yourself." In Steven P. Wheeler's review of one of the Universal Amphitheater concerts in *Music Connection*, he remarked, "Obviously stung by reviews that were critical of his 'predictable sets,' Petty went out of his way to give a looser performance than any in recent years. This improvisational slant surfaced midway through the evening during an extended string of acoustic numbers that included audience requests for 'Spike' (from *Southern Accents*) and the real surprise, 'No Second Thoughts,' from his 1977 songbook, which led Petty to ask the band if they knew the chords before giving a short but sparkling rendition that once again demonstrated just how good this band really is." The review concluded: "Another brilliant performance by the quintessential American rock 'n' roll band of this generation."

Incidentally, the Heartbreakers' lighting system came to the rescue for Rod Stewart's San Diego concert on August 1, when Stewart's system was already en route to the East Coast for the next leg of his tour due to a scheduling mishap. Since the Universal Amphitheater has its own lighting system and the band didn't need to use theirs during the three Universal shows, the Heartbreakers were able to lend their lights to Stewart for his performance.

The success of *Full Moon Fever* brought in new audiences to the concerts, with Petty telling *Rolling Stone* in 1991, "We were beginning to see the same faces for a while there. It was incredible to find so many young people who didn't know anything about us, or me, who were discovering the whole trip because they liked 'Free Fallin'' or 'I Won't Back Down.' I think I laughed for an entire year."

The Heartbreakers returned to the Universal Amphitheater on September 6 to play the finale of the 1989 MTV Video Music Awards after canceling several tour dates to fit the appearance in their schedule. The band performed two songs—"Free Fallin'" and "Heartbreak Hotel" joined by Guns N' Roses singer Axl Rose and guitarist Izzy Stradlin. Rose's more energetic performance of the not-yet-a-hit Petty single caused issues—*Musician* reported that "some viewers think Tom looks angry with Axl for taking over the song; others think he just looks bemused," while the *Los Angeles Times* said that Rose had "trouble fitting into" the song. However, *Musician* also reported, "The truth is, Petty gets a kick out of Axl's scene-stealing, though the other Heartbreakers don't."

The Heartbreakers were also caught in the crossfire of a scuffle between Mötley Crüe's lead singer Vince Neil and Stradlin and Rose after the performance. While coming off stage, Stradlin was punched by Neil over what was reported as a previous altercation between Stradlin and Neil's then-wife. Petty managed to miss the main brunt of the action, but still commented on it to *Musician*, saying, "We manage to get into shit somehow. I don't dig blindsiding somebody, if that's what happened. I didn't see it. I just saw Vince Neil go storming by and a guy running behind him with a walkie talkie going, 'Vince? Vince!' I heard a commotion but I didn't know what it was. I just kept going. I said, 'Is that any of our guys?' And they said, 'No, it's on the stage.' Stan [Lynch] was there, [Heartbreakers lighting designer] Jim Lenahan threw a couple of punches at Vince Neil. Lenahan's great. He's like, 'He's with us—at least for right now.'" The incident made headlines in the music press, though the Heartbreakers escaped most mentions.

Once the Strange Behavior Tour wrapped a week later in Chapel Hill, NC, on September 13, the Heartbreakers took a break from the road with the exception of a short set on October 28 at the Bridge School Benefit concert, an annual charity concert weekend in northern California to support the Bridge School, an academy for students with speech and physical disabilities. Petty was a semi-regular on the bill from the first edition in 1986 to 2000.

In addition to Petty's new attitude in his approach to music, the period marked a significant change in Petty's attitude towards activism. For example, Petty had in the tour riders for the Strange Behavior Tour that no Styrofoam or plastic plates or utensils could be used backstage. He told the *Austin American-Statesman*, "Boy, they think I'm crazy, but I think you've got to just do your own little bit for those things." He had come a long way from the younger man that told *Sounds* in 1978, "You don't have to throw some useless political trip on everybody that you're gonna regret three months later because you're a chump for saying it. My idea of rock 'n' roll is you don't give a fuck about politics because you're listening to records, man. I don't have time for news. If they're gonna drop the bomb, fuckin' drop it—I dare ya. Blow my ass off. But I don't wanna write songs about it. What a useless trip. Ecology? Man, I still throw Coke bottles out the window. Somebody will pick it up; in fact, somebody will make money on it. We used to go collect bottles to eat. There's a little old lady goes by here every day with a basket full. If they didn't make such a big deal about it, maybe I wouldn't, but you pass one of them 'No Littering' signs on the road, you try to hit it, right?"

Petty's opinion on ecology had certainly changed since then. Shortly after the Strange Behavior Tour ended, Petty attended a news conference organized by environmental groups asking for clarity on plans for proposed power plants in Canoga Park and concerns over nuclear power testing. Petty told the *Los Angeles Times* that he came as "a concerned citizen and resident of the San Fernando Valley," and said, "I've been reading about it in the papers, and I'm interested. I just came to hear what they had to say." Later Petty told *Rolling Stone* about his new focus on advocacy, "People are getting overly inundated with causes because the world is really fucked up. It drives me crazy, too, but out of conscience I have to sometimes at least speak out."

In July 1990, the *Los Angeles Times* reported that Petty and about one hundred other residents of Encino protested plans to build a 375,000-square-foot office tower at the intersection of Ventura Boulevard and Hayvenhurst Avenue, with Petty telling the paper, "This is sheer madness and it's being done for greed, rather than the good of the community. Encino is already prone to small businesses being wiped out and a high vacancy rate in office buildings. I don't understand why we need one that's nearly a mile long." Petty's participation brought visibility to the protest as evidenced by the article's headline: "Rock Star Joins Audience in Assailing Encino Project."

Petty wasn't just focusing on local politics, either. Throughout the Into the Great Wide Open Tour a few years later, during the outro of "Don't Come Around Here No More," Petty would be chased by individuals wearing masks of Republican Presidents Nixon, Reagan, and George H. W. Bush, whom Petty would later chase off by holding up a giant peace sign, like a cross to Dracula. While Petty always carried himself like a fighter in his various battles with the record industry, he was now equally public with his political battles. Petty would later use his celebrity to support other causes—particularly local Southern California causes—throughout the rest of his career. By the 1995 Dogs with Wings Tour in support of *Wildflowers*, the Heartbreakers had partnered with several charity organizations, including Greenpeace (which had information booths at each tour stop); USA Harvest, a food drive organization which collected cans of food from concert attendees; and Wrap It Up, an organization which took leftovers from backstage catering and delivered it to soup kitchens and homeless shelters.

In early 1990, Petty was nominated for four Grammy Awards and found himself in competition with himself when both *Traveling Wilburys Vol. 1* and *Full Moon Fever* were nominated for Album of the Year. Don Henley's *The End of the Innocence*, featuring the contributions from Campbell and Lynch, was also nominated. The eventual winner, though, was Bonnie Raitt's *Nick of Time*, which featured future Heartbreaker Scott Thurston on keyboards.

The award show was hosted by Petty's friend, comedian and actor Garry Shandling, at the Shrine Auditorium, a historic theater in Los Angeles near the University of Southern California that has served as the home of both the Academy Awards and Grammy Awards ceremonies, along with many other award ceremonies and sporting and concert events. Prior to the show, Petty spoke about the Album of the Year nomination to *USA Today*, saying, "I never pictured us as the type to be nominated. I didn't think we could even get tickets to the show! I'm pretty impressed by the company we're in, but I don't really believe in handing out awards for the 'best' record. What feels good is that your peers are saying, 'Good job, kid.' That's nice. You can't get too caught up in awards. [Pause] But I hope we win." The Wilburys took home the Grammy Award for Best Rock Performance by a Duo or Group with Vocal, which was Petty's first Grammy Award.

Despite Petty telling Hollywood columnist Marilyn Beck at the end of 1989 that he would be taking a hiatus after his past two prolific years ("I just want to live life a bit. You can't write the songs if you don't live life sometimes"), the Heartbreakers returned to the road for the More Strange Behavior Tour running from late January until early March 1990. The tour included one concert on March 1 at the Great Western Forum in Inglewood and another on March 3 at the Pacific Amphitheater in Costa Mesa. In addition to the five *Full Moon Fever* songs the Heartbreakers played the previous time they had concerts in the Los Angeles area, the Heartbreakers performed four more: "Love Is a Long Road," "A Mind With a Heart of Its Own," "A Face in the Crowd," and "Alright for Now," nearly playing the entire album live.

Both concerts featured big surprises. At the Forum, the Heartbreakers were joined onstage by both Bob Dylan and Bruce Springsteen (with the *Los Angeles Times* describing the Boss as, "looking rather Bono-esque with slicked-back hair, ponytail, stinger beard and earring") for an impromptu—and sloppy—encore of Dylan's "Rainy Day Women #12 & 35," J.J. Cale's "Cocaine" (so slapdash that many couldn't figure out what the group was attempting to play), the Animal's "I'm Crying," and Creedence Clearwater Revival's "Travelin' Band." In *Conversations*, Petty recalled of that evening, "We came back for the encore and Bob Dylan was there. And he wanted to play. And he came out. And then the next thing I looked up, and Bruce Springsteen had come out. So there's all three of us playing at once. And the crowd was just insane, they were just insane.... But none of it was rehearsed, because we didn't know it was going to happen. We literally got into a huddle, planned it out, came out of the huddle, and started the song. And huddled up again.... And I thought, 'Damn, that must have been a real treat for the audience.'"

The *Los Angeles Times* review of the concert saw it fit to place Petty on the same level as his two guests, saying, "Petty has arrived at that summit of stardom where, when he was joined on stage at the Forum by guests Bob Dylan and Bruce Springsteen—which in rock terms pretty much amounts to a visit from the gods *en masse*—he didn't seem outranked. This, as far as the crowd was concerned, was a meeting of equals." The review also praised the concert overall, remarking, "Thursday's show included the bulk of the greatest hits of Tom Petty and the Heartbreakers, as well as the bulk of his latest, biggest-selling and perhaps best album, *Full Moon Fever*." In her review in the *Santa Clarita Signal*, Karin Holtz likened Petty to "a tribal chief conducting a sacred ceremony," saying that Petty "led the Great Western Forum crowd through a mystical and haunting series of songs," and noting that the audience "screamed the names of local landmarks in the lyrics of 'Free Fallin'.'" Also reported in attendance were Jeff Lynne, Roger McGuinn, Slash, and Duff McKagan.

At the Costa Mesa concert, the Heartbreakers were joined by Roger McGuinn, who performed "Mr. Tambourine Man," "Turn! Turn! Turn!" and "Eight Miles High."

By early 1990, the Heartbreakers made another addition to their sound. Initially playing along offstage with the group was multi-instrumentalist Scott Thurston, contributing additional guitars, keyboards, and backing vocals. Thurston had been a longtime rock sideman for a variety of artists, and had worked extensively with Iggy Pop—first as a member of Iggy and the Stooges, then as a contributor to Pop's solo work—as well as the Motels, which had once also featured pre-Heartbreakers guitarist Jeff Jourard and his brother, Marty Jourard (both Thurston and Marty Jourard appeared on the Motels' 1983 album, *Little Robbers*). By the Touring the Great Wide Open Tour, Thurston was acknowledged as a sideman performing with the group, and his stature within the Heartbreakers would grow as he became an essential part of expanding the Heartbreakers' live sound. His first recordings with the group would appear on 1999's *Echo*, and by 2002's *The Last DJ* he would be officially acknowledged as a member of the Heartbreakers.

Even after the More Strange Behavior Tour ended on March 6 in Oakland, Petty still didn't take the break he said he was going to take at the end of the previous year. Almost immediately after the tour wrapped, Petty (playing bass) and Lynne (playing guitar) joined Ringo Starr (vocals and drums), Joe Walsh (guitar), and Jim Keltner (percussion) in Los Angeles at Rumbo Recorders to perform the Beatles song "I Call Your Name" for a tribute concert that aired later in the year on the tenth anniversary of John Lennon's death. Also in March, Petty attended country legend Tammy Wynette's concert at the Roxy on March 14 alongside Lynne.

Also in early spring, Petty shot the music video for "Yer So Bad," directed by Julien Temple, in which former *Saturday Night Live* actor Charles Rocket plays the lead "yuppie" depicted in the song's lyrics, as Petty creeps around—sometimes voyeuristically with a camera—to musically narrate the proceedings. The first chorus features lounge singers Marty and Elayne, a Los Angeles institution who have appeared on stage at the Dresden Room, a Los Feliz nightclub, since 1981 and have continued for over thirty-five years. This part of the video was actually shot at the Dresden, and in 2016 Elayne told KCET about the appearance in the video, "When we did the Tom Petty video the trendies came in and it got mobbed in here. It was difficult to hear what we were doing and we were shocked for a while." The video also features the yuppie staying at the El Royale Hotel, the small Studio City bungalow-style hotel that has appeared in several films and television series (including Paul Thomas Anderson's 1997 film *Boogie Nights*). Though, like many of Petty's other videos, the humor of the "Yer So Bad" video wasn't for everyone. In the *Los Angeles Times*, Chris Willman panned the video, calling it "an ugly cartoon" and labeling Rocket's character "Yer so misanthropic" for finding post-divorce comfort with a blow-up doll.

* * * * *

In 1989, Lynne, Petty, and the Heartbreakers—minus Stan Lynch—participated in sessions with Del Shannon for an album that would not be released until 1991, after Shannon's death. The album was coproduced by Lynne and Campbell. At the time, there were media reports that Shannon was being considered to replace Orbison in the Traveling Wilburys (a "fact" even mentioned years later on Shannon's official website), but Shannon told the *Los Angeles Times* in April 1989, "It's a nice rumor, and I do know Jeff, Tom and George quite well, but it hasn't been mentioned to me at all, not even hinted. And it's certainly not my business to bring it up with them. But it seems the more I deny it, the more people think I'm going to be in it." Shannon wasn't the only one that was speculated to take Orbison's place—in an interview with the *Desert Sun* that same month, rockabilly legend Carl Perkins thought he would be getting a call from Harrison to replace Orbison, saying, "I'd gladly do it. I'm just waiting on his phone call."

However, Harrison denied that anyone was ever considered to replace Orbison in the Wilburys, noting to the *Los Angeles Times*, "We didn't really bring Roy in. He just happened to be there, you know, and that's how it came about. So there was no reason to go looking for somebody [to replace him]. If somebody else happened to have been there that seemed to fit in and everybody was happy with, it would just happen like it happened with Roy. And I think to try and contrive to make some other new member, it's not worth the trouble. I mean, there's already enough of us anyway."

Starting in April 1990, the Traveling Wilburys began work on the follow up to *Vol. 1*. In *Conversations*, Petty remembered, "By the second album, we had this great big mansion up on a hill in Beverly Hills that was a Wallace Neff home [one of California's most celebrated architects]. He built it in the Twenties. It was kind of a Spanish-style, huge mansion. It was like sixteen acres up at the top of a mountain. We had a big flagpole with the Wilbury flag flying above the home. Even from the bottom of the hill, you could look up and see the flag. So that became dubbed 'Wilbury Manor.' We moved a studio into the library." When the album was released on October 29, it was perplexingly titled *Traveling Wilburys Vol. 3*. When Harrison was asked by the *Los Angeles Times* why it wasn't named *Volume 2*, he replied, "We haven't made that yet. Is that an obvious enough answer?"

The Wilburys filmed three music videos for the album, including "The Wilbury Twist," which was shot at the historic Wilshire Ebell Theatre in Los Angeles and featured celebrities like John Candy, Eric Idle, and infamous pop music busts Milli Vanilli in cameo roles.

Commercially, the album—considerably more Dylan-focused than its predecessor—was less successful than the original, though it peaked at #11 on the Billboard 200 and went platinum. The idea of the Wilburys touring came up again, though the English half of the group was even less enthusiastic than the first time the idea was proposed. Petty told *Rolling Stone* in 1991, "A lot of money was offered to us, but at the end of the meeting, we'd decided not to do it.... And I kept getting down on my knees in front of George, saying, 'Please! It's so much money.' And everybody would just start laughing. It was that kind of meeting; we'd look at each other and start giggling nervously, going, 'Nah, we can't.' Like George says, I can't see waking up in a hotel in Philadelphia and having to do a Wilburys sound check."

The various Wilburys would sometimes talk about getting together to record a third album in interviews (or by their counting, would it be *Volume Five*? Or the missing *Volume Two*?), but on December 30, 1999, Harrison was attacked in his home and stabbed over forty times by an assailant. The always-humorous Harrison released a statement about the attacker: "He wasn't a burglar, but he certainly wasn't auditioning for the Traveling Wilburys." Though Harrison survived, he rarely appeared in public in the following years, and his time in the studio was concentrated on what would become a posthumous album, 2002's *Brainwashed*.

Meanwhile, the Heartbreakers (with the exception of Epstein) participated in sessions for Roger McGuinn's 1991 solo album *Back from Rio* at Capitol Studios, including a song Petty and McGuinn cowrote and sang together on the album, "King of the Hill," a song Petty and McGuinn had demoed in 1987. When McGuinn performed an industry showcase concert at the Troubadour on January 31, 1991, Petty joined him onstage to perform the duet. In addition, Lynch backed McGuinn on drums for the whole set.

Around the time of the release of the second Wilburys album, Petty celebrated his fortieth birthday with a party at his house. In attendance were Jeff Lynne, Roger McGuinn, Bruce Springsteen, Elvis Costello, Jim Keltner, Garry Shandling, Clarence Carter, Patti Scialfa, Kathy Valentine of the Go-Gos, and members of the Heartbreakers. With so many musicians in attendance, the party naturally turned into a jam session. According to *USA Today*, songs that were played include "Little Red Rooster," "Roll Over Beethoven," "Great Balls of Fire," "Wipeout," and "Pipeline." Petty told *Rolling Stone* in 2009, "We were having this big party, and there were a lot of players there. Elvis [Costello] wasn't there yet. It had coalesced into this jam in my living room. Roger McGuinn [of the Byrds], Jeff Lynne and Bruce Springsteen were playing. I know I'm leaving some people out. But the joke was, McGuinn went into 'Mr. Tambourine Man' right as Costello comes walking in. He said, 'If I ever had to dream up walking into Tom Petty's house, it would be the Byrds playing 'Mr. Tambourine Man.'"

CHAPTER 8

THE SKY WAS THE LIMIT

With the lengthy touring cycle for *Full Moon Fever* complete and the second Traveling Wilburys album released, Petty's attention finally turned to the long overdue Heartbreakers follow-up to 1987's *Let Me Up (I've Had Enough)*. Sessions began the day after Petty's fortieth birthday on October 20, and would continue into 1991.

Early in the New Year, Petty participated in the Los Angeles session rerecording John Lennon's "Give Peace a Chance," spearheaded by Lennon's widow Yoko Ono and fifteen-year-old son Sean Lennon (sessions were also held in London and New York). Petty joined Lenny Kravitz (who produced the session), Al Jarreau, Duff McKagan, MC Hammer, and Flea of Red Hot Chili Peppers, among others. The song was released as a statement against the Operation Desert Shield coalition, regarding its deadline for Iraq President Saddam Hussein to withdraw Iraqi forces from Kuwait, which prompted Operation Desert Storm when Hussein did not adhere to the deadline. Line Producer Rob Newman told Marilyn Beck in her syndicated column, "Tom was really tired, he'd been working all day on his own recording, but he wanted to be part of it. Everyone did. Everyone wants to do something relevant to what's happening in the world right now; this is something we could do." Petty briefly appears in the music video.

Petty and the Heartbreakers then went to work with Jeff Lynne at Rumbo Recorders, Studio C (though parts were also recorded at Campbell's home studio). Petty was nervous about combining Lynne with the band, telling *Rolling Stone* in 1991, "Now that was scary for me. There I was taking one of my new friends to meet some of my old ones. And all I can think is 'Oh, boy, these people had better get along.'"

It turned out to be a challenging fit, particularly since Petty cowrote most of the album's songs with Lynne. In the liner notes to *Playback*, Petty admitted, "It was a complete mess. To me it seemed like a logical step. I was so happy working with Jeff and I thought, 'Well, let's bring Jeff and the band together and see what happens.' But really, there was always one side deferring to the other and they felt self-conscious. Jeff is a very determined person with strong views. Jeff, Mike and I were very tight; the rest of them hardly knew Jeff. I think a big mistake was that we didn't give the Heartbreakers more say. If they had had their normal amount of input I think it might have worked, but it was just impossible with the personalities. It had to happen, though, to convince me that I had brought everything out of that mine and it was time to move on."

One song that Petty wrote was inspired by the nature around his house in Encino, "You and I Will Meet Again," which features the lyric "A red-winged hawk is circling / The blacktop stretches out for days." In *Conversations*, he explained, "In Encino we lived on this wooded hill. There were a lot of big oak trees. To be in the middle of L.A., it was kind of a rural setting. You'd see these hawks all the time. I'd actually watch them dive, and come back up. And I wouldn't be surprised if that's where the reference to the hawks came from."

The album, *Into the Great Wide Open*, features two of Petty's most beloved songs, which were released as the first two singles from the album: "Learning to Fly" and the title track. The chorus of "Learning to Fly" had been inspired by a quip Petty heard from a pilot talking about flying a plane on television: "Coming down is the hardest thing."

While director Julien Temple and the Heartbreakers were filming the music video for the lead single, "Learning to Fly," at an Air Force scrapyard in Tucson, Arizona, a rainstorm halted production. During the storm, the set was visited by actors Faye Dunaway and Johnny Depp, who were filming the 1993 feature film *Arizona Dream* nearby. The meeting eventually resulted in the idea that Dunaway and Depp could star in the next Heartbreakers' video. Dunaway was a well-established, Oscar-winning actress, while Depp was a star on the rise, fresh off his television series *21 Jump Street* and film *Edward Scissorhands*. More importantly, Depp was a Heartbreakers fan and relished the opportunity to appear in a Petty video.

The second single was the title track, and it was accompanied by one of Petty's most ambitious music videos. The video tells the narrative story of Eddie Rebel (Depp), a teenager who goes to Hollywood, gets a tattoo from an artist who looks suspiciously like Tom Petty, and meets a girl (Gabrielle Anwar) who has the same tattoo. She "taught him some chords" and his landlady-turned-manager (Dunaway) begins pushing him towards stardom. Soon he's the next big thing on the Sunset Strip, a true rock 'n' roll overnight sensation. But Eddie—as many rock stars have done—arrogantly forgets the people who helped him to the top, particularly when he prevents his manager from attending a Hollywood party. She reveals herself to be something like a fairy godmother and, after waving her cigarette holder like a magic wand, Eddie's sex, drugs, and rock 'n' roll lifestyle spirals downward until he winds up back at the tattoo shop, with the artist now looking suspiciously like a down-on-his-luck Eddie tattooing another young man (played by future *Friends* star Matt Leblanc), who is perhaps the next young rock star to go through the vicious cycle of the scene. At the end of the video, Petty narrates, "And they all lived happily ever after"—but in typical Petty humor, it's very hard to believe that's actually true. While the lyrics of the song leaves Eddie's fate open-ended, the video makes it apparent that he's just another cautionary tale of the music business.

The narrative of the "Into the Great Wide Open" video was too long for the three-minute, forty-five-second song. In fact, in *Tom Petty and* the Heartbreakers: Runnin' Down A Dream, Petty recalled, "We had so much good film. The first cut of the video was eighteen minutes long. It was a four minute song. So I was working with Julien Temple, I said, 'Julian, this is not gonna fly.' And he said, 'I know, but it's so good.' I said, 'Well, you better take another pass at it.' And so I came back a few days later and he had a seven and a half minute cut."

The Heartbreakers created an extended version of the song to fit the video's length. But in that era, a seven-and-a-half minute video was still too lengthy for MTV airplay for any artist not named Michael Jackson. Petty solved that issue by simply playing dumb. "Somebody says MTV is never gonna play a seven and a half minute song. And I said, 'Just don't say anything about it, just send it.' And so we did and they played it in heavy rotation for months. And I don't know to this day if they knew it was seven and a half minutes long."

Temple told the *Los Angeles Times*, "We just wanted to capture the song's depiction of the perils of rock stardom. There's such a universal quality to it. Johnny Depp could be James Dean or Sid Vicious or Axl [Rose]. In fact, Johnny's a huge Sex Pistols fan—and I think you can see a lot of Sid in his performance."

The plot of "Into the Great Wide Open" was likely close to Petty's heart. Since their 1976 debut, the Heartbreakers had seen countless bands come and go—some that even charted singles and albums above the Heartbreakers—and the late '80s era of hard rock "hair bands" coming out of the same Southern California scene that produced bands that inspired Petty likely had an influence on the song. In *Conversations*, Petty spoke about the song's repeated line that reflected Eddie's potential: "The sky was the limit." "That's what people think when they come out to California. Strike it big. Some people hit it, some people don't."

Writing about the song in the *Los Angeles Times*, Mike Boehm pointed out that "Petty weaves a sardonic, cautionary tale about the rise of a present-day rocker on the Hollywood tattoo-band scene. Petty's 'rebel without a clue' falls into a band for no particular reason, approaches music with no particular drive for expression, and becomes

THE SKY WAS THE LIMIT

a star—an occupation that carries no particular meaning. It's a vision of rock in a fallen, twilight state, pushed forward only by the commercial imperatives of the conglomerate music business."

Another line in the song recalls MCA's initial rejection of *Full Moon Fever*. The lyrics remark that "their A&R man said, 'I don't hear a single,'" about Eddie's album. Humorously, the A&R man is played by Benmont Tench. In fact, all of the Heartbreakers have cameos—Lynch plays a club doorman, Epstein plays a Harley salesman, and Campbell plays a presenter at the "Music Video Awards." Even Tony Dimitriades and Temple play (what else?) Rebel's agent and a music-video director, respectively. The video also features cameos by Terence Trent D'Arby and Chynna Phillips as pop stars. In addition to playing the tattoo artist at the beginning of the video, Petty plays Bart the roadie and the video's bespectacled narrator. The video was shot in Los Angeles, with some wonderful sequences of Petty and Depp riding on a motorcycle on the Sunset Strip, filmed at the end of the hair-metal era.

Petty was extremely pleased with how the video turned out. In a bit of corporate synergy, MCA even slotted the highly cinematic video as a pre-movie short in its Cineplex Odeon Theatres nationwide. The video was later awarded "Best Concept Video" at the inaugural Music Video Producers Association Awards held at the Troubadour on November 5, 1991. Though the video was nominated for the MTV Video Music Award for Best Male Video in 1992, it did not win. At the 2009 MTV Video Music Awards (the twenty-fifth anniversary of the VMAs), the video was nominated again in the retrospective "Best Video (That Should Have Won a Moonman)" category.

Reviews for *Into the Great Wide Open* were generally positive, but many critics expressed that it sounded too much like Petty's recent non-Heartbreakers work. In Richard Cromelin's three-star review in the *Los Angeles Times*, he remarked, "Petty seems to be shaking his Traveling Wilburys slumber. But those who miss the forceful rock he played before that teaming with Bob Dylan, George Harrison, and Jeff Lynne will find only sporadic solace," particularly criticizing Lynne's production and songwriting contributions for steering the Heartbreakers in that direction. Mark Marymont's review in *USA Today* said that "Petty's sneer is missing," for which Lynne "gets the credit or the blame," and, while generally praising the songs, noted that "longtime fans may be put off by [Petty's] mellow mood."

Into the Great Wide Open peaked at #13 on the Billboard album charts and eventually went double platinum—a success, but a significant dip from *Full Moon Fever*. In fact, on August 11, the *Los Angeles Times* reported that since hitting #13, it "has been sliding downward ever since," and called the album's performance "a mediocre showing, especially after his previous *Full Moon Fever* album's lo-o-o-o-ng run in the Top 10." Likewise, the singles were less successful than those from Petty's solo effort. Only "Learning to Fly" reached the Top 40 (#28), while "Into the Great Wide Open" peaked at #92. On the other hand, both songs, plus "Out in the Cold" and "Kings Highway" reached the Top 5 on Billboard's Mainstream Rock chart, with "Learning to Fly" and "Out in the Cold" both hitting #1 on that chart.

The support tour, Touring the Great Wide Open, began on August 29 in Denver, and the band spent the rest of the summer and early fall touring the Midwest and East Coast. The tour finally made its way to California with two dates in the Los Angeles area: November 9 at the Pacific Amphitheatre in Costa Mesa and November 11 at the Forum.

Mike Boehm's review in the *Los Angeles Times* of the Costa Mesa concert questioned the addition of Scott Thurston as a sideman, accusing him of only being there to add "an extra layer of guitar, keyboards or backing vocals, the better to replicate the lush Lynne sound." In particular, he criticized the rendition of "I Won't Back Down" as being "soaked in the same silky sound-processing heard on the record, [and] those looking for some ferocity and brawn instead of the Petty Light Orchestra might have felt like screaming, 'Let me up, I've had enough.'" However, Boehm admitted the band improved as the concert went on as each Heartbreaker got his chance in the spotlight. In fact, Boehm concluded his review of Petty's portion of the review by noting, "That was a pretty good band Petty had up there making noise with him. Maybe he'll even try recording an album with it someday." As many album reviews stated, many critics felt the sound of *Into the Great Wide Open* was even a further step away from the classic Heartbreakers sound than *Full Moon Fever* had been.

In April 1992, rumors of Petty leaving MCA for a "secret deal" with Warner Bros. hit the media. In fact, the *Los Angeles Times* revealed that Petty had signed the deal three years previously, shortly after Petty played "Free Fallin'" for Mo Ostin with the Wilburys at a 1988 house party. The article featured an anonymous quote from a critical executive saying, "It's a free country and everyone has the right to look out for themselves, but for an artist to secretly negotiate a deal like this, most everybody in this business believes it's extremely deceptive. To [do something like this] injects all kinds of bad signals and false elements into a working relationship." The deal was reported to be $20 million for six albums. Nonetheless, while Petty had long been established as a firebrand when it came to an artist's relationship with his record label, the general consensus in the industry media was that Petty was wrong for not giving MCA fair warning about the deal. Of course, it was very much like Petty to not care what the industry media thought about his career.

Shortly after the announcement, the Los Angeles riots began. On April 29, four Los Angeles Police officers were acquitted of assault and using excessive force in the arrest of Rodney King, an African American man who had led police on a high-speed chase. When King finally stopped, the four officers severely beat King. The beating was videotaped by an onlooker, and the story became national news. The officers were charged, but the jury found them not guilty. The verdict served as a breaking point for tension over criticism of the LAPD that had been building from minority communities for decades. Over the next five days, Los Angeles was engulfed by rioting in response to the verdict, which resulted in sixty-three deaths and over $1 billion in property damage. The riots and their aftermath made national headlines.

The violence and unrest in the city Petty had called home for nearly two decades troubled him. He told *Time*, "I was watching the TV. I was upset by it. I could either pace around the room or write a song." He began writing a charity single, "Peace in L.A.," the night of Thursday, April 30. The Heartbreakers—minus Epstein, who couldn't make it—recorded it the following afternoon at Campbell's house. Though Epstein did not play on the track, his voice is heard on the "Peace Mix" of the song from a phone call saying "What's burning? Is there smoke everywhere?" (According to Petty, this was not a reference to the riots but to something that was burning on the stove at Epstein's home.) The next day, Saturday, May 2, the song was already on radio. Petty said, "I left the mastering lab and heard it over the air driving home." Petty donated all profits to various Los Angeles charities.

From a compositional standpoint, "Peace in L.A." isn't one of Petty's stronger songs. But the sheer accomplishment of writing, recording, and releasing the song in a matter of two days for charitable purposes is one of the more impressive accomplishments in Petty's career. He was especially pleased that the song kept generating donations, since it was later included on the Heartbreakers' 1995 box set *Playback*. In *Conversations*, he said, "To this day I still get letters of thanks from missions in East L.A. because the money keeps coming in...they still keep getting royalties. So it was something I felt good about because it did some good. And I was going down the road, and I saw somebody had graffitied the wall, and it said, 'Peace in L.A.' And I thought, 'Damn, that's something. [Laughs] We had an idea, got it on the air, and now it's painted on the wall.' So I felt really good about it."

The music video for "Peace in L.A." was created by Wayne Isham, who was best known for directing videos for a variety of artists, including the Rolling Stones, Judas Priest, Bon Jovi, and Mötley Crüe. The video presents a montage of footage from the riots and debuted on MTV on May 4, which was the day Los Angeles Mayor Tom Bradley lifted the mandatory curfew that was imposed on the main areas of rioting on April 30.

The Heartbreakers recorded another charity song that year under much more positive conditions. In 1987, Jimmy Iovine released a charity Christmas album, *A Very Special Christmas*, with proceeds going to the Special Olympics. The album, which featured holiday hits like

Run-DMC's "Christmas in Hollis," U2's version of "Christmas (Baby Please Come Home)," Madonna's "Santa Baby," and Bob Seger's "The Little Drummer Boy," was a smash multiplatinum hit. Iovine had asked Petty to contribute a song to that album, but the opportunity fell through. Iovine again reached out to Petty to contribute a song to the 1992 sequel. Petty agreed to it with two conditions: first, it would be an original song, which Petty wrote and titled "Christmas All Over Again;" and second, it would emulate the famed "Wall of Sound" production from Phil Spector's classic Christmas album, 1963's *A Christmas Gift for You from Phil Spector*.

Petty wrote the song on a ukulele given to him by George Harrison during the summer of 1992. "I told Jimmy what I wanted to do and he said, 'Wow, okay.' So he booked all the musicians. There's a really good film that's quite long of us doing that session and you'll see the whole thing, me taking five people aside at a time and teaching them their part and then going to the next four and teaching them. We had a harp and a harpsichord, Jim Keltner and Stan playing drums as well as a percussionist, we had two bass players, four acoustic guitars, just crazy shit going on. Michael on the 12-string. Just like we heard it could be done." The session occurred at A&M Studios in Hollywood, the former Charlie Chaplin Studios where the Heartbreakers had recorded "Mystery Man" for their first album.

Unfortunately, while Petty wanted the song to sound like Spector's production, he found that what he was left with was "pretty much a mess." He asked Jeff Lynne to step in on the track to "tidy it up just a little bit." The result has become a perennial Christmas favorite and is featured in the Christmas movies *Home Alone 2: Lost in New York*, *Jingle All the Way*, and *Four Christmases*. In addition to the album sales benefiting the Special Olympics, Petty also annually donated the publishing royalties he received from the song to the organization.

On December 9, Tom Petty appeared at the Universal Amphitheater at the Billboard Music Awards to present George Harrison with the inaugural Century Award for lifetime achievement. *Billboard* later reported that sales of both Traveling Wilburys albums "doubled" in the two weeks following the award ceremony.

The initial sessions for the follow-up to *Into the Great Wide Open* began in late 1992 with the Heartbreakers riffing on song ideas at Mike Campbell's house for about a month. Unfortunately, as the initial rehearsal sessions turned into recording sessions, the process hit a roadblock in the studio, with Petty being profoundly unhappy with the results. The Heartbreakers did record several songs at those sessions, including "God's Gift to Man" and "You Get Me High," both of which appeared on *Playback*. From various accounts, the trouble from the sessions stemmed mainly from the deteriorating relationship between Petty and Lynch.

In response to the failure of those sessions, Petty turned to another option. And so, shortly after Petty had recorded a Heartbreakers album in part to prove that he wasn't planning on going solo permanently—albeit one that didn't sound completely like a Heartbreakers album—he made the decision to make another solo album.

CHAPTER 9

TIME TO MOVE ON

In 1993, Rick Rubin was the most sought-after producer in the music business. Rubin founded Def Jam Records, a rap label that released albums by Run-DMC, Public Enemy, and the Beastie Boys. At the same time, Rubin began developing a reputation as a producer and, by the late 1980s, had been branching out from rap and hip hop. Over the next decade, Rubin produced albums by Slayer, the Cult, Danzig, Red Hot Chili Peppers, and Mick Jagger, many of which were released on the second label that Rubin had founded, Def American Recordings.

Interestingly, Rubin had begun seeking out work with Petty after the release of *Full Moon Fever*. In 2017, Rubin explained to *Rolling Stone* that he had wanted to record with Petty because he had been listening to *Full Moon Fever* non-stop, saying, "The consistency and quality of songwriting on the whole album sucked me in. I listened to it all day every day in my car for a year." Rubin reached out to Al Teller, president and chief operating officer of MCA, and told him that he wanted to work with Petty. Teller told Rubin that Petty would be working with Jeff Lynne at MCA for the foreseeable future. What Teller and Rubin didn't know at the time, however, was that *Into the Great Wide Open* would be the last album Petty recorded for MCA, as well as his last record with Lynne for more than a decade.

Several months later, Rubin was having lunch with Mo Ostin, who revealed to Rubin the secret contract that Petty had signed with Warner Bros. Rubin continued his story in *Petty: The Biography*, saying, "I said, 'Tom Petty made my favorite album. I love Tom Petty. That's incredible.' Mo is like, 'He's making one more record for MCA, and then he's coming over to Warners.' I said I thought this was great and that if they ever needed someone to work on a record with him, I'd love to." Rubin was recommended to Petty for his next album by Ostin during a meeting with Petty, and Petty was interested.

Now that Rubin had the opportunity to work with Petty, he wanted to know exactly who Petty wanted to play with, noting that his favorite album by Petty wasn't a Heartbreakers album. The end result would be a "solo" album that was largely recorded by the Heartbreakers with key special guests, including the man who would become the newest Heartbreaker on drums. In addition, like *Full Moon Fever*, the album would not feature Stan Lynch, whose relationship with Petty had greatly deteriorated.

However, while Petty wanted to focus on recording his second solo album, the Heartbreakers had a final contractual obligation to MCA. Dimitriades had revealed to MCA's Teller that Petty had signed a new deal with Warner Bros. prior to the April 1992 announcement, and had successfully negotiated it so that the Heartbreakers would not need to record another original album for the label. As a tradeoff for releasing Petty from the contract one album early, the Heartbreakers would have to deliver two new songs for an upcoming *Greatest Hits* album. Per Petty's usual attitude toward record label decisions, he wasn't happy, recalling in the liner notes of *Playback*, "I was actually really annoyed about it and didn't want to stop what I was doing. I said, 'I hate the whole idea that you have the Greatest Hits and then you have two new things on the end.' Rick Rubin said, 'Well, I think we should stop and you go away and write something specifically for the Heartbreakers and then we'll bring all of them in, we'll go to another studio, and we'll have another session.'" Rubin's idea was that although he would be producing both the new Heartbreakers songs for the *Greatest Hits* album and the new songs for Petty's second solo album, he would do whatever he could to create distinction between the sessions.

In February 1993, the Heartbreakers began recording with Rick Rubin at Sound City Studios and recorded several covers, including Elvis' "Baby, Let's Play House" and "Wooden Heart," and Thunderclap Newman's 1969 hit "Something in the Air." (Rubin estimated that the band recorded forty to fifty songs during these sessions, most of them covers). Still annoyed at the idea of including new material on a *Greatest Hits* record, Petty did not want to use any of the new songs that he was writing for his Warner Bros. debut. Several of the originals they recorded in the session were songs based on older outtakes, like "Come on Down to My House" (released later on the *Playback* box set), "Lonesome Dave" (released later on the *An American Treasure* box set), and what would become one of the band's most popular songs, "Mary Jane's Last Dance." The latter was not even recorded until July 1993, just four months before *Greatest Hits* was set to be released. It was recorded at Cello Studios in Hollywood, where the Heartbreakers would later record *The Last DJ*.

"Mary Jane's Last Dance" began its life as an outtake from the *Full Moon Fever* sessions at Campbell's house. Rubin had been going over Petty's outtakes for song ideas for the *Greatest Hits* album and suggested that he try working on that song, which was then tentatively titled "Indiana Girl." Petty wrote new lyrics for the song and, after a productive session with Rubin and the Heartbreakers, an unfinished song from five years prior would make the Heartbreakers' *Greatest Hits* album—with Petty unhappy about it the entire time.

"Mary Jane's Last Dance" was released as a single on July 22, 1993, almost four months before the release of *Greatest Hits*. Both releases were big hits—"Mary Jane's Last Dance" peaked at #14 on the Billboard chart, Petty's highest-charting song since "Free Fallin'," while *Greatest Hits* would peak at #2 on the album charts. It would reach #2 again after reentering the charts shortly after Petty's death in October 2017. In total, *Greatest Hits* spent nearly three hundred weeks on the Billboard 200 chart. The album eventually became the bestselling album of Petty's career by a significant margin, selling over twelve million copies in the United States alone. Petty would later joke about the success of the album and the single in the liner notes of *Playback*, saying, "The funny thing was how hard I fought against putting anything new on it. Rubin will never let me forget it that I complained about that so much. But I'm really glad I did it now."

One of the reasons why "Mary Jane's Last Dance" performed so well on the charts was its memorable music video starring Petty and actress Kim Basinger. Directed by Keir McFarlane, who would later become a popular music video director, the video depicts Petty as a medical examiner who unzips one of the body bags in the morgue to discover a deceased beautiful woman (Basinger). The medical examiner abducts the corpse, takes her home, dresses her in a beautiful gown, and prepares a candlelit dinner for the pair. In a memorable sequence, the examiner dances with the corpse in a room lit by hundreds of candles. Eventually, it appears the examiner comes to his senses and takes the body to the beach (shot at Leo Carrillo State Park near Malibu) and drops her in the ocean—but after the examiner leaves, the woman mysteriously opens her eyes. Unlike the other Heartbreakers music videos, the other members of the band do not appear in the video for "Mary Jane's Last Dance."

As to why Basinger was cast as the corpse, Petty explained to *Billboard* in 2005, "'She's got to look really good, or why would he keep her around after she's dead?' I thought, 'Kim Basinger would be good, I'd probably keep her a day or two, let's go see if she would do it.' You can make a joke about it, but you do have to act a bit to be dead. It's not easy."

For her part, Basinger was up for the macabre idea. "Now that was one of the coolest things I've ever done in my life," she said to the *Daily Beast* in an interview years later. "It was classic, wasn't it? [Petty] was a doll, and he was so sweet and asked me to do it, and both of us are extremely shy so we just said three words to each other the whole time.

I'll never forget how heavy that dress was! And I had to be dead the whole time. You know, it's really one of the hardest things I've ever done in my life, because I had to be completely weightless to be in his arms the way I was."

Though the music video was extremely popular, not everyone was a fan of the ghoulish idea. In the *Los Angeles Times*, Chris Willman wrote "Not since Alice Cooper's 'Cold Ethyl' have the joys of necrophilia gotten such an earnest airing in the pop mainstream, and the utterly purposeless perversity place this one high in the all-time music video what-the-hell-were-they-thinking? pantheon, ruining a perfectly good little Petty tune." Nonetheless, the following year, the video won Best Male Video at the MTV Video Music Awards. That same year, Petty was also awarded the Video Vanguard Award for his career achievement in music videos. Reflecting on the quality of his videos over the years, Petty remarked, "I just try to put something on the screen every time that's a little different, something for you to look at, something to make you smile."

For his next solo album, Petty was especially focused on songwriting, working with an 8-track recorder to create a number of demos in a prolific songwriting period, often recording them with Rubin shortly afterward. In 1995, Rubin told *Rolling Stone*, "I just hoped we could have songs as good as *Full Moon* but with a more rock 'n' roll, more personal approach, as opposed to a pop presentation." Many of the lyrics on the album appear to be influenced by the troubles in Petty's marriage, with song titles like "Time to Move On," "Only a Broken Heart," and "Crawling Back to You" (the last song featuring a reference to Los Angeles in its opening lines: "Waiting by the side of the road / For day to break so we could go / Down into Los Angeles / With dirty hands and worn out knees").

Petty would involve the Heartbreakers heavily in the recording of what was officially a solo album—although, as he indicated to Rubin in their initial meetings, with the exception of Stan Lynch. Though Lynch would officially remain a member of the Heartbreakers until just before the album's release, he didn't play on it. The other

Heartbreakers appeared on almost all of the album's tracks. Taking Lynch's place behind the drums for most of the sessions was Steve Ferrone, an English-born drummer who had been a longtime member of the Average White Band, a one-time member of the *Saturday Night Live* band, and a popular session player who had appeared on songs by George Harrison, Eric Clapton, Peter Frampton, and many others. Ferrone had first entered the Heartbreakers' circle when he performed with Campbell in George Harrison's backing band for a 1992 benefit concert at the Royal Albert Hall. Ferrone wasn't even told who the session was for when he received the call for Petty's session. Of the drummers they auditioned, Ferrone won the job after auditioning on the song "Hard on Me." The take he auditioned with at Sound City was so solid that it ended up on the final mix.

Petty and Rubin did not use synthesizers or computers on any of the tracks. Guests on the album included the Beach Boys' Carl Wilson, Ringo Starr, and orchestral arranger Michael Kamen. The sessions were recorded at Sound City and Village Recorders, and the album was mixed in the Andora Studios, located in the Cahuenga Pass.

Nonetheless, while sessions for Petty's solo album were ongoing and Lynch was on his way out of the band, the Heartbreakers were not on ice. In June, the two-day Troubadours of Folk Festival was held at UCLA's track-and-field venue, Drake Stadium, which included folk legends like Arlo Guthrie, Peter, Paul and Mary, the Kingston Trio, and Ramblin' Jack Elliott alongside some acts on the periphery of folk music like Jefferson Starship and Spinal Tap's goofy folk alter egos the Folksmen. The festival was headlined by Joni Mitchell, in her first public performance in a number of years. Petty had previously worked with Mitchell when he recorded vocals along with Billy Idol for her song "Dancin' Clown" on her 1988 album *Chalk Mark in a Rain Storm*.

Also on the bill was Roger McGuinn. During McGuinn's set, Petty joined for a few songs, including "King of the Hill." In addition, singer-songwriter John Prine was backed at the festival by Benmont Tench and Howie Epstein. Tench, Campbell, and Epstein had played on Prine's Grammy Award-winning 1991 album *The Missing Years*, which was produced by Epstein and mostly recorded at Epstein's Los Angeles home. Petty contributed some background vocals on the album as well.

On August 14, 1993, actor Johnny Depp—who since his appearance in the "Into the Great Wide Open" music video had achieved the biggest acclaim of his career so far in the film *Benny & Joon*—opened the Viper Room, a club on Sunset Strip, as a part-owner in the former space of another club called the Central (another co-owner was Depp's *21 Jump Street* costar Sal Jenco). The club became well known as a celebrity hangout and achieved particular infamy just ten weeks after it opened when actor River Phoenix died of a drug overdose on the sidewalk outside.

The Heartbreakers appeared as the headliner on opening night. The band used the opportunity of playing in front of less than three hundred people to debut "Mary Jane's Last Dance" and a song recently recorded for Petty's solo album that wouldn't be released for over a year, "Crawling Back to You." The band was reportedly fired up after the performance, with even Lynch remarking, "We should do this once a month." The opening night of the Viper Room raised $14,000 for the Starlight Children's Foundation, a Los Angeles-based charitable organization that provides aid to children in hospitals.

The Heartbreakers wouldn't play the Viper Room or other club gigs once a month, but Petty found similar inspiration when he attended the December 30, 1993, Nirvana concert at the Forum, which was the last Southern California concert for the band before leader Kurt Cobain's death in April 1994. In the linear notes of *Playback*, Petty would recall how Nirvana influenced his songwriting for his solo album, noting, "I was just trying to do something a little wilder than we'd been doing. I'd just heard Nirvana and was taken over by that. I thought, 'Damn, we've really got to catch up to this shit!' It just floored me, I thought it was the first significant thing I'd heard in a decade and it really did straighten out a lot of us older guys. Really threatened us, kicked us in the ass. I thought, 'Yeah, let's just try letting it go and see what happens.'"

The January 17, 1994, Northridge earthquake, one of the strongest ever to hit Southern California, killing more than fifty people, interrupted work on the album. Petty later told *USA Today*, "The studios were screwed up for months. The aftershocks were nerve-rattling, and we spent hours discussing whether we should leave L.A. You take the ground you walk on for granted, and to not even have that as a given really enraged me." Nevertheless, Petty reaffirmed his love for Los Angeles and what drew him there almost twenty years earlier. "L.A. is certainly not without its huge problems and disgusting factors, but I'm attached to it. People who watched too much TV or had too many dreams all come here to resist a more orderly, normal life. L.A. had the Byrds, the Beach Boys and Buffalo Springfield. I thought, that must be the greatest place on earth. And it was. I can't believe I didn't come sooner."

At sixty-two minutes, Petty's new album, *Wildflowers*, was the longest studio album of his career so far. It was twenty minutes longer than *Into the Great Wide Open* and only nine minutes shorter than the double live album *Pack Up the Plantation: Live!* Since Petty had recorded more songs than ended up on the final album, he considered releasing *Wildflowers* as a double album. Warner Bros. Records President Lenny Waronker (who would leave the company shortly before the album's release) convinced Petty and Rubin instead to make the best single album they could. Petty and Rubin trimmed the release from two dozen songs to fifteen (although Rubin estimates the original number is closer to twenty-six or twenty-eight). In a 2018 episode of the *Broken Record* podcast about the making of *Wildflowers*, Rubin noted that Petty didn't push back about leaving so many songs off the album. "He cared very much about his audience and doing what he thought was right by them," he remarked. "I was a little surprised that he decided, but I guess he thought, 'Maybe this would be better for the audience,' which is why he went along with it."

The *Wildflowers* outtakes included "Leave Virginia Alone," a song later recorded by Rod Stewart for his 1995 album *A Spanner in the Works*, and "Girl on LSD," which was used as the B-side of the *Wildflowers* single "You Don't Know How It Feels." Other songs would be reworked for Petty's next album and a few others appeared in other forms, but the full set of finished *Wildflowers* tracks has not yet been released despite Petty often discussing in his later years about reissuing it in its original two-album form.

Wildflowers debuted at #8 on the Billboard chart, its peak position, and the first single, the Dylan-esque "You Don't Know How It Feels," peaked at #13 on the singles chart, one position higher than "Mary Jane's Last Dance" (both hit #1 on the Album Rock Tracks chart). In another example of Petty trailblazing in the industry, he previewed "You Don't Know How It Feels" on the online services American Online and CompuServe, and what the *Los Angeles Times* called at the time "the Internet's Worldwide Web."

"You Don't Know How It Feels" became an instant anthem for Petty—despite the fact that, much like "Mary Jane's Last Dance," he didn't think it had single potential. In 1999, he told *Guitar Player*, "I thought the record company made a terrible mistake releasing 'You Don't Know How It Feels' as a single, but I was wrong." The album eventually went triple-platinum in the US.

The music video for "You Don't Know How It Feels," which was directed by Phil Joanou (who had previously shot several videos for U2), features Petty performing the song on a rotating stage with color-ful scenes behind him involving dancers, acrobats, gun target practice, and an illicit office affair, among several other scenes. At one point, a woman in a gown (portrayed by actress Raven Snow) intimidates Petty to step away from the microphone and sings part of the song herself (but in Petty's voice), until Petty returns to make it a one-voice duet. The video was shot as a single take and was not edited. The fol-lowing year, the video was awarded the MTV Video Music Award for Best Male Video, making Petty the winner in that category for two consecutive years.

Infamously, MTV and VH1 censored the song's lyric "Let's roll another joint" by reversing the word "joint" and making it into an unintelligible word (a radio edit played by some stations kept "joint" but replaced "roll" with "hit," which was apparently supposed to mask the drug reference). Petty later told *Musician* magazine that he never intended the song to be pro-drug, saying, "I don't want to be seen as some advocate for dope. It just seemed like something the character in that song would say."

In addition to "You Don't Know How It Feels," *Wildflowers* features some of Petty's most-loved songs, including the title track—a ballad with lush orchestrations by Michael Kamen. Petty later described the song to *Performing Songwriter* in 2014 as something that came out of him almost automatically, revealing, "I just took a deep breath and it came out. The whole song. Stream of consciousness: words, music, chords. Finished it. I mean, I just played it into a tape recorder and I played the whole song and I never played it again. I actually only spent three and a half minutes on that whole song. So I'd come back for days playing that tape, thinking there must be something wrong here because this just came too easy. And then I realized that there's probably nothing wrong at all." The description sounds remarkably similar to a story Rubin told *Rolling Stone* shortly after Petty's death about how in tune Petty was with his songwriting during this period. Rubin said, "I remember when Tom lived in Encino and I would go to his house to listen to demos he was working on. One day, between cassette recordings of songs he was working on, he began strumming the guitar. After a couple of minutes of strumming chords, he played me an intricate new song complete with lyrics and story. I asked him what it was about. He said he didn't know it just came out. He had written it or more like channeled it in that very moment. He didn't know what it was about or what the inspiration was. It arrived fully formed. It was breathtaking."

On the other end of the spectrum, Petty also stayed in touch with his more lighthearted side on *Wildflowers*. An example is "Honey Bee," which namechecks Pomona, a city in eastern Los Angeles County. In *Conversations*, he remembered, "It's got very funny lyrics: 'She give me her monkey hand and a Rambler sedan / I'm the king of Milwaukee / Her juju beads are so nice / She kissed my third cousin twice / I'm the king of Pomona...' [Laughs] Where does it come from? I don't know where I got, 'I'm the king of Pomona.' But I wanted it to be like that. I wanted it to be one part gibberish. Where it would be clear to anyone that I'm not taking this too seriously, I'm just having some fun here. So it was just a little fun with words."

In the *Los Angeles Times*, Chris Willman gave *Wildflowers* three stars, calling it "inconsistent" and remarking that it "doesn't offer any new songs that rank with Petty's greatest." However, he also added, "Yet the mixture he's going for here has such an interesting, subtle kind of resonance you may not bemoan the lack of instant anthems."

Critical opinion would shift in a more positive direction in the years following, and in Petty's estimation, *Wildflowers* was his magnum opus. Yet on a darker level, Petty also felt that *Wildflowers* represented a level of excellence that he wasn't able to match. According to Rubin in a 2017 interview with *Rolling Stone*, shortly before Petty's death, he had said to Rubin regarding *Wildflowers*, "I'm afraid of that album." Rubin continued, "I thought it was a strange comment. I asked what he meant. He said it's daunting for him to think about it because it's insurmountable. He didn't think he could do it again, so it reserved a haunted place in his psyche."

CHAPTER 10

CALIFORNIA'S BEEN GOOD TO ME

In late October 1994, Lynch finally announced that he was leaving the Heartbreakers, releasing a statement that said, "It feels strange, but I think it'll be a real good change for everybody.... Over time, people have such different desires, musically, and mine are becoming more apparent to me. I've moved away from them as a person as well as a musician. I've moved apart from them." A few weeks later, Petty had similar remarks to *USA Today*, saying, "Stan just grew away from us. I've seen it coming for years," and that after his departure "we felt freer because it was getting uncomfortable." To that he added, "I really hope nobody else quits. If I didn't have the rest of them, I don't think I'd perform anymore and I'd be very afraid of making records. I really treasure the fact that we don't sound like a bunch of session players." For a bandleader that recorded two albums presented as solo albums and two other albums with a superstar side project over the preceding five years, it was a remarkable statement endorsing group stability.

On a more positive note, as *Wildflowers* was growing into one of the biggest hits of Petty's career, the Heartbreakers chose a unique way to sell tickets to the band's upcoming tour. On January 20, 1995, VH1 started selling tickets—four hundred per show—to the Heartbreakers'

Dogs with Wings Tour via a 1-800 telephone number. It was the first time concert tickets were sold on live TV. According to *Billboard*, the roughly nineteen thousand allotted tickets sold out in a matter of hours. Adding to the anticipation for the tour was a special tribute concert held in Petty's honor on January 9 at the House of Blues in West Hollywood, where artists featured on the compilation *You Got Lucky: A Tribute to Tom Petty* (released in September 1994) performed some of Petty's greatest hits. Some performances, including Everclear's rendition of "American Girl," were broadcast on ABC's *In Concert* in February.

The Dogs with Wings Tour started on February 28 in Louisville, Kentucky. On April 28, the Heartbreakers played their first Los Angeles-area concert on the *Wildflowers* support tour at the huge Blockbuster Pavilion in San Bernardino, a 65,000-seat amphitheater that is the largest outdoor music venue in the United States (discounting venues built for other purposes, like sports stadiums). The venue opened in 1993 at the site of the 1982 US Festival, where the Heartbreakers had performed (after several name changes, the venue is currently known as the Glen Helen Amphitheater). Like most performances at the venue, Petty's season-opening performance was significantly scaled back from the venue's maximum capacity, but still drew over fifteen thousand. In fact, the *San Bernardino County Sun* reported that Petty's April 28 concert at the Blockbuster Pavilion caused "bumper to bumper" traffic on area freeways.

Once inside, the audience experienced a healthy selection of *Wildflowers* songs ("You Don't Know How It Feels," "You Wreck Me," "Cabin Down Below," "Time to Move On," "Wildflowers," "It's Good to Be King," "Honey Bee," and the B-side "Girl on LSD") alongside Heartbreakers classics.

Variety called the concert "an exploration of [Petty's] myriad influences and attitudes," and praised the band (particularly Campbell and newcomer Ferrone), though referred to the mid-set acoustic segment as "sleepy" and "draggy." In the *Orange County Register*, Mark Brown declared that the packed venue was a sign "that everyone's figured out that Petty is, indeed, one of the finest songwriters, performers and artists of our time" and praised the recent focus of Petty's set compared to the classics-heavy setlists of tours by his contemporaries. In contrast to the *Variety* review, Brown praised the acoustic set as "a thrill" and "something [Petty] was doing long before it became trendy." He did admit having a "quibble" that Petty didn't play even more obscure songs in the set, but concluded, "Petty had grandparents and punkers singing along on a couple of dozen of finely crafted, thoughtful pieces of rock. Rock shows don't get much better than that."

Petty and the Heartbreakers returned to Los Angeles to perform the group's first-ever concert at the Hollywood Bowl on June 9 (a second show was added on June 10 after the first show sold out). The Hollywood Bowl, one of Los Angeles' most iconic venues, is an outdoor amphitheater located in the Hollywood Hills. Since opening as a performance space in the early '20s, the Bowl has hosted dozens of legendary figures on its stage, including the Beatles (who recorded a live album there), the Rolling Stones, the Beach Boys, the Who, the Monty Python comedy team, Louis Armstrong, Ella Fitzgerald, the Doors, Jimi Hendrix, Deep Purple, Pink Floyd, Black Sabbath, the Grateful Dead, Van Morrison, Elton John, and dozens of notable classical performers and musical theater performances; it also serves as the summer home of the Los Angeles Philharmonic as well as the Playboy Jazz Festival. With almost triple the capacity of the Universal Amphitheatre (just two and a half miles north), the Hollywood Bowl was a perfect venue for the expanding hometown audience of the Heartbreakers. The group performed nine times at the historic amphitheater in their career and ended both the Echo Tour and the 40th Anniversary Tour with performances there.

The Bowl where Petty and the Heartbreakers performed on the Dogs with Wings Tour, which was designed by noted architecture firm Allied Architects, was erected in 1929 and was patterned after previous bowls of wooden construction. After decades of various modifications to the infrastructure, the entire Bowl's shell was replaced in 2003, which resulted in far better acoustics.

According to *Billboard*, the Hollywood Bowl shows drew a combined 33,006 fans and grossed over $1 million. The *Los Angeles Daily News* reported that dozens of celebrities were in attendance, from longtime friends Jeff Lynne, Garry Shandling, Jackson Browne, Johnny Depp, Carlene Carter, Dave Stewart, and former Heartbreaker Ron Blair, to models Kate Moss and Cheryl Tiegs. In the *Daily News*, Fred Shuster accused Petty of "holding back" and being "distracted" during the first Hollywood Bowl show, but acknowledged that Petty knew how to please a crowd with his setlist of hit after hit. Like the *Variety* review of the San Bernardino concert, Shuster also criticized the acoustic set, calling it "overlong" and a "misstep in the pacing...that dragged down the middle of the show."

The Dogs with Wings Tour continued for another four months, ending on October 8, 1995, in New Orleans. The seven-month tour ended up being the longest in Heartbreakers history, and a costly one for Petty's personal life.

For an otherwise private couple, Tom and Jane Petty had been becoming more public about their relationship. Shortly before the release of *Wildflowers*, an uncharacteristic statement from Petty about his marriage appeared in various newspapers, remarking, "Jane and I had a brief separation at one point. But not counting that we're coming on 20 years.... She's great and she's still my friend and still pretty as I can find out there. I haven't needed a new model." A few months later, Jane featured prominently in a May 1995 *Rolling Stone* profile of Petty, with the author calling them "the picture of togetherness," despite "a spell or two of separation." For what it's worth, Petty himself disputed the rosy image, remarking, "We have taken some shrapnel. We do walk with a slight limp."

In reality, shortly after the end of the *Wildflowers* tour, Petty moved out of the Encino house, this time for good. The press announced that Jane filed for divorce in September 1996, but the couple had been separated for some time before that. The fallout from the divorce would result in the darkest period in Petty's life.

* * * * *

In March 1996, the *Los Angeles Times* reported that Petty and the Heartbreakers would record four new songs for a movie titled *She's the One*, written and directed by New York independent filmmaker Edward Burns. Burns became something of an overnight sensation with his 1995 comedy-drama *The Brothers McMullen*, which he had written, directed, and starred in. The film had been produced on a small budget and became a small hit after receiving great acclaim—and the Grand Jury Award—at the 1995 Sundance Film Festival, and was acquired for distribution as the debut release for Fox Searchlight Pictures, the "arthouse" distribution arm of 20th Century Fox, based in the all-too-familiar-to-Petty Century City. Based on that success, Fox Searchlight offered Burns the opportunity to make another film in a similar vein, a romantic comedy starring Burns as a New York City cab driver, along with his *McMullen* costars Mike McGlone and Maxine Bahns, opposite rising stars Cameron Diaz and Jennifer Aniston.

Burns had finished shooting *She's the One* and screened a rough cut for Petty at Petty's house. Burns would later tell the *Worcester Telegram & Gazette* that "it was cool just meeting the guy," and that Petty initially offered to write a song for the film. Petty's participation grew in the following weeks. In late April, reports (such as the one in Palm Springs' *Desert Sun*) said that Petty had recorded six songs and incidental music for the score. Petty would later tell the *Boston Globe*, "I had never scored a picture, so that was really the incentive. I thought it would be fun and a learning experience." He also decided to do it because it was a relatively small film—after jokingly calling himself "Mr. Hollywood," Petty added, "I really took the job because it was a small movie. I wouldn't be interested in doing a Steven Spielberg movie or anything like that." Another reason for scoring the whole project himself is that when Petty asked other artists to contribute songs to the soundtrack, he felt that he was offered subpar outtakes and B-sides instead of quality material.

In May, the *Daily News* called Petty's expanded role the result of a "creative spree" and revealed that Ringo Starr played drums on two of the songs. In fact, a sizable amount of the album consists of *Wildflowers* outtakes. The newest Heartbreaker, Steve Ferrone, only played drums on two tracks, with session drummer Curt Bisquera playing drums on all the songs that Starr and Ferrone didn't play on. Other guest appearances on the album include background vocals by Fleetwood Mac's Lindsey Buckingham and the Beach Boys' Carl Wilson. Like *Wildflowers*, the album was produced by the team of Rubin, Petty, and Campbell, and most of the sessions were done at Sound City Studios and Village Studios. The album includes two covers, Lucinda Williams's "Change the Locks" and Beck's "Asshole." The Williams cover came about because Johnny Cash had introduced Petty to the song during their sessions with Rubin that year, while Petty told the *Boston Globe* that he covered Beck because "I'm a huge Beck fan.... There's a freshness about him that I really like. And I really love his sense of humor."

Simultaneously, Petty was being honored all over Los Angeles by various organizations. First, Petty won a Grammy at the 38th Annual Grammy Awards at the Shrine Auditorium for Best Male Rock Vocal Performance for "You Don't Know How It Feels" (*Wildflowers* engineers David Bianco, Jim Scott, Richard Dodd, and Stephen McLaughlin also won for Best Engineered Album, Non-Classical). Petty didn't attend the ceremony, but was at home in Los Angeles when the award was presented and found out via phone call.

In April, Petty received the George and Ira Gershwin Award for Lifetime Musical Achievement at UCLA, which included a surprise solo performance and live debut of a song from the new album, "Angel Dream," using a guitar and amplifier supplied by a student. In May, Petty was presented with the Golden Note Award from the American Society of Composers, Authors, and Publishers (ASCAP) by Jimmy Iovine at the Beverly Hilton (the presentation included Roger McGuinn and Tench performing "American Girl" and "The Waiting"), and he was back at the Hilton in July with the Heartbreakers to provide music for the American Foundation for AIDS Research's "Two Steppin' for The Cure III" event, including the first-ever live performances of the songs "Walls," "Climb That Hill," and "Asshole," with Bisquera playing drums for the set instead of Ferrone. (Bisquera was a regular fill-in for Ferrone around this time.) Then, in June, the Hollywood Walk of Fame Committee announced that Petty and the Heartbreakers would be honored with a star on the Hollywood Walk of Fame in 1997. (Ultimately, Petty and the Heartbreakers wouldn't get their star until 1999.) Petty also introduced "The King of Rockabilly" Carl Perkins when he was inducted in the Hollywood Rockwalk in June, which is located outside the Guitar Center on Sunset Boulevard. (Petty and the Heartbreakers would appear on Perkins's album released later that year, *Go Cat Go!*)

The first single from the album, now titled *Songs and Music from the Motion Picture She's the One*, was released to radio in late July. Though the single itself was titled "Walls," the release featured two versions of the song—"Walls (Circus)," which was the single version, and "Walls (No. 3)"—with the B-side "Hung Up and Overdue." Lyrically, both versions of "Walls" are exactly the same, both reflecting on the ups and downs of life, and the singer admitting that the "walls" that prevent him from falling in love will one day "fall down." Musically, the two are quite different—"(Circus)" features a full band arrangement with Buckingham's unmistakable voice on background vocals, while "(No. 3)" could be called the "unplugged" version, featuring a stripped-down arrangement at a faster tempo. The *Billboard* review of the single questioned the inclusion of two versions of the same tune, speculating, "Certainly, it will make sense within the context of the movie or album." It also correctly predicted that the "(Circus)" version would be more popular on radio, and that was indeed the version used in the music video, which took the parenthetical part of the title to heart in depicting the group playing the song in the middle of a colorful Eastern-inspired circus tent (*She's the One* stars Maxine Bahns and Jennifer Aniston make brief appearances, and Burns appears at the beginning and end of the clip as a taxi driver). Phil Joanou directed the video, which was shot at Universal Studios. "Walls (Circus)" was a minor hit for the Heartbreakers, peaking at #69 on the Billboard Hot 100 and #6 on the Mainstream Rock Tracks chart. It was even more successful in Canada, peaking at #3 on the RPM chart (the album itself peaked at #15 in the US). Petty also premiered selections from the album on a national radio broadcast on July 30, which aired in Los Angeles on KSCA-FM prior to the August 6 release of the album. The day before the album was released, the Heartbreakers appeared on *The Tonight Show* and performed "Walls (Circus)."

Another standout track that also appears on the album in two versions is "Angel Dream," which was inspired by Petty's relationship with new girlfriend Dana York. Like "Walls," the album features two versions, "Angel Dream (No. 4)" and "Angel Dream (No. 2)." According to Petty, the numbers had no meaning and were just assigned jokingly.

One of the leftover *Wildflowers* cuts on the album heard in the film is "California," a breezy, bouncy rocker in which Petty sings the most deliberate ode to the state he had called home for over twenty years. The chorus speaks of love for the Golden State and the hope that the various national disasters that befall the West Coast don't put an end to the dream: "California's been good to me / Hope it don't fall into the sea." The idea of California as a place where people chase their dreams is echoed in "Hung Up and Overdue," when the singer says the girl he loves is going, "To move to California one day / Said she's going / Out on safari to stay." That last line is a lyrical nod to the Beach Boys' seminal hit celebrating California's surfing culture, "Surfin' U.S.A."

Since *She's the One* included three songs left over from the *Wildflowers* sessions ("California," "Hung Up and Overdue," and "Hope You Never"), two reworked unreleased songs from *Wildflowers* ("Supernatural Radio" and "Climb That Hill"), two versions each of "Walls" and "Angel Dream," two instrumental tracks ("Hope on Board" and "Airport"), and two covers, it is a singular album in Petty's discography that almost seems more like the seventh disc of *Playback* rather than a proper album. In fact, in *Conversations*, Petty calls the album "almost Volume II of *Wildflowers*."

Initially, Petty was extremely positive about the material and how quickly it came together, telling the *Boston Globe*, "I'm surprised at how cohesive it is. Sometimes you do better work when you're in a hurry and not analyzing everything, which I wasn't. I was just trying to get it done and hoping it had some quality to it." Yet the album did not sell up to Petty's usual standards. Though the album was certified gold by the RIAA in December, it was the first Petty album to fail to go platinum since 1987's *Let Me Up (I've Had Enough)*, a far cry from the multiplatinum success of *Full Moon Fever*, *Into the Great Wide Open*, and *Wildflowers*.

Perhaps that's why, with the exception of "Angel Dream," which he frequently cited as one of his best songs, Petty was rather dismissive of the experience, his opinion growing harsher over time. In a 1999 interview with the *New York Daily News*, Petty said of its poor commercial performance, "It was marketed as a soundtrack and put in [those kinds of] bins. And I didn't promote it. I think it's a good record, but I don't look at it as one of our normal albums." In a 2005 interview with *Billboard*, Petty reflected, "I busted my ass on it, and then you see the movie and people are talking over it. I don't have time for that. I've got other stuff to do. I really liked Ed a lot and I thank him for giving me the shot, but it taught me that [that's] not where I want to live." In a 2014 interview with *Men's Journal*, Petty said that he never listened to the album and tore into it, saying, "I hated that record—the whole idea of it offended me. I only did it because I didn't have anything else to do. I was single and living on my own, and this idea came up, and I liked Ed and thought he was pretty sharp, so I wrote him a couple of songs. And then it just kept mushrooming into, 'Do the whole thing.' So I took some stuff I hadn't used in *Wildflowers*, really crummy versions, badly mixed, and put them on there. It was terrible, really. I'm disappointed I did that."

The album is skipped over in the otherwise thorough 2007 documentary *Runnin' Down a Dream*, and no tracks from it appear on the 2000 compilation album *Anthology: Through the Years*, though a live version of "Angel Dream" appears on the 2009 box set *The Live Anthology* and both "Walls (Circus)" and "Angel Dream (No. 2)" appear on the 2019 compilation *The Best of Everything*. However, "Walls" occasionally found its way into setlists in its "(No. 3)" version for the rest of the

Heartbreakers' existence. Petty never did a movie soundtrack again and reverted to his previous stance of rarely allowing his music to be used in film or television.

Yet to dismiss *She's the One* as a throwaway album is unfair to it. The review in the *Orange County Register* acclaimed the album as "some of Petty's most compelling work of the '90s," and called it "possibly Petty's most reflective work, looking at pressures that reflect a society where there's not enough time, not enough joy, not enough relief. It's a time when society, advertising and the media have made people's expectations impossibly high and inevitably unrealistic" (of course, Petty's future work would delve even more into these arenas). The review concluded, "Music doesn't get much more honest than this." Elysa Gardner's review in the *Los Angeles Times* was almost as praiseworthy, saying, "On these songs, his flair for balancing wry humor with understated poignancy and subtle self-awareness is once again at the fore," and, "Petty has put together a collection of lyrical, atmospheric tunes that range from sweet, acoustic ballads to moody, mid-tempo rockers."

There was no tour to support the album. In fact, aside from a twenty-night stand at the Fillmore in San Francisco in early 1997, the Heartbreakers played no live shows on the road from the end of the *Wildflowers* tour until 1999.

Petty's lone Los Angeles-area appearance on a concert stage during this period was a guest appearance at the Crosby, Stills & Nash concert at the Universal Amphitheater to play on "Ohio" on September 28, 1997. Incidentally, it would mark Petty's final appearance at the once-familiar venue. It would close in September 2013 and was demolished to make room for an expansion of the Universal Studios theme park.

* * * * *

At the same time, Petty's personal life was in disarray. In the wake of the *Wildflowers* tour, he had completely moved out of his house in Encino and was currently living in a rustic—at least by Los Angeles standards—house in Pacific Palisades, which Petty dubbed the Chicken Shack. *Petty: The Biography* describes it as "like a thing ripped from an Adirondacks postcard and dropped into a redwood grove by the Pacific.... It was dark, all knotty pine, with cracks of light visible through some of the logs." Rubin explained it as "*really* cool. Like a little log cabin on a lot of land. Going there was like stepping back in time, to a hunting lodge or something. The house was all wood, not modern, with giant trees—redwoods, I think—all around. If Levon Helm walked in, you wouldn't think twice."

In *Conversations*, the musician recalled of the place, "Very funky. Chickens in the yard. But I loved it. It was really green and over-grown. It was just a small house, and I was living there alone. I thought it was a great place. I had my little 8-track studio in the back bedroom. I wrote the *She's the One* album, the newer stuff for that. I wrote 'Walls' and 'Angel Dream.' I stayed there for a few years." In a 2006 interview with *Rolling Stone*, Petty dubbed it his "bachelor pad" but noted that "it wasn't the best period in my life. But I am through that. I came out the good side."

As Petty revealed for the first time in *Petty: The Biography*, he was suffering not only from a deep depression at the time, but also from using heroin. When Petty came into the studio for recording sessions, "he was often hiding behind a pair of sunglasses, sometimes even walking with a cane."

In the book, close friend Stevie Nicks remembered it being a rough period for him. She said, "I went over to the house in Pacific Palisades. I could get there quickly because I was fifteen minutes away in Santa Monica. It was a beautiful house. You wouldn't even have imagined it was there. It was almost like a bird sanctuary. He was...you know...he was *alone*. Jane had been such a huge personality. She was one of those women that, when she was in the room, there was no one else there. And so, all of a sudden, he's in this really nice, beautiful, small house, with all these birds everywhere. But alone."

Petty's confession of his heroin addiction during this time was the biggest revelation of the 2015 release of *Petty: The Biography*. By the time of publication, Petty had long been off the drug, thanks in part to many people—but especially then-girlfriend, and later second wife, Dana York.

* * * * *

Tom Petty and the Heartbreakers recorded another album in Los Angeles in 1996, but as a backup group as the result of a unique arrangement orchestrated by Rick Rubin.

In 1994, Rubin had signed country music icon Johnny Cash to a record deal. After the commercial performance of his albums declined through the early '80s, Cash had been released from his recording contract with Columbia Records in 1986. Though he signed a deal with Mercury Records, his fortunes did not improve, and the Man in Black's long career was at its lowest ebb. Rubin and Cash recorded a demo in Rubin's living room, a back-to-basics approach that consisted solely of Cash's voice and acoustic guitar, recorded in Rubin's living room. Many of the songs were rerecordings of older country songs that Cash had previously sung, but he also performed songs written by contemporary stars Glenn Danzig, Nick Lowe, and Tom Waits. While Rubin originally intended for Cash to rerecord the songs with various backing musicians—including Mike Campbell and Benmont Tench—Rubin and Cash decided to release the powerful demos free of ornamentation as the album *American Recordings* (which was also the new name of Rubin's label, formerly Def American) in April 1994. Rubin had renamed the label in August 1993 and marked the occasion by purchasing a tombstone with the word "Def" chiseled on it in Hollywood Forever Cemetery. Petty was one of the many guests who attended the New Orleans funeral-themed afterparty for the "funeral."

Rounding out the album were two songs—"Tennessee Stud" and "The Man Who Couldn't Cry"—that were recorded live at Cash's first-ever solo performance in his career, held at West Hollywood's famed Viper Room on December 3, 1993. Johnny Depp introduced Cash to a capacity crowd—which included Tom Petty. Remembering the gig in a 2010 retrospective of Cash's work with Rubin in *Vanity Fair*, Petty recalled, "He was really nervous about it, never having relied on his own guitar, and I was nervous watching him."

American Recordings received significant critical acclaim and earned Cash a Grammy Award for Best Contemporary Folk Album, thrusting the legend back into the spotlight and earning him new fans. A follow-up with Rubin was the next step. Unlike their first collaboration, Rubin and Cash would record with a backing band for *Unchained*. In a 2016 retrospective on the album in *Rolling Stone*, Rubin explained, "After the stark nature of the first album, the idea of making a different sounding album with the same kind of song selection process was the thought.... It was about finding the right band to record with Johnny who wouldn't simply sound like the band recordings he had done for the last 50 years." For Rubin, the natural choice for the gig was Tom Petty and the Heartbreakers.

Petty and Cash had developed a friendship over the previous dozen years. "I met him I think around '82 or '83," Petty told *Uncut* in 2009. "I liked him right away. I always liked John. I was a bit in awe of him when I first met him. I think everybody is. He's very imposing, but very warm. Not quite gregarious, I'd say, but very warm." It also helped that Howie Epstein was both professionally and romantically involved with Carlene Carter, the daughter of Cash's wife June Carter Cash. Epstein and Tench were cowriters of one of Carlene's biggest hits, 1990's Grammy-nominated "I Fell in Love," which Epstein produced. Through Carlene, Epstein had become almost family to the Cash clan. In addition, Petty and Rubin attended Cash's January 7, 1995, concert at the Pantages Theatre, during which Cash played a number of songs off *American Recordings*.

In an interview with *Billboard* to promote *Unchained*, Cash revealed how Petty and the Heartbreakers came to play on the entire album. "I love Tom's music," he said. "I went to one of his concerts in New York a few months ago, and he royally entertained me. And it seemed like there was a mutual admiration there. When he found out I was starting a new album, he asked Rick if he could come by and play some on it. We hadn't even chosen musicians at that time. I think Tom was the first to volunteer to play on the album, and the other guys in the Heartbreakers came down after that." In *Conversations*, Petty recalled that it was mutually beneficial, remarking, "I think Rick knew I was going through a difficult time, and he wanted to keep me busy."

In the *Rolling Stone* retrospective, Rubin remembered the Heartbreakers' sheer enjoyment of working with Cash. He said, "It was a fun and easy creative vibe. The Heartbreakers are such a great band, especially with the added excitement of playing with Johnny and without the pressure of it being their own album. It was no risk and all fun. The players would all switch between instruments for whatever was needed for each song and it never seemed like work. The sessions felt like musician summer camp." Petty echoed those sentiments in his *Uncut* interview, recalling, "It was great fun. I think about those sessions, and they were just some of the best times I ever had in the studio. Just very charmed sessions. Everyone was so at ease but really into the project at the same time, and really, really enjoying playing. You weren't even nailed down to your particular instrument. I might wind up playing the organ, and the bass quite a bit."

They recorded much of *Unchained* over the first few months of 1996 at Sound City. In addition, Petty and the Heartbreakers joined Cash on stage on February 25—the day before Cash's sixty-fourth birthday—during the finale of Cash's concert at West Hollywood's House of Blues. The performance included a preview of the out-of-the-box cover choices that would appear on *Unchained* when Cash and the Heartbreakers performed Cash's aggressive rendition of Soundgarden's "Rusty Cage." The concert was recorded (clips of the "Rusty Cage" performance appear in the song's music video), but has yet to be released. The concert was also memorable because backstage Petty was reintroduced to Dana York, having previously met her at a 1991 concert in Houston. Before the end of 1996, Petty and York would be dating.

Though there were other contributors on the album—including Cash's longtime collaborator and one-time son-in-law Marty Stuart, Flea of the Red Hot Chili Peppers, and Lindsey Buckingham and Mick

Fleetwood of Fleetwood Mac—Petty and the Heartbreakers performed on every track. The song selection was even more eclectic than *American Recordings*, and the album features covers of "Rusty Cage," Beck's "Rowboat," Lucky Starr's "I've Been Everywhere," and Petty's own "Southern Accents."

Unchained was released on November 5, 1996, and the *Los Angeles Times* gave the collaboration three-and-a-half out of four stars, writing, "Cash blends his complex sensibility with the sympathetic vibrations of young writers and musicians to create a work of intimate moments and epic reach." The album would earn Cash another Grammy Award, this time for Best Country Album (in *Conversations*, Petty joked that winning a Grammy Award for Best Country Album was "pretty good for a rock 'n' roll band").

Years later, several other tracks from the *Unchained* sessions were released on Cash's 2003 posthumous box set *Unearthed*. One of those tracks was a cover of Chuck Berry's "Brown Eyed Handsome Man" recorded with Carl Perkins. The session was the result of a memorable night. As Petty recalled in *Conversations*, Perkins "dropped in and we had the best night of my life, I think. One of them, anyway. We just never laughed so hard. You know when you laugh to where your gut just hurts? The music was all so good, and so effortless. I was really pleased later on when I read the liner notes to *Unearthed*, where [Cash] mentions that night, and said it was one of the greatest nights of his life. Which made me feel good, because it was for me, too."

Petty would reunite with Cash and Rubin for the pair's third album in the series, *American III: Solitary Man*. In addition to Campbell and Tench playing all over the album (both would go on to play in some capacity on the rest of Cash's American Recordings albums), Petty played with Cash on the first two tracks on the album—a cover of Petty's own "I Won't Back Down" and a cover of Neil Diamond's "Solitary Man." In particular, Petty was impressed with Cash's rendition of his *Full Moon Fever* hit, telling *Vanity Fair* in 2010, "When I heard his version, it was like I'd never done it. It dropped my jaw—something about the authority his voice carried." This version was later used in commercials for the US Army, which Petty—who rarely allowed his music used for commercials—allowed. He added, "When the Army and C.I.A. people called me and asked me to use it in their training programs, they wanted to use the Johnny Cash version. I guess it sounded more American."

Years later, Petty reflected on his time playing with Cash in *Conversations*: "These are the things that are the real bonuses to being in The Heartbreakers.... That was a man who we really loved. We loved him deeply. That record is certainly some of the best playing the Heartbreakers ever did. It's funny that it's not one of our records, but if you go and listen to that album, you really hear what we're about as a band."

* * * * *

Unchained would mark the last new music released by Petty—with or without the Heartbreakers—for over two years. During the interim, Petty made yet another one of his unexpected career turns by taking a role in the 1997 Kevin Costner film *The Postman*. In a 1999 interview with *Rolling Stone*, Petty explained, "Kevin called me up and asked me to play the mayor of a post-apocalyptic city. And it was at a time when I really needed to do something. I was, like, lost. The band had stopped touring. I lived alone. I needed to do something with my time, and this sounded perfect, so I took off and went up to Washington, in the middle of the woods somewhere, bald eagles going over and freezing cold in July."

The film was a box office bomb, but it is memorable for an exchange between Costner's and Petty's characters (neither character is given a name in the film). It is implied that Petty is playing, well, himself:

Costner: "I know you. You're...famous."
Petty: "I was once...sorta. Kinda. Not anymore."

The following year, Petty also appeared as himself in a cameo in the final episode of *The Larry Sanders Show*, a show created by and starring his old friend Garry Shandling. On the series, Shandling played Los Angeles late night television host Larry Sanders, and the show depicted the backstage drama behind producing the late-night series. The star-studded finale featured Petty arguing with country music singer Clint Black over who would get to be the "Bette Midler" on the finale of Sanders' talk show (a reference to Midler singing on the penultimate episode of *The Tonight Show Starring Johnny Carson*). The abrasive Petty ends up getting into a shoving match with both Black and actor Greg Kinnear. Ultimately, Black would be the one to play the Bette Midler role.

During a premiere program for Petty's next album on the SFX Radio Network hosted by Jim Ladd, Petty said he wasn't planning on doing much more acting: "I don't want to be a musician that turns into an actor. It's just something to do if there's nothing else to do. It's kind of fun and I like film a lot, so I get to learn and hang around." After all, Petty's first memorable encounter with rock 'n' roll was meeting Elvis on a movie set, and his music heroes included others who also acted in films, like fellow Wilburys George Harrison, Bob Dylan, and even Roy Orbison, so acting was in a lot of ways part of the fabric of Petty's idea of rock 'n' roll. However, these two performances represented the last live-action acting roles for Petty.

The same month that Petty appeared on the finale of *The Larry Sanders Show*, the *Los Angeles Times* reported that Petty bought a house in Malibu "for about $3.7 million." The three-acre property included a four-bedroom main house and a two-bedroom guest house (Dana would move into the new house shortly afterward). Curiously, the house was located across the street from a house where Denny Cordell had once lived. The property would remain Petty's home for the rest of his life. Unsurprisingly, Petty converted the garage into a recording studio (dubbed Shoreline Recorders) and would use that as a backdrop for much of his media interviews. Starting in the early 2000s, well-known rock 'n' roll tailor Glen Palmer—who has dressed stars like Petty, Bob Dylan, George Harrison, Ringo Starr, and Fleetwood Mac—took residence in Petty's guest house for several years. Palmer and Petty had met after one of the Heartbreakers' gigs opening for Blondie at the

Whisky A Go Go in 1976, and Palmer offered to dress him. The two remained collaborators, and Petty invited Palmer to live on his estate after Palmer went through some personal issues.

In a revealing interview with the *New York Daily News* in 1999, Petty talked about this period, recalling, "I took a year off for the first time since my 20s. I was worn out. I had done so much in the five years before. I'd put out so many records and toured 10 months behind *Wildflowers*. Also, I thought it wouldn't hurt us to vanish for a while. [But] it was a challenge—how to fill my days? I reflected on how orderly my life had been. You know every day where you're going to be at 4 o'clock. Suddenly that's gone."

CHAPTER II

ROOM AT THE TOP

In the Fall of 1998, Petty, the Heartbreakers, and Rubin reconvened to begin work on a new album at Mike Campbell's home studio. Rubin helped the Heartbreakers sift through the two dozen songs they had recorded and finished what they considered to be the best ones for the album. Petty had been writing material during the break between albums, but as he told the *New York Daily News*, "I'd sit and write and put stuff on tape but I'd always think, 'That's not really a song.'" The Heartbreakers thought better of the material than Petty did. In order to prevent him from second-guessing himself too much, the Heartbreakers cut the songs quickly. Petty gave an example of the fast-moving process to *Pulse* magazine when he recounted how one of the album's singles was recorded, explaining, "It's a little scary. I'll show them a new song and 20 minutes later, it's done. And they're saying, 'OK, what else you got?' There's a song on the new album called 'Swingin'' that was written right on the spot. I was sitting with the band and we were supposed to be doing another song. I just came up with this new song and they followed me. I called out the chords and ad-libbed the words. They said, 'We oughta do this for the record.' I said 'Really? OK.' We played it again with the tape rolling, and that was it."

Both "Swingin'" and "Billy the Kid" were essentially recorded live-to-tape in a minimum of takes almost as swiftly as Petty wrote them.

As a result, the album, *Echo*, was one of the quickest the Heartbreakers had ever recorded. In *Petty: The Biography*, Rubin said that they had used magnetic poetry sets placed on a music stand to help Petty write lyrics because he was writing songs quicker than he could put words to them. "I could show you specific lines he wrote that were words from the poetry set. It was remarkable and beautiful. He could draw on this pool of information to create the stories. His mind works *very* fast." Unfortunately, Petty and Rubin had something of a falling out when Rubin stopped working on the album prior to the mixing sessions to produce the 1999 album *Californication* with his frequent collaborators the Red Hot Chili Peppers. Petty was offended by Rubin leaving before the album was completed, so he changed the production credit to "Produced by Tom Petty and Mike Campbell with Rick Rubin." Years later on the *Broken Record* podcast, Rubin confessed that he didn't even know that Petty had been bothered by this until he read about it in *Petty: The Biography*. "I think he felt like I abandoned him, which I don't think was the case," Rubin said. "I think we had already done what we were supposed to do."

Perhaps because of how quickly it was written and recorded, the lyrics on *Echo* represented an almost stream-of-conscious window into Petty's personal challenges over the previous few years. He explained to Jim Ladd on the SFX Radio Network World Premiere of *Echo*, "It's very personal. It just kind of fell out of me. I didn't do second drafts. I didn't correct anything. I didn't even worry if things didn't rhyme. I just went with what was there, so I guess, in retrospect, you look back and go, 'Oh, I see what I was thinking.' But I think if I knew what I was thinking about, I would have been too embarrassed to write them." And while the album did reflect Petty's current mindset, he insisted to *Rolling Stone* that it was not about his divorce. He explained, "People say, 'Is the album about your divorce?' And it's not really. It's more about recovering from that, having your whole life completely changed—wham, you know? *Wildflowers* was more about my divorce, this is more about living through a lot of pain, and getting through it." Given that Petty was affected by his heroin use, his words make even more sense in retrospect. "Those were beautiful sessions," said Benmont Tench in *Petty: The Biography*, "But they were dark. I have very vivid memories of them. A lot of really beautiful music got made. But there was some kind of dark energy going on."

Yet years later in *Conversations*, Petty thought back on the period of writing *Echo* with more perspective and saw it as a result of both the positive and negative experiences in his life at the time. He explained, "That's the paradox. I was happy, but I was sad as well. I had been through a huge divorce. I kind of crashed through a wall in my life. Even though I knew things were going to work out, and I had found my true love, there was a lot of wreckage behind me. And it takes a lot of sorting out when something like that happens, and there's a lot of guilt that you have to deal with and figure out. Am I a good person or a bad one? And I think I did figure all that out. And part of the therapy there was writing that record."

Unfortunately, while Petty found the record therapeutic in retrospect and was able to seek treatment for his heroin use before the *Echo* tour, Epstein's own heroin use was making him increasingly unreliable. He did not show for the scheduled photo session for the album cover and, as a result, isn't shown in the group photo.

After wrapping *Echo*, Petty and the Heartbreakers returned to the Fillmore to perform another residency, this time for eight shows from March 7 through March 16. The shows included the live debuts of several songs including "Room at the Top," "Swingin'," and "Free Girl Now."

As with other times in his career, Petty sought new ways to promote his music. In early March, Petty and the Heartbreakers announced that they would be offering the first single from *Echo*, "Free Girl Now" (a song Petty wrote about sexual harassment that Dana had faced at a previous job), as a free download on MP3.com. Initially, the promotional stunt was reportedly supported by Warner Bros., which said MP3.com "allows for many hundreds of thousands of simultaneous downloads in near CD quality." Petty viewed the promotional stunt—one that would soon become relatively common in the industry—as a way to promote a single in an era of declining single sales, and he became one of the first major-label artists to offer a free song for download to promote an album.

Two days and a reported 157,000 downloads later, Petty's label changed its tune and ordered the song yanked from the website. While Petty told *Rolling Stone* that he and Warner Bros. "had a laugh over the whole thing," he admitted that he was intrigued by the power the internet had in building a band's reputation. He said, "It gives these artists a huge outlet—you can have a little band and just get on the computer and sell your stuff and build all these fan bases for things that are completely outside the music industry. I love the fear it strikes into the hearts of these moguls who have shit on us all." As in many other instances, Petty's instincts on the direction of the music business eventually proved to be right as digital music became standard and traditional media outlets like radio and MTV declined in influence.

The initial support and almost immediate reversal by Warner Bros. of the release of "Free Girl Now" on MP3.com was representative of how the music industry would struggle with the digital release and distribution of music for the next several years. A number of services would emerge in the early 2000s that would allow users to share files on their personal computers with other users. Many of these file-sharing networks—most notably Napster—became the subject of lawsuits when they were extensively used to share media files, primarily music files, though some of them briefly became incredibly lucrative companies. For example, three months after the "Free Girl Now" episode, MP3.com went public with a record-breaking $370 million IPO. Less than a year later, MP3.com would close its digital streaming service, My.MP3.com, after a lawsuit by Universal Music Group (over the service's primary function of creating unauthorized duplicates of CDs that users could access from any computer with an internet connection) cost the company $53.4 million. Months later, the company—whose stock was now worth less than a fourth of its

IPO share price—was acquired by media company Vivendi Universal, which was a subsidiary of the very company that had sued MP3.com.

Many artists became outspoken critics of these services and some, such as Metallica, even went as far as to sue services like Napster, while the RIAA itself sued the developers of services like Kazaa and Morpheus. Eventually, those services that did not get sued out of existence found a legitimate way to survive, mostly following the dollar-per-song download model pioneered by Apple's iTunes Music Store, which was the first service to legally offer digital downloads of music from all five major record labels. In Napster's case, its name and logo were bought out of bankruptcy after numerous lawsuits, and it became a legitimate music download service in 2003.

For his part, Petty said little publicly about file sharing but found his own way to take advantage of the new distribution model. In January 2004, Napster made a deal with Universal Music Group to sell Petty's MCA albums exclusively for two weeks before release on other download services. Two months later, Petty offered two live tracks from the Heartbreakers' July 2003 appearance on the TV series *Soundstage*, "Born in Chicago" and "Red Rooster," exclusively on iTunes. Years later, Petty would even give away a free download of the entire 2010 *Mojo* album to ticketbuyers for the Mojo Tour.

* * * * *

The music video for "Swingin'" was shot at Johnie's Coffee Shop, a historic coffee shop at the corner of Wilshire Boulevard and Fairfax Avenue in Los Angeles that has a famed neon light marquee. Though Johnie's closed in 2000, it has since been landmarked as an example of California's 1950s Googie architecture and is in use as a political office. The interior has been featured in numerous films, including *Reservoir Dogs* and *The Big Lebowski*. The video depicts Petty and the Heartbreakers as patrons in the coffee shop on a rainy day as a woman (played by Robin Tunney) enters with a suitcase and her pet cat. In flashbacks, the video shows the trials and tribulations that the woman faced before walking into Johnie's, including the death of her lover (played by Luke Wilson), with several of these scenes having been shot in Acton, California, in northern Los Angeles County, not far from where the Heartbreakers had filmed the "You Got Lucky" video seventeen years earlier. Back at the coffee shop, ghosts from the woman's past look over her from the ceiling. Unfortunately, despite all of its creativity, the video received little airplay on MTV, the network that previously reaped the benefits of Petty's imaginative music videos.

In addition to all the changes in Petty's private life, the industry had changed dramatically in the four and a half years between the November 1994 release of *Wildflowers* and the April 1999 release of *Echo*—or to be more accurate, the way the industry perceived Petty and the Heartbreakers had changed. For one thing, the former MTV-favorite group received virtually no promotion from the network. MTV was undergoing a radical shift away from music-related programming, and in the music programming that remained the focus was firmly on pop and hip-hop artists. The few rock bands supported by the channel's programming were much younger than Petty, indicating that after a nearly fifteen-year reign as one of the flagship acts of the MTV generation, Petty and the Heartbreakers had aged out of the MTV demographic. Not even two years earlier, MTV had regularly played the video for "Walls" from the *She's the One* soundtrack in rotation. On the other hand, Petty's videos for *Echo*—"Swingin'," "Room at the Top," and "Free Girl Now"—as well as his classic videos were in regular rotation on MTV's sister network VH1. In fact, VH1 embraced Petty and the Heartbreakers warmly to support the release of *Echo*, including recording the Heartbreakers for an appearance on the channel's popular show *VH1 Storytellers*, in which artists performed their songs and talked about the inspiration behind them.

On March 31—the night of a blue moon, as Petty pointed out—Petty and the Heartbreakers played to a crowd even more intimate in size than their recent shows at the Fillmore when they recorded their episode of *VH1 Storytellers* before a small group of invited guests and fan-club members on a soundstage in Burbank. In a small, makeshift set that simulated a theater, the Heartbreakers played for close to two hours as Petty spun tales about the background of recording the songs performed—at least, as much as he could. In the opening, Petty admitted, "I'm gonna talk a lot and tell you about these songs...but I'm not gonna tell you what they're about because I don't really know what they're about. But I know what was happening when I wrote 'em." Petty joked with the audience, and included a funny ditty that he wrote about the *Titanic*, since, as he sang, "Everybody likes the *Titanic*," in a reference to the enduring popularity of the 1997 film. At one point, he quipped that songwriting is "kind of like an orgasm...you don't know how you did that," and said explaining how a song was written is like a magician explaining how he sawed a woman in half. He also made sure to point out that the following day would be the twenty-fifth anniversary of when Mudcrutch left Florida for Los Angeles. MTV reported that Petty requested to reshoot two songs, "Free Fallin'" and "Mary Jane's Last Dance," explaining to the audience, "They said I could do this" (the latter was not included in the broadcast). Petty and the Heartbreakers were declared "Artist of the Month" for May 1999 as a way to promote the broadcast of their episode of *VH1 Storytellers*, which aired on May 16.

The changeover of attention from MTV to VH1 wasn't lost on Petty, who in an interview to promote *Echo* with *Rolling Stone* called his MTV Awards "good doorstops" and said, "MTV has been very good to me...but I think it's dead—more dead than rock, let's put it that way... VH1 is a much more musical medium right now. I think the video is, like, the tiredest idea going today. There may be a few commercials on TV as tired as that, but the rock video, let's face it—it's a worn-out, tired idea, and it needs a rest." The Heartbreakers themselves took a rest from narrative music videos, and the music videos for the rest of their career were primarily performance-based.

The shift of tone in Petty's career was also plain to see from the content of *Echo*, which was focused on introspective songs that were a cross between Petty's warm *Wildflowers* sound and the harder rock songs of the early years of the Heartbreakers with seemingly minimal studio tinkering. Elysa Gardner gave the album three out of four stars in her *Los Angeles Times* review, yet filled the copy with backhanded compliments like, "If Petty is one of the most predictable artists around, he's also among the most reliable," and the songs "are as instantly familiar, utterly unsurprising and easily satisfying as a good steak dinner." Fred Shuster's three-star review in the *Daily News* was more positive, saying that the album "is packed with superior material and the sort of rootsy, emotive playing that makes the Heartbreakers one of rock's great back lines," citing "Room at the Top," "Swingin'," and "Free Girl Now" as standout tracks.

Following the April 13 release of *Echo*, Petty and the Heartbreakers finally received their star on the Hollywood Walk of Fame that had initially been announced back in 1996. On April 28, Petty, Campbell, Tench, and Epstein were on hand for the unveiling of the 2,133rd star, located at 7018 Hollywood Boulevard, next to the Hollywood Roosevelt Hotel. The City of Los Angeles also declared it "Tom Petty and the Heartbreakers Day."

Though *Echo* charted higher than *She's the One*, debuting at #10 on the Billboard albums chart with 81,000 copies sold, that was the chart peak for the album. Less than a week after the release, the *Los Angeles Times* quoted a Musicland retail chain executive on April 19 that the album was "off to a somewhat sluggish start," though he called it "the strongest release of a very weak week." Of the album's singles, only "Free Girl Now" charted on the main Billboard chart (peaking at #120), though "Free Girl Now," "Room at the Top," and "Swingin'" were all Top 20 hits on the Billboard Rock chart. Like *She's the One*, *Echo* quickly went gold but shortly afterward dropped out of sight (though unlike *She's the One*, *Echo* also went gold in Canada). Both albums were more-or-less equal in their lukewarm commercial status.

However, *Echo* proved to be much more successful on the road. For better or worse, the Heartbreakers were falling firmly into "classic rock" status—as with many acts from the '60s and '70s, the public was showing diminishing interest in new music from the Heartbreakers and instead looked to the group as the greatest-hits concert jukebox that so many of their contemporaries were fast becoming. Yet with deep-cut driven shows at smaller venues like the Fillmore and New York's Irving Plaza (where Petty and the Heartbreakers warmed up for the *Echo* tour with three shows in April in the days after performing on *Saturday Night Live*), the Heartbreakers were resisting that label. In fact, it's worth noting that in the airing of *VH1 Storytellers*—a show that for most other artists acted as a "Greatest Hits Live" program— only songs recorded from 1989's *Full Moon Fever* to *Echo* were featured. Older songs they played at the performance, like "Breakdown," were not in the broadcast.

That's not to say that the Heartbreakers didn't play the hits on the *Echo* tour—typically half of the songs featured on the *Greatest Hits* album, plus about three songs from *Wildflowers*, were played each night. Nonetheless, the Heartbreakers got creative with the remaining third of the setlist with songs from *She's the One*, *Echo*, and various covers. Compared to other classic rock bands performing at the time, the *Echo* tour setlists demonstrated remarkable variety.

The *Echo* tour made two stops at the Irvine Meadows Amphitheatre on August 13 and August 14, and after a roundabout route through much of the US, returned to Southern California for a tour-ending performance on October 16 at the Hollywood Bowl. Continuing Petty's brief association with MP3.com, one of the concerts at Irvine was opened by a Pasadena band that won a contest on the website, Red Delicious. Mike Boehm reviewed the August 13 performance at Irvine Meadows for the *Los Angeles Times*, noting that perhaps because of the sluggish sales of *Echo*, "instead of steaming full-speed-ahead into his glorious present Friday, Petty chose a balanced, middle way suitable for a veteran rocker whose most prudent tactic is to please the fans with well-rendered favorites, thereby ensuring their ticket-buying loyalty into the future," while also writing, "The new stuff came across with a special spark. Some of the old stuff sounded thin." Yet the review complimented the band in saying, "There was nothing tired about the recitation of hits; songs such as 'Don't Come Around Here No More,' 'Free Fallin',' 'American Girl' and 'You Got Lucky' are sturdy and reliable, and Petty and the Heartbreakers fired many of them up with long jams that were models of what rock classicism should be: precision married to passion." The overall-positive review noted Epstein's nearly-inaudible bass as the lone disappointment. Unbeknownst to Boehm, that may have been a sign of Epstein's status in the group.

The *Echo* tour finale on October 16 marked the first of two times that the Heartbreakers ended a tour at the Hollywood Bowl. It was a star-studded affair—the *Los Angeles Times* reported that Kevin Spacey, Edward Norton, Phil Everly, Jenna Elfman, George Thorogood, and Lindsey Buckingham were all in the audience. As with the Irvine concerts, the final concert leaned heavily on the hits, with a mix of new material. *Variety* was effusive in its praise for the Heartbreakers' tour-ending Hollywood Bowl performance, noting it offered "hit after familiar hit in a two-hour-plus program that affectionately visited all facets of Petty's impressive 20-year recording career."

After the end of the tour, the Heartbreakers rarely played songs from *Echo* live, except for "Billy the Kid" (on both of the short 2001 tours), until the band's 40th Anniversary Tour, when "Swingin'" was occasionally featured in the set. In a 2002 interview with the *Los Angeles Times* to promote the band's induction into the Rock and Roll Hall of Fame, Petty admitted that he was uncomfortable with the material. "That *Echo* album was one of the dark times. I can't even play it. It scares me because I was so down when I made it. It was the toughest period of my life.... It was the time of my divorce and the aftermath, when I was having to rebuild a lot of relationships, including those with my daughters. There was a lot of misunderstanding. I probably spent a year withdrawn from everyone, just staying home. It was a lonely, weird time."

The successful *Echo* tour—which made $14.4 million in revenue—couldn't disguise the fact that the album sold a fraction of what *Wildflowers* had sold. Petty didn't blame the fans—after all, they packed arenas and amphitheaters to see the Heartbreakers play live. Which is perhaps why, when Petty opened up about the target of his ire for his declining sales, he once again pointed his finger at the music business.

Petty was fed up with radio stations for not supporting his new music. In an interview with *Guitar Player* magazine, Petty said, "I hate the prejudicial way that music is presented these days. Everything is broken down into categories, and stations just play this or that. I remember a time when you could hear everything on one station. It was so great to go from Frank Sinatra to the Yardbirds. You didn't think twice about it."

Another target of Petty's anger was the rising costs for his fans to attend his concerts. Prior to the kick-off of the *Echo* tour, Petty complained about increasing concert ticket costs to the *Boston Globe*, saying, "I don't want to wind up just playing to the elite. I see some people that don't mind that, but I don't think my fans would appreciate it too much. I think sometimes we're fools for not going for the dough, but I don't want to feel that we're taking advantage of people. We're not at the point where we're trying to cash in and retire or anything." He repeated that sentiment to Jim Ladd, declaring, "Let's break the news: it ain't worth it. There ain't no damn rock band worth $150. Don't pay it, baby. And them prices will come right down." These criticisms would have a significant influence on the direction of the Heartbreakers' next album.

* * * * *

Following the *Echo* tour, Petty and the Heartbreakers went quiet for a bit. On April 30, 2000, Petty was in the audience at the small Canon Theatre in Beverly Hills (a former cinema that was converted into a live performance space in the late '70s, until it was demolished in 2004) for the opening night performance of *Bill Graham Presents*, a one-man show starring actor Ron Silver as the renowned concert promoter who promoted concerts at the Fillmore, which had in recent years become the Heartbreakers' home base in San Francisco.

Despite not releasing anything new, Petty and the Heartbreakers hit the road again in spring 2001 for two short tours, the Way out West Tour (which featured two shows at the Santa Barbara Bowl on May 24 and May 25) and the East Coast Invasion Tour.

For the Heartbreakers, who had last played the Hollywood Bowl in the area, the Santa Barbara Bowl was an intimate show. The amphitheater, which holds 4,500, was built by the WPA during the Great Depression. The Heartbreakers played essentially the same set at both shows, but as per usual changed up the covers they played ("Green Onions" and "Little Red Rooster" at the first show, "Thirteen Days" and "Lucille" at the second).

Most notably, following the first tour's stops in Las Vegas (June 1 and 2), Petty and Dana got married in Sin City. The two followed that with a ceremony on June 21 at their Malibu home, which was conducted by rock 'n' roll legend Little Richard and featured an all-female mariachi band. In March 2002, Petty bought another house in Malibu for around $2.5 million. The house, which was right on the Pacific Ocean, became the Pettys' "vacation" home. In *Conversations*, Petty revealed that the second Malibu house served as a convenient place to get away: "We had bought another house. Though we kept the big house, and bought kind of a cottage on the ocean. And we were spending more and more time there. We did that to get away from this place. Because this house can get so busy, and there's always so many people in and out of it. A number of people work here. My personal office is here. It can get busy. Sometimes it's good—we go there, and you have to make your own bed, and it's an escape. So we were spending more and more time there. And the ocean is there, and the ocean is great. Both of us love the ocean. That's why we live out here."

All the while, Petty continued to stew about the recording industry and its treatment of fans and artists. Petty was one of several artists, including Don Henley, Merle Haggard, and Tom Waits, who established a coalition of musicians that hoped to lobby congress for more rights for musicians. In a March 29, 2001, *Los Angeles Times* article on musicians' rights, Petty was quoted saying that among the biggest issues faced by musicians fighting against record companies was the intimidation that scared off other musicians from supporting each other. He said, "It's really hard to get artists to do anything together for the collective good. When I was out there fighting my battle, it was very lonely.... The fact is once you decide to try to set a precedent, you're no longer just fighting the company that hired you. You're fighting all of them. This kind of thing could end up costing some very powerful people a whole bunch of money. And these aren't the kind of guys who just roll over.... They keep an entire legal team on staff and attorneys on retainer just to scare folks like us off.... It's going to be a long, hard fight ahead."

On Tuesday, February 26, 2002, Petty again showed support for the cause by guest-starring during the Concert for Artists' Rights at the Forum—a benefit concert for the Recording Artists' Coalition that featured short sets by the Eagles, Billy Joel, John Fogerty, Stevie Nicks, and Sheryl Crow—during Nicks's set to sing "Stop Draggin' My Heart Around." It was one of four concerts that took place during the evening in the Los Angeles area (the other concerts were at Universal Amphitheatre, the Wiltern Theatre, and the Long Beach Arena). It was surprising, considering Petty's history, that he didn't participate more in a concert that was specifically dedicated to raising money for the rights of artists. On the other hand, despite raising about $2.5 million from the four concerts, the Recording Artists' Coalition made no significant public moves for years afterwards—perhaps because of all the major changes to come in the music business as the internet increasingly became the primary distribution method for music—before merging with the National Academy of Recording Arts and Sciences (the organization that awards the Grammys) in 2009. Of course, Petty continued the push for artist rights without any sort of organized movement behind him. In fact, he was just getting started.

After the terrorist attacks of September 11, 2001, the Heartbreakers participated in "America: A Tribute to Heroes," a telethon that took place in Los Angeles, New York, and London and that aired on all four major US television networks. The Heartbreakers performed at CBS Television City, playing a forceful version of "I Won't Back Down." Petty also joined in on the finale, singing "America the Beautiful" with all of the Los Angeles performers, led by Willie Nelson.

In late 2001, Tom Petty and the Heartbreakers were announced as inductees for the Rock and Roll Hall of Fame class of 2002, the band's first year of eligibility. The original Heartbreakers lineup plus Howie Epstein were to be honored as inductees at the ceremony at the Waldorf Astoria Hotel in New York City. The Heartbreakers saluted all the inductees in the group by featuring Epstein on bass for their first song, "Mary Jane's Last Dance," and Ron Blair on bass for "American Girl," with Lynch playing drums on both songs. The Hall of Fame ceremony was the final time that Lynch and Epstein would play in the band. On the 2001 tours, Epstein proved to be increasingly unreliable and nearly missed several shows—he played several in poor condition—and was unable to overcome his heroin addiction despite repeated promises to get clean. "He'd show up five minutes before a gig, and then we wouldn't see him again until five minutes before the next gig," Petty told the *Orange County Register* in October 2002. "Eventually we realized that we were just contributing to the problem. When you're living a life where you really don't have any responsibilities, it's easy for evil forces to take over." Epstein did not complete any of the rehab programs that the other Heartbreakers attempted to get him in.

Epstein was no closer to recovery when he arrived for the Hall of Fame rehearsals, while Blair—who was also being inducted—played with the band as if no time had passed. When the rehearsals went poorly with Epstein, Petty realized he needed to make a change to save the band and, more importantly, to try to save Epstein's life.

Unfortunately, Epstein passed in February 2003. His friends and bandmates had a memorial for him at McCabe's Guitar Shop, a legendary Santa Monica music store, which also has a small but renowned performance space for mostly acoustic acts. "It was full of people," said Campbell in *Petty: The Biography*. "It was friends, the band, everyone. It was spiritual. I felt better afterward, taking the time to remember, to say good-bye. I don't usually speak in public, but I felt moved to get up and speak. It was bittersweet."

CHAPTER 12

CAN'T STOP THE SUN

For the band's 2002 summer tour, Petty again went against the grain of his contemporaries and other classic rock acts in order to keep ticket prices down. In particular, Petty and his manager, Tony Dimitriades, spoke out against the idea of "gold circle" ticketing that charged top-dollar prices for front row seats that included VIP treatment. Speaking to *Billboard*, Dimitriades said, "That smacks of segregation in Tom Petty's mind and is totally against what rock 'n' roll is all about." In fact, the working title for the Heartbreakers' next album, which was to be a loose concept record critical of the music industry, was *The Golden Circle*. Instead, tickets for the Heartbreakers tour ranged from twenty-two dollars to eighty-five dollars.

The Heartbreakers played one Los Angeles area concert during the 2002 Summer Tour on August 24 at the Blockbuster Pavilion (later renamed Glen Helen Amphitheater in San Bernardino). The setlist for the show was largely the same as the setlists the Heartbreakers had played at the Santa Barbara Bowl the previous summer, relying heavily on the hits and a dose of classic rock 'n' roll covers. The biggest change was that the Heartbreakers had dropped all *Echo* songs from the set and instead played three songs from their forthcoming album—"Have Love Will Travel," "Lost Children," and "Can't Stop the Sun."

Petty's August 24 concert at the Blockbuster Pavilion coincided with a Bruce Springsteen concert just seventy miles away at the Inglewood Forum, an odd coincidence of scheduling two artists that drew from much the same audience. The competition hurt Petty—while the Springsteen show was sold out, *Billboard* reported that Petty's show was attended by 16,883, over 8,000 shy of a sellout (though the show still grossed nearly $700,000).

Nonetheless, the *Daily News* review of the Pavilion show said it demonstrated "what it takes to have a career that lasts three decades," and gleefully noted that "each song sounded just as timeless and current as the last, and the fans—who ranged in age from 12 to 60—sang." Staying in line with the theme of the upcoming album, the review also noted that Petty took a shot at the Pavilion's luxury boxes, quoting Petty as saying, "It's hard to be a rock 'n' roll band in 2002 and not play to corporate boxes."

Those three new songs—which the Heartbreakers played throughout the summer tour—were indicative of the concept behind the forthcoming album, which had already been announced as *The Last DJ*. The resulting album would become the only concept album of Petty's recording career, and in a career spent standing up for artists' rights, *The Last DJ* (and its title track, which was the album's first single) served as Petty's most blatant musical criticism of the music business in his career.

After spending large swaths of his almost thirty years in the music business in conflict with various aspects of the industry, Petty felt particularly fired up by the state of radio in the early 2000s. In *Conversations*, Petty explained, "[The idea for *The Last DJ*] came to me when I kept seeing these billboards for radio stations that said, 'No Talk.' And I thought, God, that's sad. There's no talk. They don't tell you who that was [playing each song]. And when I was growing up, there were disc jockeys that seemed like people you knew. And they actually did a show. And they played a great range of music. And radio was so magical and so interesting. It played such a huge role in my life." Though Petty had his ups and downs with the US radio industry ever since stations were reluctant to play the singles from his first two albums, not knowing how to categorize his music in an era of disco, new wave, and punk, it was the weakening connection between the disc jockey and the radio audience (and also perhaps the reduced airplay of his new music) that pushed him to write about those changes.

The events that inspired Petty to write The Last DJ had been building for several years. The Telecommunications Act of 1996 deregulated radio station cross-ownership laws, and behemoth communications giants like Clear Channel (now iHeartMedia) and Infinity Broadcasting Corporation (now CBS Radio) began purchasing radio stations across the country at a rapid pace. Increasingly, the operations and playlists of these conglomerate-owned stations became standardized, and it was not uncommon for two radio stations in different markets to have nearly identical playlists. Whereas many stations once had freeform content with disc jockeys that would choose what to play, this arrangement was increasingly become a rarity on broadcast radio, as DJs were either fired or required to stick to a set playlist with as few as five hundred songs per station. Other stations removed DJs from the air entirely, particularly with the "Jack FM" format that would emerge in the mid-2000s, which featured only pre-recorded bits between songs and commercials. Many stations that did play new music had at most twenty spots a week available for new releases. Naturally, most of that scant available airplay went to the songs pushed by the record labels with the deepest pockets.

The consolidation of media was not simply the result of corporate greed. In some ways, these takeovers were a response to the changes in the way music was being distributed. Increasingly, consumers—especially young ones—were relying on CDs and MP3 players in their cars for music instead of the radio. In 2002, Arbitron found that since the passage of the Telecommunications Act of 1996, teenage radio listeners had dropped by 11 percent, and listeners in the 18–24 age range had declined 10 percent. As sound quality and variety of internet radio and satellite radio improved, more people were abandoning traditional radio.

Petty was one of the many who noticed what had been going on—and he didn't like it. "You can't say rock radio is the center of the rock universe anymore," he told the *Chicago Tribune* in April 2002. "A lot of my audience, and the rock audience in general, has given up on radio and moved on to other things, like MP3 downloads. Radio has very little to do with rock anymore, but people still want rock."

The industry changes gave Petty a new opponent. In an October 2002 interview with the *Orange County Register*, Petty confessed, "Let me be clear: I don't have any war with the music business personally. My life with the music business doesn't really have any problems. Luckily, I'm in a position now where I can deliver albums, and they're very nice to me." After all, a record label might have rejected an album like *The Last DJ* in fear of its limited commercial appeal. In fact, Petty noted that even before *The Last DJ*, the lack of radio support for *She's the One* and *Echo* hampered his ability to sell records. He added, "It's hard for people to even know you have an album out these days.... Guys like me, we're up against all sorts of odds. On a classic rock station, they'll play a new song maybe once in 24 hours. It's not like the old days where they played it every hour. Just to spread the word that this exists? It's a lot more work on my end than it ever was."

After significantly supporting the Heartbreakers for *Echo*, VH1 showed little interest in promoting "The Last DJ" music video, which features shots of the historic KRKD radio towers in downtown Los Angeles. According to Petty, the channel was disappointed that the video simply depicted an in-studio performance of the song by the band instead of one of Petty's more typical creative music videos. The channel also passed on airing a "making-of" documentary about the production of the album. Petty told *USA Today*, "It's a land of censorship and dumb ideas. The response was, 'We can't have a film of musicians playing instruments. Can't you do a funny concept video?' I've given up on the video world. I'm bowing out, at least for now."

Though the album's title and title track specifically targeted radio, Petty didn't have just one target in mind when he wrote the album—he cast blame on a wide array of targets, all of whom he connected by greed. Speaking with *USA Today* in October 2002, he said, "I left nobody out. I pick on the artist, the audience, everyone. And not just in the music industry. It could be any business. The problem is greed, pure and simple. Never mind a healthy profit; the idea is: 'We want all the money we can get. We want every damn dime out there, and our computers can show us where every dime is.' The mom-and-pop store had to care about its customers and its products to survive. These giant corporations don't care about anything but profit."

Ultimately, Petty felt the need to express that rock music—and culture in general—is something worth fighting for. He told the Associated Press, "I really have dedicated my entire life to this music—not that I didn't want to, or even have a choice. It overcame me at an early age in a big way. I care about it, and I don't want to see it reduced to a silly caricature. Maybe that's what inspired me to write this album. I really care about this, and I don't want rock to become irrelevant."

The Last DJ had been recorded between the Heartbreakers' touring commitments throughout 2001 and 2002 at Cello Studios in Hollywood, which was opened as, and is again known as, United Recording Studios (it was also where "Mary Jane's Last Dance" was recorded). The album was produced by Petty, Campbell, and George Drakoulias, a regular collaborator of Rick Rubin's who had compiled the Tom Petty and the Heartbreakers' *Playback* box set.

Several of the songs featured orchestrations by Jon Brion, who had become well known within the Los Angeles music scene for his Friday night performances at Largo in West Hollywood, a residency that began in the late '90s and has continued ever since on a once-a-month basis, even after the club moved to the historic Coronet Theatre on North La Cienega Boulevard in 2008. In addition to his live performance and session and production work for artists like David Byrne, Aimee Mann, Fiona Apple, Melissa Etheridge, the Wallflowers, and Peter Gabriel, Brion recorded music for art house filmmaker Paul Thomas Anderson's

Hard Eight, *Boogie Nights*, *Magnolia*, and *Punch-Drunk Love*. That was where Petty first took notice of him—in 2003, Petty told the *Chicago Tribune*, "The Paul Thomas Anderson movies got me to check him out, because those are my favorite contemporary movie scores. We met a few years ago, and I thought he'd be good for achieving the kind of cinematic feel I wanted for this record, and he was." Afterwards, Benmont Tench became a semi-regular guest performing at Brion's residency shows.

Another major development was that Ron Blair made his first contributions to a Heartbreakers album in twenty years. After the short reunion of the original Heartbreakers lineup at the Rock and Roll Hall of Fame Ceremony in 2002, Blair and Campbell reconnected, and Blair participated in recordings on Campbell's demos. He also became a member of the original lineup of Campbell's side project, the Dirty Knobs, which also included Steve Ferrone. Five years earlier, Blair had also collaborated with Campbell, Tench, and Mudcrutch drummer Randall Marsh for the one-off Blue Stingrays surf-rock album. Though Petty and Campbell recorded most of the bass parts for *The Last DJ*, Campbell recommended to Petty that they bring in Blair. Blair recorded the bass on two songs, "Lost Children" and "Can't Stop the Sun." In *Petty: The Biography*, Blair commented on how the band dynamic changed: "I went down to the studio and it went pretty good. I worked a couple of nights, and I was thinking, 'Wow, this is interesting.' There was a kind of tension in the air, like a nice kind of tension, right? There I was, after so many years. By the end of the second night, Tom asked me, 'So what are you doing this summer?' 'Nothing, brother,' I tell him. 'Nothing I couldn't get out of.'" Blair returned to the group for the band's 2002 Summer Tour. Petty said, "The idea of bringing in someone new, someone we didn't really know, no matter how good a player would have been just...too many missing people. I need to be a member of a band. Or not. Ron was an answer to my concerns. Had he not appeared, I think I would have put an end to the band. I couldn't have done it with a hired gun. His appearance was almost mystical to me. And, then, the band just got better, gelled in a really good way. And I think that's when we all became friends again."

One of the more damning tracks on *The Last DJ* is "Joe," a warts-and-all take on record label executives who create and dispose of pop stars—a barb that became even more relevant when *American Idol*, a reality television contest to create pop stars, debuted in June 2002. Petty alluded to the show and the various imitators that followed when discussing the song in *Conversations*, saying, "Every word of ['Joe'] is true. And the truth hurts sometimes. I saw him also as an impresario. What I was trying to say there was something about pre-packaged pop stars. And how they come ready to assemble. And TV shows that make pop stars for you. How it's gotten so cold that they're actually just created to fit certain market demands.... My favorite line in that is, 'some angel whore who can learn a guitar lick/hey, that's what I call music.' [Laughs] And that's true. It's before our eyes." That lyric also references the title to the long-running compilation series *Now That's What I Call Music!*, which began in 1998. The series comprises CD anthologies of Top 40 pop hits, and the collections are filled with artists that were quickly dropped from their labels after one successful single, in favor of the next flavor of the month.

Petty saw these as signs that the record industry was returning to some of the prefabricated tactics that they were using as Petty was growing up in Gainesville. He continued, "It's insane. It's Fabian. It's worse than Fabian. We've gone full-circle back to the days of the early Sixties when pop stars were just created, when all the Bobbys were out, and they went from leather jackets to sweaters, and they tried to say that they aspired to be something more than rock. That they weren't just rock, but they were aspiring to be more. Be real entertainers and actors. And we didn't learn a lesson from that? That it's just suddenly swung right back into that. That's your popular entertainment."

He went into more detail in an article named "10 Things That Piss Off Tom Petty" that appeared in *Rolling Stone*. Petty pointed out, "An act like ours wouldn't even be around today if someone hadn't brought us along and let us make mistakes and grow at our own pace. Today it seems that if you don't have a hit—or even if you do—they have no use for you the next time. It's like, 'Well, why wait for these guys to come back with another hit when we can bring in somebody else?' It's an asinine way to conduct yourself. These people are looking at balance sheets, not music. Most people involved in putting this music on the air or bringing it to us aren't really listening to it."

Upon the release of *The Last DJ* on October 8, reviews of the album were mixed, with many outlets supporting Petty's message but feeling that the concept wore thin over an entire album. Petty fared better in the Los Angeles media. The three-star review in the *Los Angeles Times* said *The Last DJ* "works on a number of levels.... On the surface, several numbers are straight-out poison-pen letters to the commercial forces that compromise the art—and the fun—of rock 'n' roll," and praised the album's songs as a series of "pastiches" to Petty's personal pantheon of rock music—citing "Like a Diamond" as John Lennon-like, "Blue Sunday" as Rolling Stones-like, and so on. The *Billboard* review also commended the album's lyrical content, saying, "It's always sort of tough to rally behind an artist dissin' the music industry—I mean, how do you support someone who's living a rock star's life but still complaining, right? But Tom Petty makes it all too easy here, slyly balancing bitter references to modern-day payola, shifty execs, and even the struggles of artists over 40 with wistful imagery of rock 'n' roll dreams."

Naturally, many radio stations weren't thrilled with the title track, which was released as the album's first single. In fact, some stations—like New York's WAXQ—initially refused to put the song on their playlists. Petty took the refusals in stride and saw them as ironic, telling the Associated Press, "I've never heard a more pro-radio song in my life. I think that just illustrates my point. There are no naughty words in it. That just shows that they're afraid of an idea."

On October 15 and 16, the Heartbreakers played the Grand Olympic Auditorium in downtown Los Angeles, a venue much better known for historic boxing (such as the boxing matches for the 1932 Olympics) and professional wrestling events than for music performances, though the venue did have a lengthy association with punk music during the '80s, featuring concerts by Public Image Ltd, Black Flag, Fear, Bad Religion, Circle Jerks, the Dickies, and Dead Kennedys. The Grand Olympic Auditorium ceased hosting concerts in late 2005, and has since largely been succeeded by the 7,100-seat Nokia Theatre LA Live (now the Microsoft Theater), which opened in October 2007 just one mile northeast of the Grand Olympic.

In a rare move for the Heartbreakers, on both nights the band performed *The Last DJ* album in its entirety as a first set and played an encore of classics afterward ("Change of Heart," "I Need to Know," "Mary Jane's Last Dance," and "You Wreck Me" on both nights, while October 16 also featured brief renditions of Big Joe Turner's "Shake, Rattle and Roll" and Chuck Berry's "Around and Around"). The performance also featured a forty-piece orchestra conducted by Jon Brion.

The auditorium, which held about 6,300 for Petty's concert, was likely chosen for the two-night event because the October 15 performance was broadcast live to forty Regal movie theaters around the US, as well as several hundred radio stations, including Los Angeles' KLOS. Movie theater tickets cost ten dollars, and the *Los Angeles Times* reported that about 40 percent of the seats were sold out nationwide, which was considered a big success on a Tuesday night (normally a slow night at movie theaters). The Grand Olympic Auditorium has had a long history of filming, including live sports broadcasts, appearing in movies like *The Manchurian Candidate* and *Rocky*, and music videos for Survivor, Bon Jovi, Air Supply, Janet Jackson, and Kiss. Two years earlier, Los Angeles rock band Rage Against the Machine recorded a live DVD there. The Heartbreakers' live broadcast was later released on DVD in September 2003 as *Live at the Olympic: The Last DJ*. The broadcast was directed by Martyn Atkins, who directed the Heartbreakers' 1999 live DVD, *Tom Petty and the Heartbreakers: High Grass Dogs, Live from the Fillmore*. The band was introduced by Jim Ladd, the famed Los Angeles freeform DJ who was already the subject of speculation that Petty had based "The Last DJ" on him.

In a concert review in *Variety*, which also critiqued *The Last DJ* album, Steven Mirkin called Petty "an imperfect vessel" for the message of *The Last DJ*, and noted that of all the shots Petty gives out on the album, "The heart of Petty's problem is that his audience is made up of people who attended their senior prom in 1979, and are no longer pop culture's driving force." Mirkin praised the encore of classics, remarking, "It made what came before sound like the work of a man upset because the parade has passed him by." The *Los Angeles Times* review was from a contrasting point of view, arguing, "Petty put on sunglasses to further caricature that evil businessman, but that was the only time his crusade seemed heavy-handed. The strokes may be broad, but Petty instills a real sense of betrayal into his narratives, making palpable the sense that something precious has indeed been lost," and that "this is the grand, heartfelt, gimmick-free rock whose demise Petty mourns, so he had added incentive Tuesday to make it sound good, and in that he never failed."

Ben Wener's review in the *Orange County Register* was also positive, praising the group by saying, "Whether breezing through symphonic Beatlesque passages, whipping up a little soft-shoe fun or doing what they do best—in this case, extending 'When a Kid Goes Bad' and 'Lost Children' into frazzled guitar workouts that spat hellfire—they remain a well-oiled machine capable of so much more than its patented spin on rock 'n' roll.... In the end, that's all that matters: That they rock as strongly now as ever before, maybe more. Debate Petty's current subject matter all you want. Five years from now, all anyone will remember is that *The Last DJ* contained some good tunes played superbly."

Eleven days later, The Last DJ Tour properly began on October 27 at the Santa Barbara Bowl. While the concert began with "The Last DJ," the band quickly demonstrated that it wouldn't repeat the stunt of playing the new album in its entirety when the second song was "Love Is a Long Road." Nonetheless, the Heartbreakers still played a majority of the album—"Have Love Will Travel," "Dreamville," "Joe," "When a Kid Goes Bad," "Like a Diamond," "Blue Sunday," "Lost Children," and then ending the concert with "Can't Stop the Sun"—balanced with

Heartbreakers standards ("Free Fallin'," "You Don't Know How It Feels," "I Won't Back Down," among others) and a surprising gem in "Shadow of a Doubt (A Complex Kid)," which the band hadn't played in years. The Heartbreakers also performed "Have Love Will Travel" on *The Tonight Show* in Burbank on November 13.

By the time the tour looped back to the Los Angeles area for a November 23 concert at the Forum, the tracks from *The Last DJ* had been pared down to five, "The Last DJ," "Have Love Will Travel," "Joe," "When a Kid Goes Bad," "Can't Stop the Sun," and "Lost Children," freeing up space for more Petty classics like "Refugee" and "Kings Highway." The Heartbreakers also played a cover of George Harrison's "Isn't It a Pity" (the band would play three songs—but not that one—on November 29 at the Concert for George at the Royal Albert Hall). In its review of the concert, the *Hollywood Reporter* wrote that Petty "delivered his sneering vocals with notable conviction and seemed absolutely involved with the music and his audience. His longtime backing unit, the Heartbreakers, supported the songs with firm, driving emotion, using a tasteful, minimalist approach that packed a powerful punch." According to *Billboard*, The Last DJ Tour averaged $468,767 per show and average ticket sales of 15,490, with the Heartbreakers playing to 681,592 fans.

* * * * *

It's doubtful that Petty thought a controversial album like *The Last DJ* would return the *Heartbreakers* to the top of the charts, and it didn't. Though it was the first Petty album since Wildflowers to break into the Billboard Top 10—it peaked at #9 in its first week after selling 74,396 copies—it was Petty's first album to fail to go gold. The title track failed to chart on the Top 200, though it did peak at #22 on the Mainstream Rock chart, the lowest peak positioning on that chart for Petty since 1992's "Makin' Some Noise."

Though Petty was particularly proud of the album, the band rarely revisited the material live. Both "Have Love Will Travel" and "When a

Kid Goes Bad" were played by the Heartbreakers at the two Cal State University, Northridge benefit shows in 2011, and both tracks were revisited at the Heartbreakers' smaller-scale Fonda Theatre shows in Hollywood and Beacon Theater shows in New York in 2013.

Surprisingly, one of the more enduring aspects of *The Last DJ* was debate over who (if anyone) the title track was written about. The most obvious answer was Jim Ladd, the freeform radio legend whom had interviewed Petty several times and who had introduced him at several Los Angeles area shows over the years. Ladd had been a Los Angeles radio institution from the end of the '60s and heard nationwide on his syndicated interview show *Innerview*. Though generally popular throughout his career with listeners, Ladd had been chased off several stations because of changing formats and his refusal to adhere to a strict playlist. While the lyrics of "The Last DJ" don't completely follow the narrative of Ladd's life, his notoriety as one of the most famous DJs who "plays what he wants to play" in Southern California made him an obvious candidate. Also, the liner notes of the album include a note of thanks to Ladd, which seemed like a clear clue for those sleuths who treated the track like a mystery.

Initially in interviews Petty insisted that the DJ was fictional, pointing to the lyrics mentioning that the DJ moved to Mexico as an example that it was not representative of any particular real-life DJ. Nonetheless, the song became associated with Ladd—so much so that when Ladd was fired from KLOS in October 2011 after the station was purchased by Cumulus Media, many headlines (including those in the *Los Angeles Times* and *Rolling Stone*) in articles that reported the firing used "The Last DJ" as a moniker for him (in a coup, one month later, Ladd was hired by SiriusXM to host his own freeform show—joining fellow SiriusXM DJ Tom Petty on the Deep Tracks channel).

Unfortunately, that association ended up landing Ladd and Petty into legal trouble. In late 2004, Petty and Ladd were sued for $6 million in Los Angeles County Superior Court by California songwriter Jim Wagner, who accused the pair of working together to rip the song "The Last DJ" off a song Wagner said he sent to Ladd in 2000 titled "The

Last Great Radio DJ." The lawsuit claimed that Ladd and Wagner came to an agreement for Ladd to use the song as the intro music for his radio show, but accused Ladd of instead giving the song to Petty, who "took the idea, theme, title, and overall 'feel' of the song and wrote and recorded his 'version' of the song, which he entitled 'The Last DJ.'"

Petty denied the allegation and, in a statement posted on his website, said, "To this date, I have never heard the recording the lawsuit claims influenced my song. The plaintiff is accusing me of stealing. I do not take kindly to such accusations, as the plaintiff and his attorney for hire will find out." More than two years later, Wagner wrote a lengthy open letter to Petty posted on Underground.fm and noted he was seeking representation to continue his legal battle over his claims of plagiarism. If the lawsuit went anywhere, terms were not reported to the media.

At the end of 2002, Petty appeared as himself in the long-running Fox animated sitcom *The Simpsons*. The episode, titled "How I Spent My Strummer Vacation," features family patriarch Homer Simpson attending rock 'n' roll fantasy camp, where Petty is an instructor alongside Mick Jagger, Keith Richards, Elvis Costello, Lenny Kravitz, and Brian Setzer (all also voicing themselves). "The Last DJ" played over the credits of the episode, which featured clips of the rock stars recording their lines in the studio. Petty told *USA Today*, "My family went ape when I was asked to do an episode. It's as if I'd never accomplished anything in my life. For them, this is the absolute pinnacle of my career."

Two years later, Petty began what became a long-running guest role on another Fox animated sitcom, *King of the Hill*. In a 2004 episode, Petty voiced "Lucky," a redneck who earned his moniker from his "windfall" settlement of $53,000 from slipping on "pee-pee" in the bathroom of a Costco. Though very much a background character in his initial appearance, Lucky became a regular presence on the show when he began dating one of the main characters and frequently shared his low-rent, but somewhat insightful, philosophies on life. Petty and his unmistakable Florida drawl would voice Lucky in twenty-eight episodes of the series that aired from 2004 to 2009. "It's too much fun," he told *Rolling Stone* in 2007. "It's maybe the only show I like on television. They called me down out of the blue to do it, and then [show creator] Mike Judge really liked the character, so they kept calling me back."

In a 2009 *Chicago Tribune* retrospective of the series before its final episode aired, Judge spoke about how Petty's recurring role came about, revealing, "John Altschuler, who ran the show for the last seven/eight years, had written this character named 'Lucky' and described him as looking like 'Tom Petty without the success.' And we thought, what if we tried to get Tom Petty? And he said, 'Yeah, I'll do it.' And he was great, just killed at the table read. Then he said, 'Any time you want me to do it, I'll do it.' Turns out he really meant it."

After wrapping up The Last DJ tour at the end of 2002, the Heartbreakers took a break before reconvening in April 2003 to play a five-show residency at the Vic Theatre in Chicago, and then in June they kicked off a tour (dubbed the Lost Cities Tour) of cities they hadn't played in some time (or ever), starting with Sioux Falls, South Dakota, on June 26. Since the Heartbreakers were virtually a "house band" of the state of California when it came to their performing history, there were no California dates (though they did appear on *The Tonight Show* in Burbank on August 7, performing an incredible version of the Animals' "I'm Crying" on an outdoor stage as part of the show's Summer Concert Series). After that, the Heartbreakers went back to quiet.

Petty did make headlines throughout the state in October 2003 after getting in a car accident in Malibu. Naturally, it being Tom Petty, it was no normal car accident. Petty was driving on Pacific Coast Highway when he was distracted by what he thought was a UFO in the sky. Afterwards Petty recalled, "I'm clean and fairly sober and I thought this was a flying saucer. Helicopters were circling it. I thought, 'They're landing in Malibu. So I make a bad turn and I hit this poor college kid's car in the left lane." Petty was almost instantly greeted by a swarm of dozens of photographers.

The photographers and the "UFO" were all there for something that had nothing to do with an extraterrestrial invasion. Actor and comedian Adam Sandler was getting married in Malibu, and the "UFO" was one of several weather balloons deployed to keep paparazzi helicopters away from the ceremony. The photographers had been there to try to get shots of the wedding and just so happened to get shots of Petty's car accident instead. Incidentally, Petty's "You Don't Know How It Feels" appeared in Sandler's 2002 comedy *Mr. Deeds*, and "American Girl" would later appear in Sandler's 2012 comedy *That's My Boy* (Petty and Sandler were also both guests on the same episode of *The Tonight Show* in November 2002). Curiously, Petty later told *Men's Journal* that it wasn't this incident, but one that happened later that night, which made him largely give up driving. "Later that night we went somewhere else, and I backed up and hit the car behind me. I've been a passenger ever since," he said, calling himself too "spaced out" to drive. A song titled "Night Driver" on Petty's next album, *Highway Companion*, seems to reference this experience with Petty singing, "High tide rumbles, PCH / My tires losing track / Helicopter circling, wiping overhead."

The Heartbreakers played just one date in all of 2004, a benefit concert on February 7 at the St. Regis Monarch Beach Resort in Dana Point, California, in Orange County. The benefit, which had nine hundred attendees, including Jackson Browne, Stephen Stills, Olivia Harrison, and Carrie Fisher, was titled Arts for AIDS III and supported the AIDS Services Foundation Orange County and Laguna Art Museum. Petty was asked to perform the benefit by Dr. Arnold Klein, his dermatologist, in memory of Stephen Costick, Dana Petty's brother, who had died of AIDS. "This one involves my family, and I'm glad to be able to do it. It's not a lot of trouble for a good cause, and it will help my wife work through her loss," Petty told the *Los Angeles Times*. The Heartbreakers played an eclectic set, mixing covers (Elmore James' "Done Somebody Wrong," and the Animals' "Don't Bring Me Down"), Heartbreakers favorites, and some of the band's rarities ("What Are You Doin' in My Life," "Melinda," "Makin' Some Noise," and "Angel Dream"). The Heartbreakers helped the event raise more than a half-million dollars.

Though once again without an album to support, the Heartbreakers hit the road for the summer in 2005 playing a greatest-hits-heavy setlist. Once again, Petty made headlines for keeping his concert tickets low in comparison to his classic rock contemporaries. The *Los Angeles Times* wrote about how Petty's top tickets, at seventy dollars, were less than half the price of the top tickets for the Eagles and U2, less than a third of the top tickets for Paul McCartney, and less than a sixth of the top tickets for the Rolling Stones. *Billboard* magazine's Ray Waddell told the paper it was a strategy that was paying off, saying, "His shows are averaging about 17,000 people a night, and he'll end up playing to about 730,000 people by the time the tour ends.... He's a rock 'n' roll player and the Heartbreakers is a rock 'n' roll band—their whole thing is to play in front of a lot of people." The article also noted that Petty's camp normally booked tours through local promoters rather than having a large national promoter as a middleman negotiating an entire tour for the band, which helped reduce costs.

Petty told *Rolling Stone* that the 2005 tour stage set was inspired by a Hollywood design legend, noting, "It's the greatest stage set we've ever had. It was inspired by Saul Bass, who did screen titles in the Fifties and Sixties, like *Anatomy of a Murder*. I can't describe it—you gotta see it. It's gonna crack your head."

The 2005 tour featured two Los Angeles-area concerts—August 14 at the Verizon Wireless Amphitheater in Irvine and August 21 at the recently renamed Hyundai Pavilion in San Bernardino.

The review of the Irvine show in *Variety* commented on the "Greatest Hits" aspect of the setlist, remarking, "With no new album to support, it seems as if Petty's offering a career retrospective almost as a plea to be taken seriously as an artist and to continue having a blast onstage as a performer. He succeeds admirably at both.... He may be running a victory lap right now, but it's clear that this career-long marathon isn't quite over yet." Similarly, Ben Wener's review in the *Orange County Review* declared in its headline that the Heartbreakers had "aged better than wine," and, "Tom Petty reminds with Irvine bash that he and the Heartbreakers are among few still-viable touring legends." In particular, Wener praised Petty's low-priced tickets for the tour's success, adding, "Petty and cohorts are among that rare breed of veteran rockers who still sound as good as they did way back when, who are almost as respected for recent work as they are for staples, and whose ticket prices remain under $100." The *Los Angeles Times* review also mentioned Petty's low ticket prices, and asked rhetorically, "Is this the world's best bar band? An arena-rock war horse? Tom Petty & the Heartbreakers flashed a bit of both identities at their Verizon Wireless Amphitheater concert, but mainly they came across as a classic-rock band that's stayed on this side of the nostalgia frontier."

Even with no new material—and not having had a Top 40 hit in over a decade—the 2005 tour was the most successful in Heartbreakers' history up to that point according to *Billboard*, averaging just under $600,000 per night and 15,763 in ticket sales per show. In total, the Heartbreakers played to over a half-million fans. While Petty didn't intend for the Heartbreakers to morph into an annual greatest-hits touring machine like many of the band's contemporaries, the Heartbreakers managed to follow that model in their own fashion. Just a few weeks after the 2005 tour concluded, *Billboard* announced that Petty would be the 2005 recipient of the Century Award, the same award that Petty presented in its inaugural year to George Harrison in 1992. Petty received the award on December 6 in Las Vegas.

* * * * *

In December 2004, XM Satellite Radio aired the first episode of *Tom Petty's Buried Treasure*, an hour-long program hosted by Petty on the US and Canadian satellite radio service, in which Petty broadcast selections from his own collection of music and, in between, spoke about the influence of his selections or simply goofed off with his trademark humor.

On the surface, Petty hosting a radio show on a paid subscription radio network ran contrary to the lyrics of "The Last DJ" ("All the boys upstairs want to see / How much you'll pay for what you used to get for free"). Yet the opportunity on XM Satellite Radio gave Petty a chance to fulfill the song's main call to action. (In fact, in a 2010 interview in *Parade*, Petty flat out said, "I play what I want to play and say what I want to say.") On his *Buried Treasure* show—which ran for 251 episodes, until his death—Petty would play anything he fancied under his expansive definition of "rock, rhythm, and blues," from obscure recordings by early American blues artists to B-sides of British Invasion bands and everything in between, including new music from current artists he admired. The program was a labor of love for Petty (he told *Rolling Stone* in 2011, "Even when the Heartbreakers are really busy, I'm up all night putting this together"), and a project that he regularly returned to in between his other commitments. Petty even hosted a special broadcast of the show before a live audience on April 14, 2011, at East-West Studios in Hollywood—incidentally, the same studio where *The Last DJ* had been recorded when it was known as Cello Studios.

Lee Abrams, then XM chief creative officer, was inspired to approach Petty after hearing Petty's take on the industry in "The Last DJ." In 2006, Abrams told *Billboard*, "Tom obviously wasn't thrilled with the state of terrestrial radio at the time of the song's release. So, I thought maybe he should show us how he'd like to do radio.... It's radio, as Tom likes to do it. That was one of the prerequisites he had for it, and we were more than happy to honor it; anything he wants to do, anything he wants to say, he just lets it flow. It's the music he would play in his living room."

Petty went into detail about how he put together his *Buried Treasure* show in *Conversations*, calling the whole experience "a gas." He said, "The way I do it is that I have this large collection of CDs. And I've downloaded a lot of it, at least a few thousand songs, into my iPod library on my computer. And so I just make files and with that equipment, with the computer, it's really easy. It's the only time it's gotten me into using the computer, because I never have before. And that's a really good way to assemble your shows, because you can move things around and see what flows. So I look around the library, and pick out things I like, and throw them into the files. See if they segue together nicely. And try to make a nice balance."

While many classic rock artists flirted with satellite radio hosting gigs—fellow Wilbury Bob Dylan hosted a show from 2006 to 2009 on XM, then on SiriusXM—few stuck with it as long as Petty did. In November 2015, Petty's radio show expanded to an entire channel on SiriusXM (the result of competing satellite radio networks merging after Sirius purchased XM in 2008). Tom Petty Radio not only featured new and rerun episodes of Petty's *Buried Treasure* show, but also occasionally featured shows hosted by Benmont Tench, Steve Ferrone (the latter affectionately titled "The New Guy Show"), and many other friends and acquaintances of both Petty and the Heartbreakers.

* * * * *

The Heartbreakers rang in 2006—their thirtieth year as a band—jamming at Mike Campbell's Woodland Hills home in front of a small crowd (Campbell told *Billboard*, "About 50 were invited and 150 weren't"). The year became one in which the Heartbreakers would both look forward and reflect on the past. Petty had recently met with Oscar-nominated filmmaker Peter Bogdanovich at Geoffrey's, a popular restaurant in Malibu, to discuss whether Bogdanovich would be interested in directing a documentary about the Heartbreakers. The meeting lasted four hours, and Bogdanovich agreed to work on the film. Curiously, the name of Bogdanovich's most famous film, *The Last Picture Show*, appears as a lyric in the Heartbreakers' song "All Mixed Up." Admittedly, Bogdanovich knew little about Petty or his music. However, what the two had in common was their deep appreciation for classic films, and Bogdanovich began to see a distinctly American journey in the Heartbreakers' story.

The writing and recording of Petty's next album, *Highway Companion*, actually began in mid-2004, in the aftermath of Petty's reunion with Jeff Lynne to induct George Harrison into the Rock and Roll Hall of Fame early that year in New York. In 2006, Petty told *Guitar Player* that the album was largely written in Lynne's Los Angeles home studio (dubbed Bungalow Palace), saying, "Mike and I went over to Jeff's house, showed him a tune, and he wanted to cut it right there in his studio. We didn't have a band, so Jeff said, 'You play drums don't you?' So I wound up being the drummer. Anyway, that first track went really nice, so we just pitched camp at Jeff's studio. I kept dragging out songs, and the next thing we knew, we'd recorded ten tracks. It was just the three of us. Jeff played bass, Mike played all the solos, and each one of us would fill in wherever we could on keyboard and guitar."

Unsurprisingly, the rest of the Heartbreakers used the band's downtime to work with other artists. For example, Rubin called on Campbell and Tench to work on albums he was producing, including Neil Diamond's 2005 album *12 Songs* and the Dixie Chicks' 2006 album *Taking the Long Way*. In addition, Tench played on John Fogerty's 2004 album *Deja Vu All Over Again* and his 2007 album *Revival*. As with most of the Heartbreakers' session work, all four projects were largely recorded in Los Angeles studios.

Petty began to feel like Warner Bros. no longer had his best interests in mind after multiple regime changes, telling *Billboard* several months before the release of *Highway Companion*, "It was a very confused place at the time and, you know, I could feel that I don't have anyone here who understands me or who really understands what we're trying to do." Though Petty had been previously annoyed with Rick Rubin over Rubin leaving the *Echo* sessions before mixing, *Highway Companion* was released on Rubin's American Recordings label, then under the Warner Bros. umbrella.

Highway Companion was something of a small rebound for Petty in terms of sales and chart performance. The album peaked at #4 on the US Billboard charts, his highest-charting album either solo or with the Heartbreakers since *Full Moon Fever*. The first single, "Saving Grace," peaked at #100 on the US Billboard Top 200, his highest-charting single since "Walls (Circus)." While it took nearly three years, *Highway Companion* was certified gold by the RIAA, which suggests that in the long run it has outsold *The Last DJ*, which has not received a sales certification. Overall, *Highway Companion* received better reviews (and, not surprisingly, more radio support) than *The Last DJ*.

Unlike *The Last DJ*, *Highway Companion* doesn't have an overt theme. However, Petty did feel the songs had a subtle theme, telling *Billboard*, "I think it does have an underlying theme of time and what it does to you." Fred Shuster began his review of *Highway Companion* in the *Los Angeles Daily News* by pointing out Petty's LA pedigree: "Even though he hails from the wrong coast, Petty writes about Los Angeles' losers and dreamers as effectively as though he'd spent a lifetime being cut off on the 101 by Hummers driven by junior agents from William Morris." Shuster praised the album as a collection of "haunting, sparingly fleshed-out songs that find Petty facing down mortality and wondering where all the years went." In the *Los Angeles Times*, Randy Lewis's three-star review reflected on the themes of the album and called the album's lyrics "overwhelmingly oblique, snatching imagery and memories at will with nary a linear narrative."

After tour rehearsals at the Sony Pictures lot (which were filmed by Peter Bogdanovich for his in-the-works documentary), the Heartbreakers began the Highway Companion Tour on June 9 in Charlotte, North Carolina. In the pre-press for the tour, Petty openly spoke to several outlets about how it could be the band's last major tour. Naturally, that answer got parroted as "this is the last Tom Petty and the Heartbreakers tour" in subsequent reports, meaning that Petty later had to walk back his comments to several reporters. Obviously, regardless of Petty's initial intent, the Highway Companion Tour was far from the band's swan song.

The tour made its way west until July 3, when the band took a nearly month-long break. The only interruption was a July 20 performance of "Saving Grace" on *The Tonight Show* in Burbank—the last time the Heartbreakers would perform on the show—and a private album-release party at the Malibu Performing Arts Center on July 26. Then the Heartbreakers returned to the road for the second leg of the Highway Companion Tour, picking up on July 29 in Ridgefield, Washington.

The band played just one public concert in the Los Angeles area on the 2006 tour on September 26 at the Hollywood Bowl. The sold-out Hollywood Bowl concert featured two special guests—Stevie Nicks, who had been joining the Heartbreakers on several shows on the tour, accompanied them for "Stop Draggin' My Heart Around," "I Need to Know," and "Insider," and performed background vocals on several others; and Jeff Lynne, who performed "Handle with Care" with the Heartbreakers. The band had been playing the Traveling Wilburys song throughout the 2006 tour, but Lynne performing it with his fellow Wilbury was a rare occasion. From the new album, the Heartbreakers played "Saving Grace" and "Down South." The review of the show in *Variety* was stellar, remarking, "The Bowl show had a lovely organic feel to it as Petty jumped through his life, playing the 30-year-old rocker one moment, the pensive middle-aged balladeer the next and, for a few tunes, a bar band leader who just came of age. The band, too, went along for the ride, especially Mike Campbell, whose assured and appropriate guitar solos are as familiar as Petty's unchanged, nasally voice." In Ben Wener's review for the *Orange County Register*, he cast suspicion on Petty's remarks about this being the band's final tour, yet still concluded, "Should this really be their last local appearance—and somehow I doubt it will be—then at least they went out smashingly. In any case, it's one to savor if you were there. We aren't likely to get a replay anytime soon."

Petty seemed to agree with that assessment of the concert. He would later tell a reporter for the *Los Angeles Times* that he was disappointed that the paper didn't review the Hollywood Bowl concert ("That night was one of our best shows. That's why we're upset it wasn't reviewed in The *Times*"). The Heartbreakers did swing back on October 21 to play their first (and only) concert at the Indian Wells Tennis Garden, a complex located outside of the resort city Palm Springs, which features one of the largest tennis stadiums in the world (at 8,100 seats), and has served as the home of the Indian Wells Masters tennis tournament since it opened in 2000. For a brief period, the stadium also hosted concerts, including three shows by the Eagles in 2005. The Heartbreakers were one of two bands to play the venue in 2006 (the other was the Who). When it comes to live music, the Palm Springs area is better known for the annual Coachella Valley Music and Arts Festival and the Stagecoach Festival—neither of which the Heartbreakers ever performed at, despite their standing as a Southern California institution. The near-sellout Indian Wells show was virtually a repeat of the Hollywood Bowl show, minus Lynne's appearance. Nonetheless, the *Desert Sun* declared, "Tom Petty did the impossible Saturday night—he lived up to the hype."

The Heartbreakers ended their thirtieth year by celebrating with an invite-only party and gig at Harvelle's, a historic music club in Santa Monica established in 1931 that has hosted a lengthy list of blues legends, including Etta James, Albert King, and Keb' Mo'. The Heartbreakers jammed for much of the night, especially with special guest Bo Diddley.

Despite all those rumors that 2006 would be the last full-scale tour for Petty, Petty released only two albums in a six-year period of touring (2001–2006). It seemed that Petty and his band might join many of his '70s contemporaries in becoming a group that eschewed recording new music in favor of making money on the road playing their classic hits. Reflecting on his incredibly successful year to the *Los Angeles Times* in an article that appeared in the paper's December 31 edition (in which he conclusively revealed he was *not* retiring), Petty confessed, "I really couldn't have imagined a year like this happening. I didn't see this coming, especially with the way things were just a few years ago." At the end of the article, he speculated, "You never know how things are going to turn out...maybe next year will be even better."

But 2007 was a relatively quiet year for the Heartbreakers, in which they played only three scattered gigs. They did join together on the Warner Bros. Studios lot on October 2 for the world premiere of Bogdanovich's four-hour *Runnin' Down a Dream* documentary, and then in December it was announced the band would play the Halftime

Show at the 2008 Super Bowl. On the other hand, 2007 was a big year for Petty, Campbell, and Tench in another way when they pulled off perhaps Petty's strangest career move in a career full of them.

CHAPTER 13

PACIFIC OCEAN BETWEEN THE ROCKS AND THE SKY

In a move that perplexed just about everyone—even those involved—in August 2007, Petty, Campbell, and Tench joined with Randall Marsh (drums) and Tom Leadon (guitar) to resurrect Mudcrutch in something of a "best of" version of the old Gainesville group (Leadon had left the original Mudcrutch before Tench joined full-time).

Both Leadon and Marsh had remained involved in music after the dissolution of the original Mudcrutch. Leadon, the younger brother of Eagles musician Bernie Leadon, had left Mudcrutch in 1972 to move to Los Angeles and become a session musician, and had a minor hit record in "Wham Bam" with the short-lived band Silver. When Petty called him, Leadon had spent the previous several years teaching music in Brentwood, Tennessee. In 2008, Leadon told the *New York Times*, "I was driving home from getting groceries at Kroger's, and my cellphone rang. He said, 'Hey, it's your old pal Tom Petty.' My first thought was that it was one of my friends pulling my leg. I wasn't going to fall for that."

Marsh's life had taken a similar route—after coming to Los Angeles with Mudcrutch in 1974 and staying with the band until it lost its record deal, Marsh formed a band called Code Blue with future Motels guitarist Dean Chamberlain. However, long after the breakup of Mudcrutch, Marsh remained part of the Heartbreakers' family. He had previously reteamed with Campbell and Tench when, along with Ron Blair, they formed the short-lived side project Blue Stingrays, which released one surf rock album in 1997, *Surf-N-Burn*. Marsh was also teaching music when he received Petty's call about getting Mudcrutch back together. Marsh, who had moved back to Florida, got an inkling about the possibility of a reunion when Peter Bogdanovich mentioned it while filming an interview with Marsh for *Runnin' Down a Dream*. But as Marsh told the *New York Times* in 2008, "I didn't make too much of it. Months went by, and then finally Tom called me."

In August 2007, Petty invited Marsh and Leadon to stay at his house in Malibu so they could record the album that Mudcrutch never had a chance to release ("My wife told me having Mudcrutch in the house was like living with a bunch of old pirates," Petty would later tell *Uncut*). Leadon told *The Tennessean*, "It was just entirely unexpected. It was like a dream, the whole thing. Tom couldn't have been nicer. It was great to hang out with him again." The band recorded four songs in their first session, and two of them—"Crystal River" and "Shady Grove"— ended up on the final album. "Crystal River" was even recorded in one take. "When we listened back we saw no reason to do it again. It was one of the greatest nights of my life," Petty remembered in *Petty: The Biography*. "I went home and started writing more songs while the other guys slept. That's always a good sign."

The group recorded eighteen new songs in ten days over two weeks at the Heartbreakers' Clubhouse—a Van Nuys warehouse located between an auto shop and an upholsterer that Petty used to store his guitars and other Heartbreakers gear, and which soon became a hangout for the band—for a planned album. Petty, Tench, and Leadon shared lead vocals and Petty played bass. All members except for Marsh contributed to the songwriting (one of the songs, the bouncy "Topanga Cowgirl," was written by Petty and inspired by how his driver would take him through Topanga Canyon, a very bohemian area of Los

Angeles, on his way to the Clubhouse each day). Almost all the songs were recorded live in the studio with the band facing each other in a circle. Mudcrutch later recorded two music videos, "Scare Easy" and "Love of the Bayou," showing the band playing in this fashion at the Heartbreakers' Clubhouse.

After coming off the Heartbreakers' biggest show of all time at the 2008 Super Bowl, Petty's revival of a band—one that he once said had "one of the worst names ever in show business"—usually mentioned as a footnote in articles about his career was surprising. As Petty would say to the *Los Angeles Times* in the midst of Mudcrutch's first tour of California, "You wouldn't exactly call it a career move, would you?" Yet the reformation of Mudcrutch didn't come out of nowhere—Petty brought it up as something he wanted to do in a 2006 interview with *Rolling Stone* prior to the Highway Companion Tour, but he wasn't sure then that it could be pulled off. But even Petty would admit the reunion was downright puzzling—why would one of the most famous bands in rock 'n' roll history jettison half its members to reunite a thirty-year-old band that never came close to success? Even *Rolling Stone*, a longtime Petty supporter, referred to the move as the "Least-Requested Reunion" in rock 'n' roll. Petty gave the magazine the simplest reason why he did it: "It was the most fun I've had in years. I had to calm myself down at night I was having so much fun."

The revived Mudcrutch had no record deal when they recorded the album, but Petty's label, Warner Bros., eagerly accepted it for release. Label Chief Operating Officer Diarmuid Quinn told the *New York Times*, "We feel like we should support Tom whatever he does. With this kind of artist you go with their instincts because they're usually right." Warner Bros. released the album on its Reprise record label, a label that had been established by Frank Sinatra in 1960 and had been owned by Warner Bros. since 1963, which made Petty labelmates with Stevie Nicks and Eric Clapton. The Heartbreakers would also end up signing with Reprise, which Petty credited to the label's willingness to release *Mudcrutch*, telling Warren Zanes later in 2008, "Because of that good experience with Mudcrutch on Reprise, the Heartbreakers have signed with Reprise, a label we've always admired, which has that rich history from Sinatra to the Kinks to Hendrix to Neil Young. So here we are, in the midst of a terrible time in the industry, having a great experience with our label."

The end of 2007 also brought up not-so-welcome memories for Petty when, in late October, he had to evacuate his Malibu home because of a canyon fire that accidentally started when power-line poles blew over and sparked a blaze. Unlike the unsolved arson that destroyed his Encino home, thankfully Petty didn't lose a second home to flames. Petty would later use the evacuation experience as inspiration for the song "All You Can Carry" on the Heartbreakers' 2014 album *Hypnotic Eye* ("I saw the flames come across the ridge / Falling ashes in the northern wind"). In 2014, Petty revealed to *Billboard* that he did grab one possession on his way out with Dana—"It was a Hohner bass that I've used on every record, and you can't find another one. I grabbed that and I went, 'Hell, is this going to happen to me twice in my life where everything I own is just wiped out?' And then I thought, 'Well, I'm OK with that.' Because things come back, but people don't."

When Mudcrutch's self-titled debut album was released on April 29, 2008—featuring fourteen of the eighteen songs recorded, with a fifteenth ("Special Place") appearing as a bonus track on iTunes—Petty's instincts on the group's abilities were indeed proven right. In the *Los Angeles Times*, Geoff Boucher said that *Mudcrutch* "has more swamp, stomp and twang than records that made the Heartbreakers famous, and there's a dappled, Southern psychedelic feel to parts of it." Randy Lewis' three-star review in the *Times* called the album "a breath of fresh air. It's rock the old-school way—born of real-time collaboration and realized with heaps of joy and sweat," and noted that, "The instrumental interplay, particularly among guitarists Campbell and Leadon, extends beyond the Heartbreakers' signature corner of pop into Allman Brothers Band, Crazy Horse, even Grateful Dead territory." Reviewer Sam Gnerre also praised the album in Long Beach's *Press-Telegram*, writing, "Imagine being able to hear an extremely talented bunch of musicians unconstrained by fame who are playing music they love for the joy it brings them, and you'll have a good handle on where Mudcrutch is coming from." *Mudcrutch* sold 38,000 copies in its first week, peaking at #8 on the Billboard chart—higher than the peak position of *The Last DJ*.

Petty endeavored to take Mudcrutch on the road, but to piggyback off the Heartbreakers' Super Bowl performance, Petty's main group had booked a 2008 summer tour that was set to begin May 30 in Grand Rapids, Michigan, and run through August 29 in The Woodlands, Texas. As a result, Mudcrutch booked a short series of California dates that started with a charity concert to raise money for Midnight Mission at the Malibu Performing Arts Center on April 12. The performance was the third installment in a charity series titled "From Malibu With Love" organized by Norman Harris, owner of the iconic Norman's Rare Guitars music shop in Tarzana. Petty was a long-time customer of Norman's and the store had even received a "thanks to" credit in the liner notes of *Hard Promises*. Harris told the *Malibu Times* that he gave Petty extra incentive to do the show beyond the charity aspect: "I had a guitar he really wanted—a Rickenbacker, very rare, made for export in England [and] I agreed to sell it to him [if he did the concert]." According to the *Los Angeles Business Journal*, the guitar was valued at $60,000 to $100,000 and was Petty's only payment for the gig. Harris had given Petty the guitar a few months before the gig, and he had even used it during the Heartbreakers' performance at Super Bowl XLII. Nonetheless, Harris believed that the charity-minded Petty would've done the concert anyway, adding, "He's doing it out of the goodness of his heart. He is a Malibu resident and wants to set an example for other residents, to do something good for the needy."

The Mudcrutch tour ran from San Francisco south to Alpine and ended with a six-night stand at the Troubadour in West Hollywood. While the Heartbreakers had played numerous small-scale residencies in their recent history, Petty, Campbell, and Tench hadn't undertaken a tour of venues this size in decades. Per Petty's sometimes quixotic nature, he played before one of the largest combined live and television audiences in his career in February at the Super Bowl and then, just two months later, played some of the smallest club shows he had in decades.

In *Variety*'s review of the first Troubadour show, reviewer Steven Mirkin drew a distinction between Petty on stage with the Heartbreakers and Petty on stage with Mudcrutch, pointing out, "While Petty is definitely Mudcrutch's leader, he gets to be more of a member of band than usual. He leaves most of the talking to Leadon...and gives both Leadon and Tench time in the spotlight." He then concluded, "The question on everyone's mind is, Could Mudcrutch have achieved the success of the Heartbreakers had they stuck at it? The answer is probably no. Their country rock, fine as it is, was already on the wane by the mid-'70s; the poppier elements Petty added to the Heartbreakers mix gave that band a more contemporary sound (and allowed his label to sweep him in with the then-ascendant new wave). But it was certainly worth the wait to check out a seemingly lost part of Petty's history, and that should put a smile on his many fans' faces."

On that first tour, Mudcrutch featured all the material on their album plus several covers—however, none were covers of songs by Petty. Campbell told *Entertainment Weekly*, "It's nice, to get to go out and play and not have to do 'Runnin' Down a Dream' and 'Refugee' every night," although the magazine noted that a woman at Mudcrutch's debut Malibu concert repeatedly (and annoyingly) shouted for the band to play "Breakdown." While it would've been easy for the band to have slipped in a few of the Heartbreakers' greatest hits—especially since *Mudcrutch* wasn't even released until midway through the tour-ending Troubadour run—it was clear that Petty wanted to establish Mudcrutch as its own entity on this short tour.

In an interview with Warren Zanes that was posted on the Tom Petty website in October 2008, Petty revealed that because Leadon and Marsh were staying at his home during the tour dates in the Los Angeles area, the group had a lot of time to bond after the gigs. He explained, "We'd get home, and then Tom [Leadon] would cook. He's a very healthy, very careful eater. So he'd go make some meal for himself that seemed to take forever to cook. And we'd all wind up sitting in the kitchen talking about the shows, old times, and so forth. Tom has a memory like a steel trap. He really can remember everything that ever happened to him. Sometimes he'd just take us back down memory lane—he could dive back into the sixties like it was yesterday. Randall and I were in awe. It would be like, 'I forgot that guy completely.' And Tom would say, 'Oh no, let me tell you...' It was endless fun having someone around with a memory like that. Randall and I were missing some big chunks of time that Tom gave back to us [Laughs]."

Once the tour ended with the final Troubadour show, Petty, Campbell, and Tench took one short weekend off before leaping into rehearsals for their next tour—except this one was with Petty's far more commercially successful band and was booked in far bigger venues. However, considering how much fun he had with his old group, Petty left the door open for future work with Mudcrutch (in fact, later that year, on November 11, Mudcrutch released *Extended Play Live*, an EP featuring four songs recorded live during the tour, including an extended version of "Crystal River" recorded at the Troubadour).

And so, just seven weeks after Mudcrutch wrapped up its first tour at a 500-capacity club in West Hollywood, Petty returned to Los Angeles to play the 17,500-capacity Hollywood Bowl on June 25 with the Heartbreakers. On the 2008 tour, the band dug a little deeper than previous summer tours with the setlist—the Hollywood Bowl performance included the B-side "Sweet William," a cover of the Traveling Wilburys' "End of the Line," and "A Face in the Crowd" from *Full Moon Fever*. Keeping in line with Stevie Nicks's regular onstage appearances during the Highway Companion Tour, this time around, tour opening act Steve Winwood frequently joined the Heartbreakers onstage to perform Blind Faith's "Can't Find My Way Home" and Spencer Davis Group's "Gimme Some Lovin'."

The *Hollywood Reporter* gave the concert positive marks, but knocked it as "markedly similar" to the 2006 Hollywood Bowl stop, noting it featured the "same length, 13 of the same songs and Petty's word-for-word intonation that 'I've come to rock Hollywood'...Half of the set's 20 songs are on the 10-times-platinum *Greatest Hits* album;

a half-dozen others, including the three covers, are staples of classic rock radio." While praising the musicianship of the Heartbreakers, it ultimately concluded, "The staid set list is the only major gripe about Heartbreakers shows these days, though, and this one had plenty to enjoy." The *Los Angeles Times* also noted the lack of variety in the setlist, but cast it in a more positive light, saying, "Even if Petty spent much of the night looking back, it was with a journeyman's confidence, not nostalgia." Avowed Petty fan Ben Wener, writing for the *Orange County Register*, questioned the need for another Heartbreakers performance so close to the last one that was amid rumors of the band's retirement (asking, "Didn't that Stevie Nicks-studded show underneath this shell in the hills play like some sort of farewell?"), yet praised the performance as "so masterful—smooth like well-aged Scotch," and asked, "Of all the so-called heritage acts still touring every other summer or so, who can rival these guys at this point?" He concluded, "It sounds even better this time than the time before...which was better than the time before that...which was better than the time before that."

The Heartbreakers returned to the Los Angeles area to perform a sold-out concert at the Verizon Wireless Amphitheater in Irvine on August 22, and Ben Wener's review in the *Orange County Register*—under the title "Petty Doesn't Deviate"—was much more critical than his Hollywood Bowl review from two months earlier. The review opened with an acknowledgment that the Heartbreakers again did not stray from the standard set, and joked that then-California Governor Arnold Schwarzenegger should pass legislation to outlaw that practice, saying, "Note: Slap him and his Heartbreakers on the wrist for scarcely altering the set they played two months ago at the Bowl. There oughta be a law about this sort of thing. Hustle it through the Legislature, hurry it to the Governator before it happens again and dub it Live Music Ordinance 90125.5150: All classic rockers with at least 20 years of staples to draw from who schedule more than one show in the Southern California region within a six-month period are required to swap out a minimum of a half-dozen songs from gig to gig. More would be preferable." Wener noted that the Irvine performance was shorter than the Bowl performance, had no Winwood jam (while Winwood opened the Irvine concert, he did not perform with the Heartbreakers), and both "You Don't Know How It Feels" and "Sweet William" were removed from the set. The band added "Breakdown" and swapped Northern Irish rock group Them's "Gloria" with "Mystic Eyes," but Wener (and perhaps other Heartbreakers fans in the audience) was left disappointed with the sameness.

Nevertheless, *Rolling Stone* reported that the Heartbreakers' 2008 tour was the highest-grossing US tour of the summer. Yet perhaps because of the repetition on stage, Petty and the Heartbreakers took 2009 off from the road and instead concentrated on compiling a career-spanning live box-set, *The Live Anthology*, as well as recording the first Heartbreakers album since *The Last DJ*. In demonstrating how much Southern California had become the Heartbreakers' home base, nearly a fourth of the songs on the *Live Anthology* were culled from concerts in the Los Angeles area, and the Deluxe Edition also included a recording of the Heartbreakers' New Year's Eve 1978 show in Santa Monica in its entirety.

Petty made a public appearance on April 14 at the unveiling of George Harrison's star on the Hollywood Walk of Fame, alongside fellow Wilbury Jeff Lynne, as well as Paul McCartney, Joe Walsh, producer T-Bone Burnett, actors Tom Hanks and Eric Idle, and Harrison's widow Olivia and son Dhani. Harrison's star is located outside of the Capitol Records building. Petty, Campbell, and Tench also took the stage of the Greek Theatre—a historic Los Angeles venue that Petty had never previously performed at in his career—on May 19 to guest at an Allman Brothers Band concert. The 5,870-seat outdoor venue, which is located in Los Angeles' Griffith Park, originally opened in 1930 and was designed after a Greek theatre. Sitting in a canyon, the Greek is noted for having extraordinary acoustics.

Tench joined the Allman Brothers on keys for a performance of the Elmore James blues standard "The Sky is Crying," and then Petty and Campbell joined the band for two Bob Dylan covers, "It Takes a Lot to Laugh, It Takes a Train to Cry" and "Highway 61 Revisited." Perhaps even more surprising was that the concert also featured an appearance by actor Bruce Willis, who played harmonica on the Willie Cobbs cover "You Don't Love Me."

Playing with the Allman Brothers Band may have been part of the influence that led Petty and the Heartbreakers to pursue a less single-driven album as they recorded their first album together in seven years. Petty would even compare the new music to the Allman Brothers in several promotional interviews. Another influence on the album was J.J. Cale, after Petty had run into his former Shelter labelmate at McCabe's Guitar Shop in Santa Monica. He told *Parade* in 2010, "I had a thing not long ago with J.J. Cale at McCabe's. 'Come on down.' He knew Mike Campbell, our guitarist. We practiced a number, and J.J. said, 'When you come up there, stay there; don't leave.' We stayed and had this marvelous time. I left there feeling really great about things, and I think it had a lot to do with this new album. He played with such a loose structure to everything, but it worked like crazy. So I found myself playing songs for the first time but really getting a big bang out of it. I looked at the way he structured his songs, and I took a lot of that back to my record. He plays a song once, verse and chorus, and everybody falls into it. And the rest of it is how you express yourself."

Perhaps most importantly, Petty no longer felt like he had to write for radio airplay. Petty told the *Wall Street Journal* in 2009, "Whether you wanted to admit it or not, that was always a factor. Letting that go, it's very freeing." But the biggest influence on the recordings for the next Heartbreakers album was the sessions for *Mudcrutch*. Petty told Warren Zanes, "One thing that's on my mind right now, though, is that I want to do the next Heartbreakers' record in that same fashion. I don't want to get into overdubbing and production as much. I just want to take them in and do the thing live, very much like we did the Mudcrutch. There's an energy and a purity you get that way. I think it will be interesting to do that with the Heartbreakers." As a result, the Heartbreakers recorded their next album at the Clubhouse playing live, with the band recording from April 2009 to January 2010. Much like how Petty brought Jeff Lynne and his production style into the

Heartbreakers fold after his solo album *Full Moon Fever*, Petty was taking the production style he learned from the *Mudcrutch* sessions and bringing that to the Heartbreakers. Also, similar to the music videos shot for *Mudcrutch*, three of the videos for the new album—for the songs "Jefferson Jericho Blues," "I Should Have Known It," and "Something Good Coming"—were shot with the Heartbreakers performing the songs at the Clubhouse.

Petty spoke highly of the recording process to Tribune News Services, explaining, "We got into a comfortable space in our rehearsal room which we call our clubhouse. We don't have headphones. We sit in a semi-circle, and recording doesn't feel much different than a rehearsal would feel. One odd thing about the Heartbreakers, they have never rehearsed for an album. Each album has been created on the studio floor. That's what we did this time to an even greater degree. I didn't have demo tracks. I'd come in and teach them a song on guitar, just the skeleton structure, and then we'd work it up. As soon as we had something working as group, there was a recording of that event, and that became the record."

In what must have seemed like the final leg of Petty's career retrospective period before jumping into promotion for the first Heartbreakers album in eight years, in early March 2010, Petty, Jeff Lynne, Jim Keltner, Olivia Harrison, Barbara Orbison, Ringo Starr, Joe Walsh, Eric Idle, and Gary Wright attended a party celebrating the self-titled Traveling Wilburys book released by Genesis Publications at James Perse Beverly Hills (hosted by Perse).

The new Heartbreakers album, titled *Mojo* and clocking in at a lengthy sixty-five minutes, took a bit longer to finish than Petty initially anticipated, and the first nine dates of the Mojo Tour—including May 22 at the Hollywood Bowl and June 3 at the Verizon Wireless Amphitheater in Irvine—were postponed until the fall and came at the end of the tour instead of the beginning. In addition, Petty continued to be a trailblazer in ways to get his music to fans—eleven years after the debacle of offering "Free Girl Now" as a free MP3 download, the Heartbreakers gave all ticketbuyers for the 2010 tour codes to first download two songs from *Mojo* ("First Flash of Freedom" and "Good Enough") and then the entire *Mojo* album when it was released. Doing so must have given Petty and the Heartbreakers the confidence that audiences would be more familiar with the new material and more open to hearing the band play new songs instead of more of the band's classics. In fact, when the tour began the Heartbreakers were playing as many as six songs from *Mojo* in their nightly sets. "We have no intention of turning into an oldies group," Petty told *USA Today*. "It's very lucrative, and everyone has a great time if you play hits for two hours, but I'm not done and I want people to know it."

That had changed somewhat by the time the Mojo Tour finally made it to the Hollywood Bowl and Verizon Wireless Amphitheater in early October. Both nights, the Heartbreakers played four tracks from *Mojo* ("Jefferson Jericho Blues," "Good Enough," "Running Man's Bible," and "I Should Have Known It") back-to-back in the middle of the set, and "American Girl," which had surprisingly been absent in the early shows on the Mojo Tour, was back in its semi-traditional spot as the band's final encore. The setlists were identical except for the Heartbreakers performing Chuck Berry's "Carol" at the Verizon Wireless Amphitheater in the place of "King's Highway."

As to why the band had scaled back on its strong showing of new songs in the set, longtime Petty supporter Ben Wener remarked in his Irvine concert review in the *Orange County Register*, "*Mojo* has got to be the worst-reviewed Heartbreakers album out of the dozen studio jobs they've officially made," and quoted several of the harshest reviews, which mostly viewed the "live in the studio" nature as lazy rather than Petty's view of it being invigorating. Wener didn't have that issue, calling *Mojo* "neither dynamite nor abysmal, just a fine slab of in-the-moment rock 'n' roll made by masters who probably couldn't care less what any boob with a blog has to say about it," and he largely lavished his usual praise on the October 2 Irvine concert ("The Heartbreakers are such a well-oiled machine at this point, it's hard to tell when, if ever, they're having an off night anymore"). Where he criticized the band—as he did in his review of the Heartbreakers' performance in the same venue of the 2008 tour—was in the rest of the setlist. "Consider instead," Wener wrote, "that Petty & Co. played a very similar show last time they were in O.C.: 10 of 17 songs were repeated, almost in the same structure, with the same three ending the main portion." He then suggested something that Petty may have in fact taken to heart the next time the Heartbreakers performed on a tour in the Los Angeles area: "Maybe the thing to have done was to first stage a small-scale outing behind *Mojo*...perhaps a night at the Wiltern [where the band recorded *Pack Up the Plantation*] devoted to that material, with only choice covers and deep-album tracks to balance out the unfamiliar... then they could have embarked on this massive amphitheater trek, still mixing in *Mojo* selections but playing longer, favorites-filled sets."

Unsurprisingly, the reviews of the Hollywood Bowl concert were more forgiving than Wener's frank assessment of the state of the Heartbreakers' setlists, yet they didn't ignore the *Mojo* issue completely. Todd Martens's review in the *Los Angeles Times* also made reference to the less-than-stellar reviews of *Mojo*, claiming that the songs "lack the chorus, the jangle and the communal feel of much of the band's catalog. It's an album that can divide fans and critics alike," but added, "it's definitely not the sound of a band phoning it in." The review praised the performances of the new songs and criticized the audience for being impatient with the new material. In addition, the *Hollywood Reporter* review by Erik Pedersen praised the concert, writing, "Friday's sold-out show at the Hollywood Bowl was another triumph for one of rock's greatest bands—a showcase of singular musicianship, sonic clarity, killer songs and the bond between performer and fan," but didn't ignore the obvious issue: "There's really only one thing missing: surprises." Even the concert review of the Irvine show in the the *Daily Titan*, the student newspaper of California State University in Fullerton, observed, "The moment the Heartbreakers began playing songs off their latest album, listeners flocked to the restrooms and concession stands—typical for any band whose hits are decades old."

The fact that three major-outlet Los Angeles-area reviews of the Heartbreakers' 2010 tour dates mentioned the band's stagnant setlist may have given Petty pause, since over the previous few years he was adamant that after the 2006 Thirtieth Anniversary Tour he wasn't planning on doing much looking back—at least, not as much as most other classic rock bands that rarely put out new music. Yet with an eight-year gap between Heartbreakers albums and a setlist still heavy on songs that were hits two or three decades earlier, it was definitely becoming harder to believe Petty when he made statements like, "I think we've all had enough of...celebrating our past for a while," to outlets like *M Music & Musicians Magazine*, and later adding, "I do not want to ever get in that situation of only being appreciated for your past. That's not a good feeling."

On September 22, 2011, Petty attended the world premiere of the documentary *The Hollies: Look Through Any Window 1963–1975* at the American Cinematheque Aero Theatre in Santa Monica, a historic movie theater that opened in 1940. Around that time, Petty—who had little interest in sports, dating back to his youth—suddenly became a semi-regular courtside presence at Los Angeles Lakers games at the Staples Center in Downtown Los Angeles (a venue Petty surprisingly never performed in) whenever acting legend Jack Nicholson couldn't make it to his usual seats and gave Petty his tickets. Petty told *Men's Journal* in 2014, "I hardly ever even go into L.A. anymore, unless it's for business. Or to watch basketball. I never had any interest in sports whatsoever, but then suddenly, about 10 years ago, I got interested in professional basketball." During the band's downtime, Campbell and Ferrone both appeared on Stevie Nicks's 2011 album *In Your Dreams*, produced by Dave Stewart and recorded at several Los Angeles studios.

A 2011 tour was initially planned for the Heartbreakers, but was later scrapped. The Heartbreakers ended up playing just three gigs in 2011, with two of them back-to-back nights in a surprising venue—the five-hundred-seat Performance Theater at Cal State University, Northridge. The Heartbreakers played the two concerts as benefit gigs for KCSN-FM, the university-affiliated station that had recently changed to a freeform AAA (adult album alternative) format after spending two decades as a classical-music station. The station called the format "smart rock"—music from a number of genres that were selected by the station's DJs and not from a strict playlist. In other words, KCSN represented everything Petty loved about radio, which made the Heartbreakers a natural fit to play benefit concerts to support the station once the station's program director, Sky Daniels, made a public appeal to Petty for help. Although it was initially planned to be a one-night event on October 29, the Heartbreakers added a second date the following night.

While the setlists generally followed the *Mojo*-heavy setlists of the 2010 tour—including the live debut of "Lover's Touch," played at both shows—the Heartbreakers appropriately dug out two songs from *The Last DJ*, "Have Love Will Travel" and "When a Kid Goes Bad," for the first time since the end of that album's tour. The Heartbreakers also played some other deeper cuts, such as "To Find a Friend" from *Wildflowers* and "Angel Dream" from *She's the One* at both concerts, and "Spike" from *Southern Accents* and "Melinda" on the second night.

The KCSN benefit concerts took on extra meaning because the second-largest radio conglomerate in the United States, Cumulus Media, had finalized the acquisition of recently bankrupt Citadel Broadcasting (itself the third-largest radio conglomerate) just weeks before, adding over two hundred stations nationwide to the three hundred Cumulus already owned. Days before the Heartbreakers took the stage, Cumulus fired a significant portion of Citadel's Los Angeles stations' on-air staff—including the "Last DJ" himself, Jim Ladd, who had been with LA's KLOS since 1997. Ladd's final show on KLOS—which he didn't know was a farewell show—aired on October 25. During both concerts, Petty called out the firing of Ladd as an example of why he was doing these benefit performances—to support radio that was willing to take a stand against companies like Cumulus. The *Los Angeles Times* reported that during Saturday's performance, Petty said, "When we started out, people in radio took a chance on this band, and I'll tell you what—we would not have won on *American Idol*." In a move that spoke louder than any speech Petty could muster, he dedicated the next song to Ladd: "I Won't Back Down." Ladd signed a deal to work for SiriusXM six weeks later.

After taking 2011 off from touring, the Heartbreakers reconvened in early 2012 to rehearse for a handful of US dates and the group's first European tour in many years. The band rehearsed at the Culver Studios in Culver City, though unfortunately five of the group's guitars were discovered missing from the rehearsal space on April 12, just six days before the short US tour was to start in Broomfield, Colorado. The stolen guitars were Petty's 1967 twelve-string Rickenbacker and 1965 Gibson SGTV Junior, Thurston's 1967 Epiphone Sheridan, Blair's Fender Broadcaster, and Campbell's blue Duesenberg Mike Campbell Model. The band offered a $7,500 "no questions asked" reward, and after a few days, a security guard at the complex was arrested and charged with the theft after he had sold one of the guitars to a Hollywood pawn shop for $250. All five guitars were recovered by police the day before the opening night of the tour.

Though the Heartbreakers' 2012 tour dates were all far outside the Los Angeles area, the band's adopted home found a different way to salute the fan-favorite band—the first annual Petty Fest. The Best Fest launched in 2001 with a small show at a Manhattan Lower East Side bar named Manitoba's—owned by the Dictators musician "Handsome" Dick Manitoba—to celebrate Bob Dylan's sixtieth birthday. The charity benefit, which was founded by *Rolling Stone* editor Austin Scaggs and one-time Epic Records Vice President Alex Levy, thereafter grew both in size, with an increasing number of musicians joining the festivities, and scope, with an increasing number of artists being saluted. One of the first added to the rotation was Tom Petty, and New York hosted a Petty Fest in 2010 and 2011. However, in 2012, Petty Fest expanded to Petty's adopted hometown and held two shows at the El Rey Theatre on November 14 and 15. The El Rey is a 771-capacity former movie theater and nightclub that had been converted into a live music venue in the early 1990s shortly after it and its famed neon marquee were landmarked.

Scaggs and Levy were members of the house band—dubbed the Cabin Down Below Band after the fan-favorite album track from *Wildflowers*—and featured performances by members of Guns N' Roses, Eagles of Death Metal, the Black Keys, Kings of Leon, the Strokes, and even Johnny Depp, who performed "Mary Jane's Last Dance" with pop singer Ke$ha, among other songs. The concert raised money for Hurricane Sandy relief. Petty Fest became an annual tradition in Los Angeles and eventually moved to the larger Fonda Theatre, and would go on to feature performances by Dhani Harrison, Jakob Dylan, the Shelters, and Norah Jones.

As usual, while the Heartbreakers were inactive as a band, the members were pursuing other work—but this time, one original member did a personal project over session work. Over the course of ten days in January 2013, Benmont Tench recorded his first solo album—with contributions from Petty on bass—at Sunset Sound in Los Angeles and released it as *You Should Be So Lucky* in February 2014. In an interview with *Mother Jones*, Tench explained, "It took me a long time to do a record because I wasn't sure if the songs were good enough. I've spent most of my life playing with Tom Petty, and he's a damn good songwriter. It's a very high standard to hold yourself to. But I got encouragement from a lot of people." To support the release, Tench played three sold-out solo performances in February 2014 at the Largo at the Coronet. Petty attended one of Tench's performances and told *Uncut*, "I went down to see the show and I felt so proud. He was really good and he had a great little band and the audience just went mad for him. You'd have thought he had done this his whole life the way he was so comfortable onstage and being up front. I was shouting at the top of my lungs for him."

While no members of the Heartbreakers appeared at the inaugural Los Angeles Petty Fest, the successful tribute concert and Tench's solo shows may have inspired the Heartbreakers to finally bring the group's small-theater residency concerts to Los Angeles. Following in the footsteps of the band's residencies in San Francisco in 1997 and 1999, and Chicago in 2003, the Heartbreakers announced in late February 2013 that the band would play a five-night stand at the Beacon Theatre in New York City followed by a six-night stand at the Fonda Theatre in Hollywood on June 3, 4, 6, 8, 9, and 11.

The Fonda Theatre, named after Hollywood legend and Fonda family patriarch Henry Fonda in 1985, opened on Hollywood Boulevard in 1926 as the Music Box Theatre. Though it spent three decades as a movie theater, in 2012 it was purchased by Goldenvoice, the concert promoter behind the famed Coachella Valley Music and Arts Festival. Goldenvoice changed the focus of the art-deco theater (which had been briefly renamed back to the Music Box but renamed again to the Fonda Theatre after the acquisition by Goldenvoice) from a mixture of stage plays and live music to mostly live music. Though the Fonda seats 1,200, it is actually more than double the size of the venue the Heartbreakers played the last time they performed in the area for the KCSN benefit performances. Nevertheless, these six performances otherwise represented the smallest non-benefit public concerts the Heartbreakers had played in the Los Angeles area since the group played the opening night of the Viper Room in 1993.

With the exception of a handful of songs played each night—all six shows opened with the Byrds' "So You Want to Be a Rock 'n' Roll Star," followed by "Love is a Long Road," and (all except one) ended with "American Girl"—the Heartbreakers dug deep for the Fonda shows, which were wildly popular with fans. In fact, the shows were arguably *too* popular, because the June 8 concert was stopped early by the Los Angeles Fire Marshall when they determined the floor was over capacity. Initially, Petty asked if a hundred people on the floor would move to the balcony or leave the building (several of the Heartbreakers jokingly offered to go home early), but the request didn't take. Since the venue did not sell more tickets than the Fonda's capacity, *LA Weekly* placed the blame squarely on building security by claiming they were taking eighty dollars in cash from dozens of people without tickets and letting them in while not ensuring that only those with floor tickets could access the floor. The band offered full refunds to ticketholders.

The setlists featured a number of rarely played favorites, including "Billy the Kid," "Cabin Down Below," "Crawling Back to You," "House in the Woods," "Something Big," "The Best of Everything," "Time to Move On," "To Find a Friend," "Two Gunslingers," "When a Kid Goes Bad," "When the Time Comes," an acoustic version of "Rebels," plenty of covers, and perhaps the biggest surprise, the Traveling Wilburys' Bruce Springsteen satire, "Tweeter and the Monkey Man," which the Heartbreakers played at each performance. Petty told *Rolling Stone*, "That was one [of the Traveling Wilburys] songs I had a hand in writing with Bob [Dylan]. We've just never done it. No one has ever done it. So I just thought, 'This would be interesting to try.' We played it and it came off entirely different, but kind of cool. We're really enjoying playing that one."

The *Los Angeles Times* review of the first performance praised the depth of the Heartbreakers' setlist, including the California focus of the songs the band covered, and saw the concerts as a victory lap of sorts, remarking, "The sound of California permeated the band's 20-song set which delivered deep cuts from throughout Petty's career, peppered with enough hits to underscore the songwriter's universal appeal. The West Coast ran through each Rickenbacker guitar riff like a breeze through his blonde hair...the longtime Angeleno presented a hidden narrative. It's a plot that not only featured lyrics of seduction, betrayal and obsession but also the support of a devoted fan base earned through relentless early years touring the highways of California. Multiple nights at the Santa Monica Civic Auditorium in 1977, yes, but also miles spent running up the coast from Fresno and Bakersfield to San Jose and Santa Cruz, gigging inland colleges at UC Davis, Chico State, and UC Riverside. Evenings at the Whisky a Go Go and the Cow Palace begot multiple sold-out shows at the Forum. In the process, the Heartbreakers...became one of America's great rock bands."

In his review for the *Orange County Register*, Ben Wener called the first concert "tremendous" and favorably compared the Heartbreakers to the Rolling Stones by saying that Petty's band "are taking a smarter approach to late-career performances." At the end of the year, *LA*

Weekly listed the June 9 concert as number seven on "The 20 Best L.A. Concerts of 2013," while the *Hollywood Reporter* called the first concert, "assuredly the most satisfying show Petty's done in Los Angeles in about 30 years."

Petty's assessment of the intimate concerts in New York and Los Angeles was that the experience was good for the band. He told *Men's Journal* in 2014, "It did us a lot of good just to break out of the greatest hits. There's a whole tier of other good songs that we don't play. I think I needed to remind myself of that." He did have an issue with the sound quality of the shows, telling *Rolling Stone* in 2015, "At the Fonda, though, we had big electrical buzz onstage that we couldn't quite control, which kind of irritated me. Other than that, it was great. I love the whole idea of doing a different show every night." The concerts also happened while the Heartbreakers were in the midst of recording their follow-up to *Mojo*, which they had been recording at the Clubhouse since August 2011.

On April 23, Petty was awarded the ASCAP Founders Award at the organization's 31st Annual Pop Music Awards at the Loews Hollywood Hotel, which was presented to Petty by Jackson Browne. To pay tribute, musician Lucinda Williams and her band performed "Rebels" and "Runnin' Down a Dream" (Petty had covered Williams' song "Change the Locks" for 1996's *She's the One* and had her on a Heartbreakers tour as an opening act several years later). It was one event of many that would celebrate Petty's influence and career in Los Angeles over the final years of his life.

CHAPTER 14

ALL YOU CAN CARRY

Petty revealed to the *Los Angeles Times* that the initial sessions for the new album—which would be titled *Hypnotic Eye* and recorded once again at the Clubhouse—followed the path of *Mojo*. After recording several tracks, he said, "I listened to them and I thought, 'You know, we're going to end up going down the same road if we get hung in this. We should play some rock 'n' roll.' I don't like to make the same record twice."

Two of the songs on *Hypnotic Eye* were inspired by infamous natural disasters in Southern California. "All You Can Carry" had been inspired by the 2007 canyon fire in Malibu that forced Petty and his family to evacuate, while another was inspired by earthquakes. As Petty told the *Los Angeles Times*, he and Dana were getting ready to go to one of the concerts by the Rascals on their Once Upon a Dream reunion tour in October 2013 ("I wasn't going to miss that," Petty added) when inspiration hit: Dana had left a map of Southern California fault lines on the computer. Petty said, "Just for a second I looked at it and went, 'Fault lines—I've got a few of those.'" Slightly modified, that became one of the lines in the chorus of the *Hypnotic Eye* song "Fault Lines."

Upon its release on July 29, 2014, *Hypnotic Eye* became the Heartbreakers' first album to hit #1 on the US Billboard chart, and Petty and

Campbell had the distinction of also appearing on the #2 album on the chart, Eric Clapton's *The Breeze: An Appreciation of JJ Cale* (Petty sang on three of the album tracks and Campbell contributed guitar), during the chart debut week for both albums. Petty had a third album on the same chart with *Greatest Hits*, which had jumped over seventy spots to land at #71 for its 182nd week on the Billboard Hot 100.

The Hypnotic Eye Tour was the Heartbreakers' longest jaunt since the Mojo Tour in 2010 and was bookended with performances in the Los Angeles area. The band preceded the tour with a performance of three of the album's songs—"American Dream Plan B," "Forgotten Man," and "U Get Me High"—on *Jimmy Kimmel Live!* on July 31. Instead of performing at Kimmel's Hollywood Masonic Temple Studio on Hollywood Boulevard, the performance actually aired from the Heartbreakers' tour rehearsal space at Sony Pictures Studios in Culver City. The tour wrapped up in Southern California with a concert on October 7 at the Honda Center in Anaheim (the only time the Heartbreakers played the home arena of the NHL's Anaheim Ducks) and then back-to-back shows at the Forum in Inglewood on October 10 and 11. These would mark the Heartbreakers' first (and last) concerts at the Forum since it reopened in January 2014 after closing for refurbishment in 2012. According to *Billboard*, the two Forum concerts grossed a combined $2.4 million.

The band performed four songs from *Hypnotic Eye*, "American Dream Plan B," "Forgotten Man," "U Get Me High," and "Shadow People," throughout the tour, including on those three dates. The setlist featured the Heartbreakers' usual heavy dose of the classics for the arena crowds, including "Mary Jane's Last Dance," "I Won't Back Down," "Free Fallin'," "Learning to Fly," "Refugee," "Runnin' Down a Dream," "You Wreck Me," and "American Girl." The Honda Center and first Forum show also both featured "Into the Great Wide Open," and a cover of Paul Revere and the Raiders' "I'm Not Your Stepping Stone" (a tribute to Revere, who died just days earlier), while the second performance at the Forum also included "Don't Do Me Like That," "A Woman in Love (It's Not Me)," and "Don't Come Around Here No More."

The review of the Honda Center concert in the *OC Weekly* said the setlist paled in comparison to the setlists of the Fonda Theatre shows of 2013, but complimented the band on having picked up a few tricks from those small-scale performances, remarking, "While the set wasn't nearly as experimental and adventurous as the band's six-night stint at the Fonda, it felt comfortable in an arena setting. A few songs from those shows, like an acoustic version of 'Rebels' from *Southern Accents* managed to sound just as intimate in the big room as it did in the theatre. Hearing the songs off *Wildflowers* or even the underrated *Echo* would have been a treat, but wouldn't have stuck with the band's M-O of this tour, which was to simply have fun as the singer himself stated halfway through...the group effortlessly powered through the set that mixed subtle improvisation with a sense of comforting familiarity. Petty and the Heartbreakers have the rare ability to make the familiar not sound stale, while tightly gliding through their set." The *Los Angeles Daily News* likewise praised the performance, noting, "Petty seemed genuinely taken aback by the unflagging enthusiasm of the arena's capacity crowd, which roared with delight repeatedly." The *Orange County Register* said Petty "was in top form," and that "Petty was enthusiastic about presenting the latest material, but he wasn't stingy on the hits." All things considered, the reviewers clearly believed that the Heartbreakers had a better-balanced setlist than they did during the much-maligned Mojo Tour.

Petty planned to get Mudcrutch back together in January 2015 to record a sophomore album (of the band's eight-year hiatus, Petty said to *Rolling Stone* in 2016, "I honestly didn't realize it had been that long. We just kept saying we were going to do it. We were just looking for a hole in the schedule"), but Leadon had medical issues that delayed the sessions until August. In July, Petty remarked to *Rolling Stone* how much he was looking forward to it. He said, "Some of the most fun I have is those Mudcrutch sessions. It was just so much fun and I think that's one of the better albums I was ever involved in. I'm hoping it's something like that again. It's kind of intimidating to have to follow it up." The sessions were again held at the Heartbreakers' Clubhouse and took up most of the next three months, with Leadon and Marsh again staying at Petty's Malibu estate during that period. One of the songs the band recorded, "Trailer," is a remake of a Heartbreakers *Southern Accents* outtake that was the B-side of the "Don't Come Around Here No More" single. It became the single for the album, titled *Mudcrutch 2*, when it was released in 2016. Each member of Mudcrutch sang lead on at least one track, with Campbell's lone lead vocal on the highway tune "Victim of Circumstance" making a specific mention of California (Rollin' down easy Highway 49 / Out of body and out of mind / I might get lost I might be found / Ain't no way of knowin' I'm California bound).

Petty and the Heartbreakers played just one concert in 2015, and it was a special one. For the past several years, Campbell had cohosted a charity concert for the holidays called the Merry Minstrel Musical Circus. For the 2015 edition, which was held at the Troubadour in West Hollywood, the Heartbreakers took the stage minus Steve Ferrone (Los Angeles session drummer Matt Laug played drums). The Heartbreakers played a ten-song set consisting of covers ("Little Red Rooster," "I'm a Man," "Thirteen Days"), hits ("Mary Jane's Last Dance," "Runnin' Down a Dream"), and rarities ("Cabin Down Below," "Dogs on the Run"), and were joined by Jeff Lynne for covers of "Runaway," "Roll Over Beethoven," and for the only time ever, Petty and Lynne performed "The Poor House" from *Traveling Wilburys Vol. 3*.

Upon its release on May 20, 2016, *Mudcrutch 2* received strong reviews from Petty's hometown press. In the *Los Angeles Daily News*, Sam Gnerre said the album was "more tightly focused than the first album," and in particular praised the songs sung by Petty's bandmates as being as good—if not better—than Petty's songs on the album.

To support *Mudcrutch 2*, the band once again hit the road—however, unlike the 2008 tour, there was no upcoming Heartbreakers tour scheduled to limit the excursion. Because of that, Mudcrutch was able to do a number of dates outside of California, though nine of the concerts on the twenty-one-date tour took place in California. The tour started with two benefit shows on May 23 and May 24 at California

State University Northridge—the same venue that the Heartbreakers played for the two KCSN benefits in 2011. This time the benefit concerts, titled "From Northridge with Love," supported Midnight Mission, just like the first Mudcrutch concert ("From Malibu with Love") on the 2008 tour. The setlists mixed songs from the two Mudcrutch albums, including the cover of "Trailer" along with an encore featuring a cover of Jerry Lee Lewis's "High School Confidential."

After playing a number of theater and festival dates across the rest of the country, Mudcrutch returned to Los Angeles and played two shows at the Fonda Theatre on June 25 and June 26. The second concert featured two special appearances—Stephen Stills, who joined the group for the Mudcrutch debut album song "The Wrong Thing to Do," a song Stills had covered a few times in concert, and Heartbreaker Steve Ferrone, who performed with Stills and Mudcrutch during the encore "Crystal River" (Ferrone played tambourine). Two days later, Mudcrutch performed at the Observatory in Santa Ana in Orange County, a 550-capacity theater. Following that, Mudcrutch played its final show in San Diego.

In July, Mudcrutch released a music video for the Petty-sung ballad "I Forgive It All." The video was codirected by Oscar-winning actor Sean Penn, who had personally selected the track when Petty offered him the chance to make a music video for any of the album's songs (Penn's codirector was veteran music-video director Samuel Bayer). The black-and-white video opens with archival footage of Los Angeles during the Great Depression and is later juxtaposed with shots of fellow Oscar-winning actor Anthony Hopkins depicting one of those starving children of the Depression, now well-dressed in his elder years, driving and then walking around Los Angeles and taking in views of modern poverty, hunger, and homelessness on the streets, including stopping in what appears to have been the former tenement where he grew up. The video was shot in a single day.

Though by the end of the Highway Companion Tour in 2006, Petty had already walked back his initial hints that that thirtieth anniversary trip would be the last large arena tour for the Heartbreakers, when Petty expressed the same sentiments at the end of 2016 once the band's 40th Anniversary Tour was announced for 2017, the statement sounded much more concrete. The Heartbreakers reconvened in November 2016 at the Clubhouse to jam. At the time, Petty told *Rolling Stone*, "I'm thinking it may be the last trip around the country. It's very likely we'll keep playing, but will we take on 50 shows in one tour? I don't think so. I'd be lying if I didn't say I was thinking this might be the last big one. We're all on the backside of our sixties. I have a granddaughter now I'd like to see as much as I can. I don't want to spend my life on the road. This tour will take me away for four months. With a little kid, that's a lot of time." However, in the same *Rolling Stone* article, both Campbell and Tench cast doubt on that, with Campbell saying, "I've been hearing him say that of the past 10 years. It would be a shame to stop playing while we're at the peak of our abilities," and Tench adding, "I don't know what's on Tom's mind because he certainly hasn't said that to me." As with previous tours, the band did final tour rehearsals at Sony Picture Studios.

Before the 2017 tour was announced, Petty was selected as the honoree for the 2017 MusiCares Person of the Year, an annual celebration held before the Grammy Awards that honors musicians who have used their platform for charitable works.

The benefit, held on February 10, 2017, at the Los Angeles Convention Center, raised $8.5 million for musicians in medical or financial need, a record for a MusiCares benefit. Producer T-Bone Burnett served as the musical director for the evening. The house band included legends like Booker T. Jones and several Heartbreakers on select songs, and the night included performances by Elle King, Cage the Elephant, the Shelters (whose 2016 debut album was coproduced by Petty), the Lumineers, Regina Spektor, Randy Newman, Taj Mahal, Chris Hillman, Jakob Dylan, Don Henley, George Strait, Foo Fighters, Gary Clark Jr., Jackson Browne, Lucinda Williams, and Norah Jones all playing covers of Petty's songs.

In response to all the praise and celebration, Petty said during his speech, "Twenty years ago, I would have been way too cynical to do this, but I'm 66 now." During his speech, Petty referenced a note he had received from Johnny Cash on the occasion of his fiftieth birthday. Petty shared, "This morning, I was looking through a box, and a card fell out, and it was from John, on my fiftieth birthday. And it said, 'Happy birthday. You're a good man to ride the river with.' And that's all I want to be: a good man to ride the river with, and I'm gonna keep riding the river."

The celebrity-studded evening was capped by a short set from Petty and the Heartbreakers, who were joined by the Bangles on backing vocals—first on "Waiting for Tonight," the outtake from the *Full Moon Fever*-era Heartbreaker sessions, for its only live performance. They remained on backing vocals for the next song, "Don't Come Around Here No More," and also for the following song, "Stop Draggin' My Heart Around," on which they were also joined by Stevie Nicks. After Petty and Nicks performed "Insider," the Bangles returned—this time with Jeff Lynne on lead vocal and Dhani Harrison—to perform "I Won't Back Down," and then the Heartbreakers ended the set with "Runnin' Down a Dream."

Just over two months later, the Heartbreakers began their 40th Anniversary Tour on April 20 in Oklahoma City. The tour—the band's most extensive in two decades—crisscrossed the US and Canada, plus a one-off date in England with Stevie Nicks. The Heartbreakers were accompanied on the tour by two backup singers, sisters Charley and Hattie Webb, who had previously worked with Leonard Cohen. Their inclusion broke Petty's long-standing rule, as stated in *Runnin' Down a Dream*: "There are no girls in the Heartbreakers," (though, to be fair, there had been female backup singers on the Pack up the Plantation tour).

The first Los Angeles area stop occurred on June 24 for Arroyo Seco Weekend 2017, the first night of what was billed as a family-friendly, two-night music festival at the Rose Bowl in Pasadena. It was the Heartbreakers' only performance at the Southern California land-mark (Petty had appeared at Peace Sunday at the Rose Bowl in June 1982, but without the Heartbreakers). Like the rest of the tour, the show opened with the first song from the Heartbreakers' first album, "Rockin' Around (With You)," and was followed by a mix of songs from all eras of Petty's discography.

While the *Los Angeles Daily News* praised Petty's performance at the festival, writer Peter Larsen wrote, "Threatening the good vibes of Petty's set was the cluster-mess of the crowd. Festival organizers didn't book any acts opposite Petty, choosing to close down the two other stages, which is fine, but that also meant everyone on the festival grounds tried to squeeze into a space that was too narrow to accommodate them—especially given that many, many people came with blankets and lawn chairs and staked out spots—large spots—on the lawn in front of the Oaks stage." Larsen's only criticism for the Heartbreakers was regarding the songs that the band didn't perform, adding, "I've realized how many great songs the band didn't play: 'Breakdown,' 'Don't Do Me Like That,' 'The Waiting,' and a whole lot more. Come back next year, Tom! Play the rest of them and hopefully the lawn chair and blanket people will be moved into their own little corral so the rest of us can better enjoy the show." On the other hand, the *Los Angeles Times*' Mikael Wood panned the festival as a whole and wrote that Petty's set was "solid," but added, "Nothing about Petty's set disrupted or even slightly expanded my sense of what he does; the show was merely congratulating festival-goers for upholding an old-fashioned—and increasing endangered—belief in electric guitars and snare drums whacked by hand."

Immediately after the festival performance, the Heartbreakers announced that the 40th Anniversary Tour would end with a homecoming concert at the Hollywood Bowl on September 21. Due to demand, the band added two more Hollywood Bowl dates, September 22 and September 25. All three concerts sold out, with 49,217 total people attending the concerts. The three concerts featured varied setlists like the others that the band had been playing throughout the lengthy 40th Anniversary Tour, with one exception: for the seventh song the first night, the Heartbreakers played "Walls (Circus)," "Into the Great Wide Open" the second night, and "Breakdown" on the third night.

In a review that appeared in the *Orange County Register*, the *Pasadena Star*, and the *Inland Valley Daily Bulletin*, Robert Kinsler called the performance of "Walls" a highlight, saying it "featured some of Petty's most potent vocals of the night," and said that the concert "captured the magic of those four decades of spirited rock 'n' roll." Also reviewing the first concert, August Brown praised the setlist selection in the *Los Angeles Times*, remarking, "Petty looked back on Thursday, for sure. But he and the Heartbreakers also made the case that they should be considered the most invigorated almost-original-lineup classic rock act touring today. Thursday's set was a flawless collection of hits from one of the great writers of rock, backed by a band with a near-telepathic relationship to its singer," and also called the choice to perform "Walls" "a perfectly-chosen rarity."

Reviewing the final concert for the *OC Weekly*, Daniel Kohn almost prophetically wrote, "Despite him saying that he's winding down his touring days, Tom Petty didn't look like a man ready to hang up his guitar quite yet. As fans like my mom sang and danced along to the grizzled rocker, he maintained a sharp focus on the evening's intent—to celebrate the band's rich history. The inspired performance wasn't drenched in nostalgia like a 40th anniversary tour would have given him a right to be. Instead, on an idyllic night at the Bowl with a renewed vigor, Petty dazzled and if he's going to retire soon, he's going out in style." Out in style, indeed—months later *Billboard* reported that the tour grossed $61 million—a record for the band. Of that gross, $5.3 million came from just the three Hollywood Bowl shows.

The concert's opening performer, Lucinda Williams, whose song "Change the Locks" Petty covered on *She's the One*, spoke to *Rolling Stone* about her last interaction with Petty shortly after the end of her opening set. She remembered, "He had a big smile, and he was putting a cough drop into his mouth. I didn't want to stay too long. It was getting close to showtime. I said, 'Tom, the audience is rockin'. They're good to go. I've warmed them up for you.' He looked at me and goes, 'I bet you did,' with those twinkly eyes and that beautiful face."

After the final encore of "American Girl" at the September 25 concert, the Heartbreakers took what would be their final bow together on stage. One week later, Petty died at the UCLA Medical Center in Santa Monica, just a few miles from his Malibu estate where he had been found unconscious. He was just weeks away from his sixty-seventh birthday.

In the world of social media, updates on Petty's condition happened nearly in real-time, though many were filled with misinformation. Some outlets, including *Rolling Stone*, reported Petty's death too early (Petty's youngest daughter, Annakim, would criticize the magazine for reporting that her father died before he actually did). Despite all the misreporting and unconfirmed reports, one thing was certain: it was only a matter of time.

Unsurprisingly, the tributes to one of the most respected veterans in rock 'n' roll were numerous, particularly in his adopted hometown. In Peter Larsen's obituary in the *Orange County Register*, he remarked, "From the day he arrived, Petty was as much a Los Angeleno as anyone born here, so deeply did he sink his roots into its soil, never looking back from his decision to pick Los Angeles over New York City when he and the rest of Mudcrutch were looking for a bigger scene than Gainesville in which to pursue their dreams."

Just two days after what ended up being the final Heartbreakers concert, and just five days before he died, Petty sat for his final interview at his Malibu estate, which was—appropriately enough—with Randy Lewis of the *Los Angeles Times*, the outlet that had helped break the Heartbreakers, and then years later would need to issue a *mea culpa* to an annoyed Petty for not giving the Heartbreakers enough credit for being a Los Angeles band. The interview was published two days after Petty's death under the poignant title, "The Hardest Part." Lewis opened the story with the line, "This is not the Tom Petty story that I had intended to write."

Sadly, much of the interview that was published focused on Petty looking ahead. Calling 2017 "a wonderful year for us," Petty said, "This has been that big slap on the back we never got." He expressed his hope to take a rest, but envisioned the band getting back to work sooner rather than later. For example, one of the projects Petty frequently talked about in his later years but never got to release was a reissue of *Wildflowers* with all of the outtakes, followed by a small theater tour that would involve the Heartbreakers performing the expanded *Wildflowers* album in its entirety.

Petty had gotten as far on the reissue as to visit with Rubin in 2016 to review the tracks. "I had like a vague memory of [the songs]," Rubin revealed on a 2018 episode of the Broken Record podcast about the making of *Wildflowers*, "but some of them just hit me like, 'Wow, what a great song! How did we miss this?' [Laughs] ...He very much wanted to rerelease it. He thought it was really important because the legacy of the *Wildflowers* album loomed large in his career and he knew that the second half of *Wildflowers* was an important statement." Unfortunately, Petty felt the biggest roadblock to releasing the rest of the songs would be how they were presented—not as a new Petty album or a catalog "deluxe edition" like the 2010 rerelease of *Damn the Torpedoes*, but as something more befitting the treasured place the album held in his esteem. "He felt that it was too good to just put out, and was sort of looking for the right story where it would have the exposure it deserved," Rubin continued. "And he just never came up with it." With Petty swearing off large-scale arena tours after the 40th Anniversary Tour, the *Wildflowers* tour concept seemed like a perfect fit for the album's twenty-fifth anniversary in 2019. He told *Rolling Stone* in 2016, "Single album concerts often don't scan right for a concert, but with the amount of material I have for the *Wildflowers* double album, I think I've got enough tempos and types of songs that I could do a live show....And it'll be fun for the audience since there's a bunch of songs they'll know." Petty also said the 40th Anniversary Tour wasn't the right fit for that setlist, telling *Rolling Stone* in 2016, "The 40th anniversary kind of got in the way of that. I looked at the tour they booked and it was all big places. The *Wildflowers* tour will have to be in smaller places because it's just a lot of quiet and a lot of it is acoustic."

What a tour it would've been.

EPILOGUE

SOMEWHERE CLOSE TO ME

Los Angeles saluted Tom Petty's memory in much the same fashion that Los Angeles does a lot of things—both weird and wonderful.

Longtime Petty friend and mentor Chris Hillman postponed his release party for the album *Bidin' My Time*, which was coproduced by Tom Petty and also featured a cover of "Wildflowers." The concert was originally scheduled for October 16 at the Troubadour, but was pushed back to October 23 when Petty's memorial service was scheduled for that day. Hillman performed "Wildflowers" at the show and dedicated it to Petty—and had Petty not died, it's likely he would've made an appearance at the show.

Petty's private memorial service was held at Lake Shrine Self-Realization Fellowship Temple in Pacific Palisades (the same location where the memorial service for Petty's close friend George Harrison was held), and then Petty was cremated at the Westwood Village Memorial Park Cemetery.

One of the earliest tributes was the "Tom Petty Memorial Vampire Walk" on October 19, in which dozens of self-described "vampires" met at the Sherman Oaks Galleria at the corner of Ventura Boulevard and Sepulveda Boulevard—often incorrectly thought of as the location where the escalator scenes in the "Free Fallin'" music video were filmed, because of its proximity to other filming locations in the video—so they could "move west down Ventura Boulevard," as Petty sings in the lyrics. The event, which included singalongs, was perhaps as LA as rock star death tributes get.

When the Heartbreakers returned to the stage with their own projects, they paid tribute to their bandleader. Tench was the first when he played a solo concert at the Largo at the Coronet on October 28. Tench opened with "Today I Took Your Picture Down," a song from his 2014 solo album that seemed particularly poignant ("Today I took your picture down / One of us had to go"). The set ended with two Mudcrutch songs that Tench sang lead on, "This is a Good Street" and "Welcome to Hell," and finally the Heartbreakers song "You Can Still Change Your Mind," a *Hard Promises* rarity. Tench would later play organ on two tracks on Bob Dylan's June 2020 album, *Rough and Rowdy Ways*, Dylan's first album of original songs in eight years, which was recorded at the Heartbreakers' old haunt Sound City Studios.

On January 27, 2018, Campbell returned to the stage with his side band the Dirty Knobs at a charity concert, the Imperial Ball, at the Anaheim Center for the Performing Arts. While on stage, Campbell addressed his longtime friend's death and said that out of respect for him, he had never played Heartbreakers songs with the Dirty Knobs. He mentioned his sadness of never being able to play those songs *with* Petty again, but said that he now would be playing them *for* him. The Dirty Knobs played "Something Good Coming" and "Runnin' Down a Dream."

Also in January 2018, the medical examiner released Petty's cause of death: an accidental overdose of medication, including pain medication that Petty had been using throughout the 2017 tour because of issues with his knees and a fractured hip. A statement from Petty's family said that they hoped that his death would shed further light on opioid drug abuse, stating, "As a family, we recognize this report may spark a further discussion on the opioid crisis and we feel that it is a healthy and necessary discussion and we hope in some way this report can save lives. Many people who overdose begin with a legitimate injury or simply do not understand the potency and deadly nature of these medications."

Though Petty wasn't exactly a movie star, Hollywood saluted him at the 90th Annual Academy Awards, which was held just a few months after Petty's death. At the ceremony, Pearl Jam frontman Eddie Vedder played Petty's 1999 *Echo* track "Room at the Top" during the annual "In Memoriam" segment that, by extension, also served as a remembrance of the beloved Los Angeles musician. Of course, this being Tom Petty, "Room at the Top" was one of the many beloved songs that he composed of which he was rather dismissive (he told *USA Today* in 2016 that it was "one of the most depressing songs in rock history," and never performed it live after the Echo Tour).

Unsurprisingly, the musical collaborations between the Heartbreakers continue on Los Angeles stages. On March 30, 2018, both Campbell and Tench participated in "Jubilee: A Celebration of Jerry Garcia," a concert at the Ace Hotel in Downtown Los Angeles. On April 21, 2018, three of the Heartbreakers—Campbell, Tench, and Ferrone—reunited on stage at the Dolby Theatre in Hollywood for Stephen Stills's annual charity event "Light Up the Blues," a benefit for Autism Speaks. With Stills, the Heartbreakers trio performed "I Won't Back Down," in addition to performing with other artists on the program like Patti Smith.

Stills being the first musician to perform with most of the Heartbreakers after Petty's death was certainly appropriate. Just over a decade before his death, Petty referred to the Heartbreakers as the "last link" to Stills's Buffalo Springfield and other '60s California groups. In some ways, Petty is correct. Subsequent Los Angeles rock groups who achieved mainstream success—from the Sunset Strip hard rock and heavy metal bands to alternative groups like Red Hot Chili Peppers and Jane's Addiction—drew their primary influences from other artists. On the other hand, many of Petty's Southern California influences, like Roger McGuinn and Chris Hillman of the Byrds and Stephen Stills of Buffalo Springfield, are still on the road and serve as living links to that pre-Heartbreakers era. Nonetheless, in terms of a vibrant rock group that continues to release celebrated, commercially successful music, the Heartbreakers appear to be the end of that line. Beyond the music, in recent years, so many of the studios that the Heartbreakers recorded in have shuttered as the music industry still grapples with the ever-changing reality of recording and distributing music in the twenty-first century.

Sadly, LA's legacy bands and recording studios haven't been the only casualties of the changing face of the city's music business. Though Petty insisted that his nearly career-long dissatisfaction with record labels had been resolved when he became a Reprise artist with the first Mudcrutch album, Petty passed before a bombshell 2019 story in the *New York Times Magazine* that would have likely brought back Petty's fighting spirit. The story, titled "The Day the Music Burned," uncovered previously unreported details of the June 1, 2008, fire on the Universal Studios backlot. At the time, the fire was widely reported mostly because it had destroyed the popular King Kong theme park ride, though Universal claimed the fire also destroyed tens of thousands of archived copies in its film library. Regarding that damage, Ron Meyer, chief operating officer of Universal Studios, told CNN, "Fortunately, nothing irreplaceable was lost. The video library was affected and damaged, but our main vault of our motion picture negatives was not." That was Universal's explanation of the extent of the fire's destruction for the next decade.

Sadly, the *New York Times Magazine* report revealed otherwise. Also destroyed were as many as 175,000 master recordings of the Universal Music Group, the truth of which did not begin to emerge even as artists over the years contacted Universal to access their master recordings for archival and reissue projects, and were told that they could not be located.

Petty and the Heartbreakers were listed by the *Times* as one of the hundreds of artists whose work was destroyed by the fire. Presumably, it could have amounted to the master recordings of Petty's career from his Mudcrutch single to the 1993 recording sessions for *Greatest Hits*.

However, considering how much remastering and archival reissue work has been done on Petty's music from the original master tapes in the decade since the fire, it's clear that much of his work was not lost. In fact, online posts from July 2019 purported to be by Ryan Ulyate, who has mixed Petty's albums and compilations since *Highway Companion*, have noted that much of Petty's Universal albums have been accounted for and were not lost (Universal also claims that Petty's master recordings were not destroyed in the fire).

But the same can't be said for dozens of artists that Petty respected, like Chuck Berry, Ray Charles, B.B. King, David Crosby, Glen Campbell, T-Bone Burnett, Don Everly, and the Eagles, all of whom were named on an internal Universal list obtained by the *New York Times*. While it may appear that Petty got lucky, it's unlikely that the masters of many artists—including those Petty celebrated on his *Buried Treasure* radio show—escaped the flames.

It's sad to think that after decades of Petty's rantings and warnings that record labels and the music industry did not have the best interests of artists at heart, he was proven right by the inadvertent destruction of not just part of his own history, but of hundreds of thousands of hours of recorded history. The catastrophe also reflects Petty's *The Last DJ*-era concerns of conglomerate control of the music industry. Perhaps if Universal Music Group had not ballooned into such a large corporation that owned so many master recordings without a plan to store all of them properly—or had at least been willing to devote some more of the budget to figuring out how to do a better job of preserving and protecting the scores of material it owned—all of these irreplaceable works could have survived. Unsurprisingly, many media conglomerates have little interest in preserving archival material—especially if it no longer has commercial value.

One can only imagine how infuriated a musician like Petty, who had such a deep appreciation for music history and heritage, would have felt about the 2008 Universal Studios fire when the revelations of the true losses finally began to emerge two years after his death. A class-action lawsuit by artists whose work was reportedly destroyed in the fire against Universal Music Group for negligence was joined by Jane Petty, who later became the only plaintiff in the case after the others dropped out. The case was dismissed without prejudice by a Los Angeles federal judge in April 2020, who declared her claims "legally deficient." The extent of exactly what may have been lost of Petty's recordings—as well as those of hundreds of other artists—is not yet known.

No matter the status of his master recordings, Petty's musical legacy endures far beyond Los Angeles. Just a few months after Petty's death, longtime Fleetwood Mac member Lyndsey Buckingham was dismissed from the group over touring disagreements (just a few months later Buckingham would also be sidelined from his solo work by open-heart surgery). To replace him, Fleetwood Mac brought on two musicians: Crowded House singer-guitarist Neil Finn and Heartbreaker Mike Campbell.

Campbell already had a long-time connection with the band—in addition to his many recordings with Fleetwood Mac vocalist Stevie Nicks, a song that Campbell cowrote with Nicks, "Freedom," appeared on Fleetwood Mac's 1990 album *Behind the Mask* (coincidentally, it is an album that was recorded during another period when Buckingham was not in the band)—so, in a lot of ways, he was a natural fit for Fleetwood Mac.

On the Fleetwood Mac tour, the band recognized Petty's legacy. The group performed "Free Fallin'"—with Nicks on lead vocals—as the first encore, though Campbell admitted to *Rolling Stone* that he initially objected ("I love that song, but I've just played it so much. I said to [Nicks], 'Do we have to?' She said, 'The crowd will love it. It'll be a moment'"). The 2018 leg of the tour ended with three concerts at the Forum in December, marking the first time Campbell ever performed that song on stage in Southern California without Petty. In January 2019, Campbell spoke about the Fleetwood Mac tour to *Guitar World*, remarking, "It's been going phenomenally. Better than I could've hoped. The crowds have been great and we're having a blast. It's also emotional. I mean, every night I walk out onstage and look around and [Petty and the Heartbreakers] aren't there, you know? And I miss them. But that's part of the process."

Part of that "process" included Campbell and Tench assisting with compiling *An American Treasure*, a box set featuring unreleased material covering Petty's entire career (released in September 2018), and a greatest hits compilation, *The Best of Everything* (released in March 2019). Other archival projects of Petty's music have been planned, including the retrospective release of *Wildflowers* that Petty often spoke about in his lifetime, and Adira Petty previewed the potential of that collection in June 2020 by releasing her father's original 8-track demo of "You Don't Know How It Feels" for free on the internet. And yet, even with Petty gone, his musical legacy remains in high demand, even illicitly. In October 2019, a number of items, including hard drives containing unreleased music by Petty, were stolen from a storage unit owned by an unnamed engineer (the hard drives were quickly recovered by police).

Invite-only events to promote the first two posthumous releases were held at the Heartbreakers Clubhouse, which still remains in a warehouse in the San Fernando Valley, despite the club now missing its leader. Of course, the Clubhouse is far from the only place in Los Angeles that Petty left his mark in his career, and Petty's music—including new songs that will make it out of the vaults—will continue to be part of the cultural fabric of Los Angeles.

That's a good enough last laugh for a band once listed as Los Angeles' *eighth* best rock 'n' roll group.

ABOUT THE AUTHOR

Christopher McKittrick's publications include *Can't Give It Away on Seventh Avenue: The Rolling Stones and New York City* (Post Hill Press) and "The Secret History of New York Blues" in *Artefact* magazine.